Collins
World Atlas

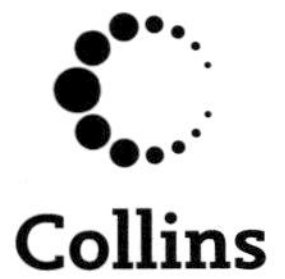

Collins

Settlements

Population	National Capital	Administrative Capital	Other City or Town
over 10 million	**BEIJING** ✪	**Karachi** ◉	**New York** ◉
5 million to 10 million	**JAKARTA** ✪	**Tianjin** ◉	**Nova Iguaçu** ◉
1 million to 5 million	**KĀBUL** ✪	**Sydney** ◉	**Kaohsiung** ◉
500 000 to 1 million	BANGUI ✪	Trujillo ◉	Jeddah ◉
100 000 to 500 000	WELLINGTON ✪	Mansa ◉	Apucarana ◯
50 000 to 100 000	PORT OF SPAIN ✪	Potenza ◯	Arecibo ◯
10 000 to 50 000	MALABO ✪	Chinhoyi ◯	Ceres ◯
under 10 000	VALLETTA ✪	Ati ◯	Palena ◯

Built-up area

Boundaries

▪▪▪▪▪ International boundary

▪▫▪▫▪ Disputed international boundary or alignment unconfirmed

──── Administrative boundary

••••• Ceasefire line

Miscellaneous

---------- National park

·········· Reserve or Regional park

✳ Site of specific interest

▭▭▭▭▭ Wall

Land and sea features

Desert

Oasis

Lava field

1234 Volcano
height in metres

Marsh

Ice cap or Glacier

Escarpment

Coral reef

1234 Pass
height in metres

Lakes and rivers

Lake

Impermanent lake

Salt lake or lagoon

Impermanent salt lake

Dry salt lake or salt pan

123 Lake height
surface height above
sea level, in metres

──── River

──── Impermanent river or watercourse

Waterfall

Dam

Barrage

Relief

Contour intervals and layer colours

metres

6000
5000
4000
3000
2000
1000
500
200
below sea level
200
2000
4000
6000

1234 Summit
height in metres

-123 Spot height
height in metres

123 Ocean deep
depth in metres

Transport

Motorway (tunnel; under construction)

Main road (tunnel; under construction)

Secondary road (tunnel; under construction)

Track

Main railway (tunnel; under construction)

Secondary railway (tunnel; under construction)

Other railway (tunnel; under construction)

Canal

✈ Main airport

✈ Regional airport

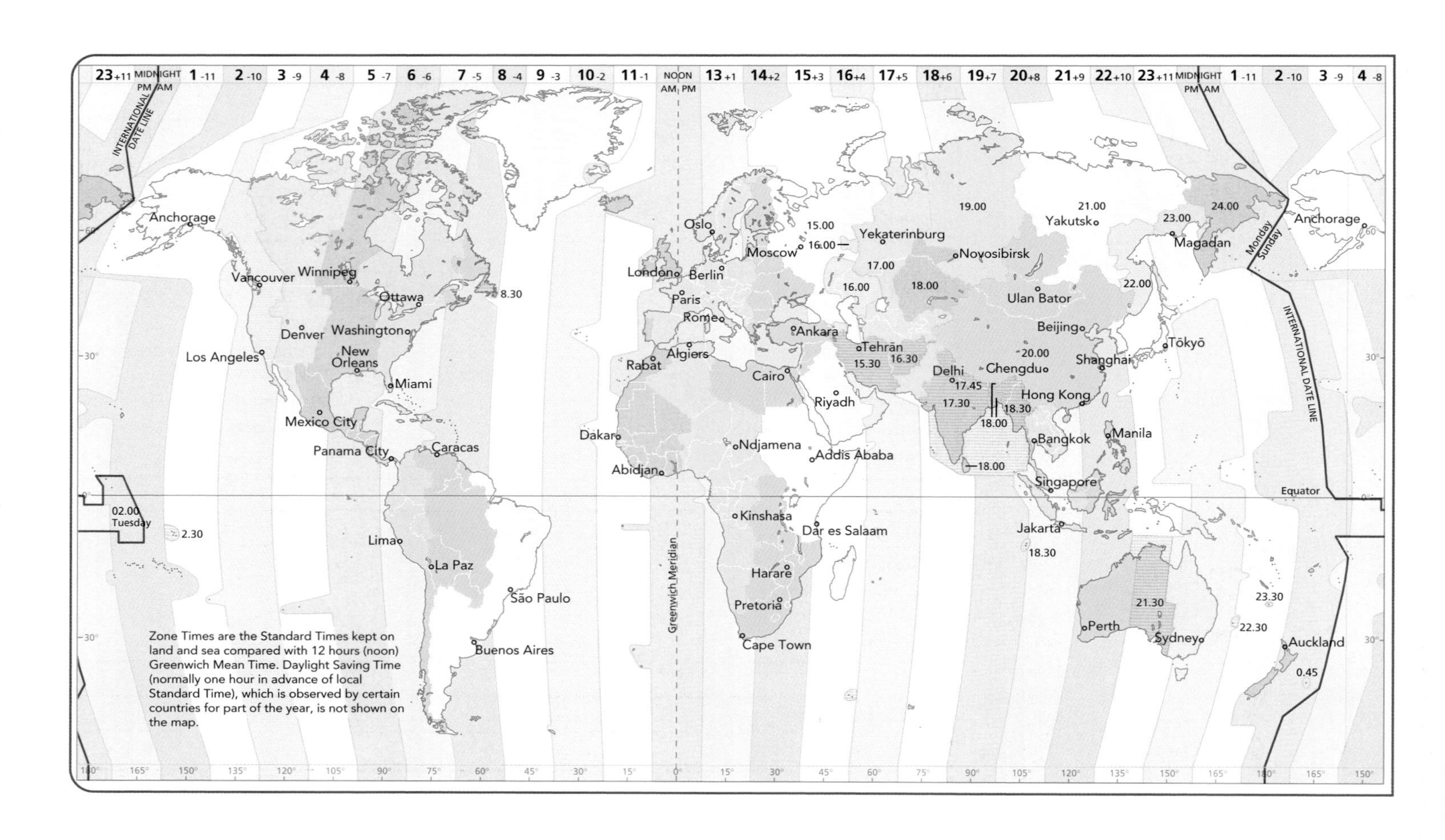

Zone Times are the Standard Times kept on land and sea compared with 12 hours (noon) Greenwich Mean Time. Daylight Saving Time (normally one hour in advance of local Standard Time), which is observed by certain countries for part of the year, is not shown on the map.

Map Symbols and Time Zones

Europe		Area sq km	Area sq miles	Population	Capital	Languages	Religions	Currency	Internet link
ALBANIA		28 748	11 100	3 166 000	Tirana	Albanian, Greek	Sunni Muslim, Albanian Orthodox, Roman Catholic	Lek	www.keshilliministrave.al
ANDORRA		465	180	71 000	Andorra la Vella	Spanish, Catalan, French	Roman Catholic	Euro	www.andorra.ad
AUSTRIA		83 855	32 377	8 116 000	Vienna	German, Croatian, Turkish	Roman Catholic, Protestant	Euro	www.oesterreich.at
BELARUS		207 600	80 155	9 895 000	Minsk	Belorussian, Russian	Belorussian Orthodox, Roman Catholic	Belarus rouble	www.government.by
BELGIUM		30 520	11 784	10 318 000	Brussels	Dutch (Flemish), French (Walloon), German	Roman Catholic, Protestant	Euro	www.belgium.be
BOSNIA-HERZEGOVINA		51 130	19 741	4 161 000	Sarajevo	Bosnian, Serbian, Croatian	Sunni Muslim, Serbian Orthodox, Roman Catholic, Protestant	Marka	www.fbihvlada.gov.ba
BULGARIA		110 994	42 855	7 897 000	Sofia	Bulgarian, Turkish, Romany, Macedonian	Bulgarian Orthodox, Sunni Muslim	Lev	www.government.bg
CROATIA		56 538	21 829	4 428 000	Zagreb	Croatian, Serbian	Roman Catholic, Serbian Orthodox, Sunni Muslim	Kuna	www.vlada.hr
CZECH REPUBLIC		78 864	30 450	10 236 000	Prague	Czech, Moravian, Slovak	Roman Catholic, Protestant	Czech koruna	www.czech.cz
DENMARK		43 075	16 631	5 364 000	Copenhagen	Danish	Protestant	Danish krone	www.denmark.dk
ESTONIA		45 200	17 452	1 332 000	Tallinn	Estonian, Russian	Protestant, Estonian and Russian Orthodox	Kroon	www.riik.ee
FINLAND		338 145	130 559	5 207 000	Helsinki	Finnish, Swedish	Protestant, Greek Orthodox	Euro	www.valtioneuvosto.fi
FRANCE		543 965	210 026	60 144 000	Paris	French, Arabic	Roman Catholic, Protestant, Sunni Muslim	Euro	www.premier-ministre.gouv.fr
GERMANY		357 022	137 849	82 476 000	Berlin	German, Turkish	Protestant, Roman Catholic	Euro	www.bundesregierung.de
GREECE		131 957	50 949	10 976 000	Athens	Greek	Greek Orthodox, Sunni Muslim	Euro	www.greece.gov.gr
HUNGARY		93 030	35 919	9 877 000	Budapest	Hungarian	Roman Catholic, Protestant	Forint	www.magyarorszag.hu
ICELAND		102 820	39 699	290 000	Reykjavík	Icelandic	Protestant	Icelandic króna	www.eng.stjornarrad.is
IRELAND, REPUBLIC OF		70 282	27 136	3 956 000	Dublin	English, Irish	Roman Catholic, Protestant	Euro	www.irlgov.ie
ITALY		301 245	116 311	57 423 000	Rome	Italian	Roman Catholic	Euro	www.governo.it
LATVIA		63 700	24 595	2 307 000	Rīga	Latvian, Russian	Protestant, Roman Catholic, Russian Orthodox	Lats	www.saeima.lv
LIECHTENSTEIN		160	62	34 000	Vaduz	German	Roman Catholic, Protestant	Swiss franc	www.liechtenstein.li
LITHUANIA		65 200	25 174	3 444 000	Vilnius	Lithuanian, Russian, Polish	Roman Catholic, Protestant, Russian Orthodox	Litas	www.lrv.lt
LUXEMBOURG		2 586	998	453 000	Luxembourg	Letzeburgish, German, French	Roman Catholic	Euro	www.gouvernement.lu
MACEDONIA (F.Y.R.O.M.)		25 713	9 928	2 056 000	Skopje	Macedonian, Albanian, Turkish	Macedonian Orthodox, Sunni Muslim	Macedonian denar	www.gov.mk
MALTA		316	122	394 000	Valletta	Maltese, English	Roman Catholic	Maltese lira	www.gov.mt
MOLDOVA		33 700	13 012	4 267 000	Chişinău	Romanian, Ukrainian, Gagauz, Russian	Romanian Orthodox, Russian Orthodox	Moldovan leu	www.moldova.md
MONACO		2	1	34 000	Monaco-Ville	French, Monegasque, Italian	Roman Catholic	Euro	www.monaco.gouv.mc
NETHERLANDS		41 526	16 033	16 149 000	Amsterdam/The Hague	Dutch, Frisian	Roman Catholic, Protestant, Sunni Muslim	Euro	www.overheid.nl
NORWAY		323 878	125 050	4 533 000	Oslo	Norwegian	Protestant, Roman Catholic	Norwegian krone	www.norway.no
POLAND		312 683	120 728	38 587 000	Warsaw	Polish, German	Roman Catholic, Polish Orthodox	Złoty	www.gov.mt
PORTUGAL		88 940	34 340	10 062 000	Lisbon	Portuguese	Roman Catholic, Protestant	Euro	www.portugal.gov.pt
ROMANIA		237 500	91 699	22 334 000	Bucharest	Romanian, Hungarian	Romanian Orthodox, Protestant, Roman Catholic	Romanian leu	www.guv.ro
RUSSIAN FEDERATION		17 075 400	6 592 849	143 246 000	Moscow	Russian, Tatar, Ukrainian, local languages	Russian Orthodox, Sunni Muslim, Protestant	Russian rouble	www.gov.ru
SAN MARINO		61	24	28 000	San Marino	Italian	Roman Catholic	Euro	www.consigliograndeegenerale.sm
SERBIA AND MONTENEGRO		102 173	39 449	10 527 000	Belgrade	Serbian, Albanian, Hungarian	Serbian Orthodox, Montenegrin Orthodox, Sunni Muslim	Serbian dinar, Euro	www.gov.yu
SLOVAKIA		49 035	18 933	5 402 000	Bratislava	Slovakian, Hungarian, Czech	Roman Catholic, Protestant, Orthodox	Slovakian koruna	www.government.gov.sk
SLOVENIA		20 251	7 819	1 984 000	Ljubljana	Slovenian, Croatian, Serbian	Roman Catholic, Protestant	Tólar	www.sigov.si
SPAIN		504 782	194 897	41 060 000	Madrid	Spanish, Castilian, Catalan, Galician, Basque	Roman Catholic	Euro	www.la-moncloa.es
SWEDEN		449 964	173 732	8 876 000	Stockholm	Swedish	Protestant, Roman Catholic	Swedish krona	www.sweden.se
SWITZERLAND		41 293	15 943	7 169 000	Bern	German, French, Italian, Romansch	Roman Catholic, Protestant	Swiss franc	www.admin.ch
UKRAINE		603 700	233 090	48 523 000	Kiev	Ukrainian, Russian	Ukrainian Orthodox, Ukrainian Catholic, Roman Catholic	Hryvnia	www.kmu.gov.ua
UNITED KINGDOM		243 609	94 058	58 789 194	London	English, Welsh, Gaelic	Protestant, Roman Catholic, Muslim	Pound sterling	www.ukonline.gov.uk
VATICAN CITY		0.5	0.2	472	Vatican City	Italian	Roman Catholic	Euro	www.vatican.va

Asia		Area sq km	Area sq miles	Population	Capital	Languages	Religions	Currency	Internet link
AFGHANISTAN		652 225	251 825	23 897 000	Kābul	Dari, Pushtu, Uzbek, Turkmen	Sunni Muslim, Shi'a Muslim	Afghani	www.afghanistan-mfa.net
ARMENIA		29 800	11 506	3 061 000	Yerevan	Armenian, Azeri	Armenian Orthodox	Dram	www.gov.am
AZERBAIJAN		86 600	33 436	8 370 000	Baku	Azeri, Armenian, Russian, Lezgian	Shi'a Muslim, Sunni Muslim, Russian and Armenian Orthodox	Azerbaijani manat	www.president.az
BAHRAIN		691	267	724 000	Manama	Arabic, English	Shi'a Muslim, Sunni Muslim, Christian	Bahrain dinar	www.bahrain.gov.bh
BANGLADESH		143 998	55 598	146 736 000	Dhaka	Bengali, English	Sunni Muslim, Hindu	Taka	www.bangladesh.gov.bd
BHUTAN		46 620	18 000	2 257 000	Thimphu	Dzongkha, Nepali, Assamese	Buddhist, Hindu	Ngultrum, Indian rupee	www.bhutan.gov.bt
BRUNEI		5 765	2 226	358 000	Bandar Seri Begawan	Malay, English, Chinese	Sunni Muslim, Buddhist, Christian	Brunei dollar	www.brunei.gov.bn
CAMBODIA		181 035	69 884	14 144 000	Phnom Penh	Khmer, Vietnamese	Buddhist, Roman Catholic, Sunni Muslim	Riel	www.cambodia.gov.kh
CHINA		9 584 492	3 700 593	1 289 161 000	Beijing	Mandarin, Wu, Cantonese, Hsiang, regional languages	Confucian, Taoist, Buddhist, Christian, Sunni Muslim	Yuan, HK dollar*, Macau pataca	www.china.org.cn
CYPRUS		9 251	3 572	802 000	Nicosia	Greek, Turkish, English	Greek Orthodox, Sunni Muslim	Cyprus pound	www.cyprus.gov.cy
EAST TIMOR		14 874	5 743	778 000	Dili	Portuguese, Tetun, English	Roman Catholic	United States dollar	www.gov.east-timor.org
GEORGIA		69 700	26 911	5 126 000	T'bilisi	Georgian, Russian, Armenian, Azeri, Ossetian, Abkhaz	Georgian Orthodox, Russian Orthodox, Sunni Muslim	Lari	www.parliament.ge
INDIA		3 064 898	1 183 364	1 065 462 000	New Delhi	Hindi, English, many regional languages	Hindu, Sunni Muslim, Shi'a Muslim, Sikh, Christian	Indian rupee	www.goidirectory.nic.in
INDONESIA		1 919 445	741 102	219 883 000	Jakarta	Indonesian, local languages	Sunni Muslim, Protestant, Roman Catholic, Hindu, Buddhist	Rupiah	www.indonesia.go.id
IRAN		1 648 000	636 296	68 920 000	Tehrān	Farsi, Azeri, Kurdish, regional languages	Shi'a Muslim, Sunni Muslim	Iranian rial	www.president.ir
IRAQ		438 317	169 235	25 175 000	Baghdād	Arabic, Kurdish, Turkmen	Shi'a Muslim, Sunni Muslim, Christian	Iraqi dinar	www.iraqmofa.net
ISRAEL		20 770	8 019	6 433 000	Jerusalem *(De facto capital. Disputed)*	Hebrew, Arabic	Jewish, Sunni Muslim, Christian, Druze	Shekel	www.index.gov.il/FirstGov
JAPAN		377 727	145 841	127 654 000	Tōkyō	Japanese	Shintoist, Buddhist, Christian	Yen	www.web-japan.org
JORDAN		89 206	34 443	5 473 000	'Ammān	Arabic	Sunni Muslim, Christian	Jordanian dinar	www.nic.gov.jo
KAZAKHSTAN		2 717 300	1 049 155	15 433 000	Astana	Kazakh, Russian, Ukrainian, German, Uzbek, Tatar	Sunni Muslim, Russian Orthodox, Protestant	Tenge	www.president.kz
KUWAIT		17 818	6 880	2 521 000	Kuwait	Arabic	Sunni Muslim, Shi'a Muslim, Christian, Hindu	Kuwaiti dinar	www.kuwaitmission.com
KYRGYZSTAN		198 500	76 641	5 138 000	Bishkek	Kyrgyz, Russian, Uzbek	Sunni Muslim, Russian Orthodox	Kyrgyz som	www.gov.kg
LAOS		236 800	91 429	5 657 000	Vientiane	Lao, local languages	Buddhist, traditional beliefs	Kip	www.un.int/lao
LEBANON		10 452	4 036	3 653 000	Beirut	Arabic, Armenian, French	Shi'a Muslim, Sunni Muslim, Christian	Lebanese pound	www.presidency.gov.lb
MALAYSIA		332 965	128 559	24 425 000	Kuala Lumpur/Putrajaya	Malay, English, Chinese, Tamil, local languages	Sunni Muslim, Buddhist, Hindu, Christian, traditional beliefs	Ringgit	www.mcsl.mampu.gov.my
MALDIVES		298	115	318 000	Male	Divehi (Maldivian)	Sunni Muslim	Rufiyaa	www.maldivesinfo.gov.mv

*Hong Kong dollar

National Statistics   3

Asia continued		Area sq km	Area sq miles	Population	Capital	Languages	Religions	Currency	Internet link
MONGOLIA		1 565 000	604 250	2 594 000	Ulan Bator	Khalka (Mongolian), Kazakh, local languages	Buddhist, Sunni Muslim	Tugrik (tögrög)	www.pmis.gov.mn
MYANMAR (BURMA)		676 577	261 228	49 485 000	Rangoon	Burmese, Shan, Karen, local languages	Buddhist, Christian, Sunni Muslim	Kyat	www.myanmar.com
NEPAL		147 181	56 827	25 164 000	Kathmandu	Nepali, Maithili, Bhojpuri, English, local languages	Hindu, Buddhist, Sunni Muslim	Nepalese rupee	www.nepalhmg.gov.np
NORTH KOREA		120 538	46 540	22 664 000	P'yŏngyang	Korean	Traditional beliefs, Chondoist, Buddhist	North Korean won	www.korea-dpr.com
OMAN		309 500	119 499	2 851 000	Muscat	Arabic, Baluchi, Indian languages	Ibadhi Muslim, Sunni Muslim	Omani riyal	www.moneoman.gov.om
PAKISTAN		803 940	310 403	153 578 000	Islamabad	Urdu, Punjabi, Sindhi, Pushtu, English	Sunni Muslim, Shi'a Muslim, Christian, Hindu	Pakistani rupee	www.infopak.gov.pk
PALAU		497	192	20 000	Koror	Palauan, English	Roman Catholic, Protestant, traditional beliefs	United States dollar	www.palauembassy.com
PHILIPPINES		300 000	115 831	79 999 000	Manila	English, Pilipino, Cebuano, local languages	Roman Catholic, Protestant, Sunni Muslim, Aglipayan	Philippine peso	www.gov.ph
QATAR		11 437	4 416	610 000	Doha	Arabic	Sunni Muslim	Qatari riyal	www.english.mofa.gov.qa
RUSSIAN FEDERATION		17 075 400	6 592 849	143 246 000	Moscow	Russian, Tatar, Ukrainian, local languages	Russian Orthodox, Sunni Muslim, Protestant	Russian rouble	www.gov.ru
SAUDI ARABIA		2 200 000	849 425	24 217 000	Riyadh	Arabic	Sunni Muslim, Shi'a Muslim	Saudi Arabian riyal	www.saudinf.com
SINGAPORE		639	247	4 253 000	Singapore	Chinese, English, Malay, Tamil	Buddhist, Taoist, Sunni Muslim, Christian, Hindu	Singapore dollar	www.gov.sg
SOUTH KOREA		99 274	38 330	47 700 000	Seoul	Korean	Buddhist, Protestant, Roman Catholic	South Korean won	www.korea.net
SRI LANKA		65 610	25 332	19 065 000	Sri Jayewardenepura Kotte	Sinhalese, Tamil, English	Buddhist, Hindu, Sunni Muslim, Roman Catholic	Sri Lankan rupee	www.priu.gov.lk
SYRIA		185 180	71 498	17 800 000	Damascus	Arabic, Kurdish, Armenian	Sunni Muslim, Shi'a Muslim, Christian	Syrian pound	www.moi-syria.com
TAIWAN		36 179	13 969	22 548 000	T'aipei	Mandarin, Min, Hakka, local languages	Buddhist, Taoist, Confucian, Christian	Taiwan dollar	www.gov.tw
TAJIKISTAN		143 100	55 251	6 245 000	Dushanbe	Tajik, Uzbek, Russian	Sunni Muslim	Somoni	www.tjus.org
THAILAND		513 115	198 115	62 833 000	Bangkok	Thai, Lao, Chinese, Malay, Mon-Khmer languages	Buddhist, Sunni Muslim	Baht	www.thaigov.go.th
TURKEY		779 452	300 948	71 325 000	Ankara	Turkish, Kurdish	Sunni Muslim, Shi'a Muslim	Turkish lira	www.mfa.gov.tr
TURKMENISTAN		488 100	188 456	4 867 000	Ashgabat	Turkmen, Uzbek, Russian	Sunni Muslim, Russian Orthodox	Turkmen manat	www.turkmenistanembassy.org
UNITED ARAB EMIRATES		77 700	30 000	2 995 000	Abu Dhabi	Arabic, English	Sunni Muslim, Shi'a Muslim	United Arab Emirates dirham	www.uae.gov.ae
UZBEKISTAN		447 400	172 742	26 093 000	Tashkent	Uzbek, Russian, Tajik, Kazakh	Sunni Muslim, Russian Orthodox	Uzbek som	www.gov.uz
VIETNAM		329 565	127 246	81 377 000	Ha Nôi	Vietnamese, Thai, Khmer, Chinese, local languages	Buddhist, Taoist, Roman Catholic, Cao Dai, Hoa Hao	Dong	www.na.gov.vn
YEMEN		527 968	203 850	20 010 000	Şan'ā'	Arabic	Sunni Muslim, Shi'a Muslim	Yemeni rial	www.nic.gov.ye

Africa		Area sq km	Area sq miles	Population	Capital	Languages	Religions	Currency	Internet link
ALGERIA		2 381 741	919 595	31 800 000	Algiers	Arabic, French, Berber	Sunni Muslim	Algerian dinar	www.el-mouradia.dz
ANGOLA		1 246 700	481 354	13 625 000	Luanda	Portuguese, Bantu, local languages	Roman Catholic, Protestant, traditional beliefs	Kwanza	www.angola.org
BENIN		112 620	43 483	6 736 000	Porto-Novo	French, Fon, Yoruba, Adja, local languages	Traditional beliefs, Roman Catholic, Sunni Muslim	CFA franc*	www.gouv.bj
BOTSWANA		581 370	224 468	1 785 000	Gaborone	English, Setswana, Shona, local languages	Traditional beliefs, Protestant, Roman Catholic	Pula	www.gov.bw
BURKINA		274 200	105 869	13 002 000	Ouagadougou	French, Moore (Mossi), Fulani, local languages	Sunni Muslim, traditional beliefs, Roman Catholic	CFA franc*	www.primature.gov.bf
BURUNDI		27 835	10 747	6 825 000	Bujumbura	Kirundi (Hutu, Tutsi), French	Roman Catholic, traditional beliefs, Protestant	Burundian franc	www.burundi.gov.bi
CAMEROON		475 442	183 569	16 018 000	Yaoundé	French, English, Fang, Bamileke, local languages	Roman Catholic, traditional beliefs, Sunni Muslim, Protestant	CFA franc*	www.spm.gov.cm
CAPE VERDE		4 033	1 557	463 000	Praia	Portuguese, creole	Roman Catholic, Protestant	Cape Verde escudo	www.governo.cv
CENTRAL AFRICAN REPUBLIC		622 436	240 324	3 865 000	Bangui	French, Sango, Banda, Baya, local languages	Protestant, Roman Catholic, traditional beliefs, Sunni Muslim	CFA franc*	www.odci.gov/cia/publications/factbook
CHAD		1 284 000	495 755	8 598 000	Ndjamena	Arabic, French, Sara, local languages	Sunni Muslim, Roman Catholic, Protestant, traditional beliefs	CFA franc*	www.tit.td
COMOROS		1 862	719	768 000	Moroni	Comorian, French, Arabic	Sunni Muslim, Roman Catholic	Comoros franc	www.presidence-uniondescomore.com
CONGO		342 000	132 047	3 724 000	Brazzaville	French, Kongo, Monokutuba, local languages	Roman Catholic, Protestant, traditional beliefs, Sunni Muslim	CFA franc*	www.congo-site.com
CONGO, DEMOCRATIC REP. OF		2 345 410	905 568	52 771 000	Kinshasa	French, Lingala, Swahili, Kongo, local languages	Christian, Sunni Muslim	Congolese franc	www.un.int/drcongo
CÔTE D'IVOIRE (IVORY COAST)		322 463	124 504	16 631 000	Yamoussoukro	French, creole, Akan, local languages	Sunni Muslim, Roman Catholic, traditional beliefs, Protestant	CFA franc*	www.pr.ci
DJIBOUTI		23 200	8 958	703 000	Djibouti	Somali, Afar, French, Arabic	Sunni Muslim, Christian	Djibouti franc	www.odci.gov/cia/publications/factbook
EGYPT		1 000 250	386 199	71 931 000	Cairo	Arabic	Sunni Muslim, Coptic Christian	Egyptian pound	www.sis.gov.eg
EQUATORIAL GUINEA		28 051	10 831	494 000	Malabo	Spanish, French, Fang	Roman Catholic, traditional beliefs	CFA franc*	www.ceiba-equatorial-guinea.org
ERITREA		117 400	45 328	4 141 000	Asmara	Tigrinya, Tigre	Sunni Muslim, Coptic Christian	Nakfa	www.shabait.com
ETHIOPIA		1 133 880	437 794	70 678 000	Addis Ababa	Oromo, Amharic, Tigrinya, local languages	Ethiopian Orthodox, Sunni Muslim, traditional beliefs	Birr	www.ethiopar.net
GABON		267 667	103 347	1 329 000	Libreville	French, Fang, local languages	Roman Catholic, Protestant, traditional beliefs	CFA franc*	www.un.int/gabon
THE GAMBIA		11 295	4 361	1 426 000	Banjul	English, Malinke, Fulani, Wolof	Sunni Muslim, Protestant	Dalasi	www.statehouse.gm
GHANA		238 537	92 100	20 922 000	Accra	English, Hausa, Akan, local languages	Christian, Sunni Muslim, traditional beliefs	Cedi	www.ghana.gov.gh
GUINEA		245 857	94 926	8 480 000	Conakry	French, Fulani, Malinke, local languages	Sunni Muslim, traditional beliefs, Christian	Guinea franc	www.guinee.gov.gn
GUINEA-BISSAU		36 125	13 948	1 493 000	Bissau	Portuguese, crioulo, local languages	Traditional beliefs, Sunni Muslim, Christian	CFA franc*	www.odci.gov/cia/publications/factbook
KENYA		582 646	224 961	31 987 000	Nairobi	Swahili, English, local languages	Christian, traditional beliefs	Kenyan shilling	www.kenya.go.ke
LESOTHO		30 355	11 720	1 802 000	Maseru	Sesotho, English, Zulu	Christian, traditional beliefs	Loti, S. African rand	www.lesotho.gov.ls
LIBERIA		111 369	43 000	3 367 000	Monrovia	English, creole, local languages	Traditional beliefs, Christian, Sunni Muslim	Liberian dollar	www.liberiaemb.org
LIBYA		1 759 540	679 362	5 551 000	Tripoli	Arabic, Berber	Sunni Muslim	Libyan dinar	www.libya-un.org
MADAGASCAR		587 041	226 658	17 404 000	Antananarivo	Malagasy, French	Traditional beliefs, Christian, Sunni Muslim	Malagasy franc	www.madagascar-diplomatie.ch
MALAWI		118 484	45 747	12 105 000	Lilongwe	Chichewa, English, local languages	Christian, traditional beliefs, Sunni Muslim	Malawian kwacha	www.malawi.gov.mw
MALI		1 240 140	478 821	13 007 000	Bamako	French, Bambara, local languages	Sunni Muslim, traditional beliefs, Christian	CFA franc*	www.maliensdelexterieur.gov.ml
MAURITANIA		1 030 700	397 955	2 893 000	Nouakchott	Arabic, French, local languages	Sunni Muslim	Ouguiya	www.mauritania.mr
MAURITIUS		2 040	788	1 221 000	Port Louis	English, creole, Hindi, Bhojpurī, French	Hindu, Roman Catholic, Sunni Muslim	Mauritius rupee	www.gov.mu
MOROCCO		446 550	172 414	30 566 000	Rabat	Arabic, Berber, French	Sunni Muslim	Moroccan dirham	www.mincom.gov.ma
MOZAMBIQUE		799 380	308 642	18 863 000	Maputo	Portuguese, Makua, Tsonga, local languages	Traditional beliefs, Roman Catholic, Sunni Muslim	Metical	www.mozambique.mz
NAMIBIA		824 292	318 261	1 987 000	Windhoek	English, Afrikaans, German, Ovambo, local languages	Protestant, Roman Catholic	Namibian dollar	www.grnnet.gov.na
NIGER		1 267 000	489 191	11 972 000	Niamey	French, Hausa, Fulani, local languages	Sunni Muslim, traditional beliefs	CFA franc*	www.delgi.ne/presidence
NIGERIA		923 768	356 669	124 009 000	Abuja	English, Hausa, Yoruba, Ibo, Fulani, local languages	Sunni Muslim, Christian, traditional beliefs	Naira	www.nigeria.gov.ng
RWANDA		26 338	10 169	8 387 000	Kigali	Kinyarwanda, French, English	Roman Catholic, traditional beliefs, Protestant	Rwandan franc	www.rwanda1.com
SÃO TOMÉ AND PRÍNCIPE		964	372	161 000	São Tomé	Portuguese, creole	Roman Catholic, Protestant	Dobra	www.uns.st
SENEGAL		196 720	75 954	10 095 000	Dakar	French, Wolof, Fulani, local languages	Sunni Muslim, Roman Catholic, traditional beliefs	CFA franc*	www.gouv.sn
SEYCHELLES		455	176	81 000	Victoria	English, French, creole	Roman Catholic, Protestant	Seychelles rupee	www.virtualseychelles.sc

*Communauté Financière Africaine franc

Africa continued		Area sq km	Area sq miles	Population	Capital	Languages	Religions	Currency	Internet link
SIERRA LEONE		71 740	27 699	4 971 000	Freetown	English, creole, Mende, Temne, local languages	Sunni Muslim, traditional beliefs	Leone	www.statehouse-sl.org
SOMALIA		637 657	246 201	9 890 000	Mogadishu	Somali, Arabic	Sunni Muslim	Somali shilling	www.odci.gov/cia/publications/factbook
SOUTH AFRICA, REPUBLIC OF		1 219 090	470 693	45 026 000	Pretoria/Cape Town	Afrikaans, English, nine other official local languages	Protestant, Roman Catholic, Sunni Muslim, Hindu	Rand	www.gov.za
SUDAN		2 505 813	967 500	33 610 000	Khartoum	Arabic, Dinka, Nubian, Beja, Nuer, local languages	Sunni Muslim, traditional beliefs, Christian	Sudanese dinar	www.sudan.gov.sd
SWAZILAND		17 364	6 704	1 077 000	Mbabane	Swazi, English	Christian, traditional beliefs	Emalangeni, South African rand	www.gov.sz
TANZANIA		945 087	364 900	36 977 000	Dodoma	Swahili, English, Nyamwezi, local languages	Shi'a Muslim, Sunni Muslim, traditional beliefs, Christian	Tanzanian shilling	www.tanzania.go.tz
TOGO		56 785	21 925	4 909 000	Lomé	French, Ewe, Kabre, local languages	Traditional beliefs, Christian, Sunni Muslim	CFA franc*	www.republicoftogo.com
TUNISIA		164 150	63 379	9 832 000	Tunis	Arabic, French	Sunni Muslim	Tunisian dinar	www.tunisiaonline.com
UGANDA		241 038	93 065	25 827 000	Kampala	English, Swahili, Luganda, local languages	Roman Catholic, Protestant, Sunni Muslim, traditional beliefs	Ugandan shilling	www.government.go.ug
ZAMBIA		752 614	290 586	10 812 000	Lusaka	English, Bemba, Nyanja, Tonga, local languages	Christian, traditional beliefs	Zambian kwacha	www.zambiatourism.com
ZIMBABWE		390 759	150 873	12 891 000	Harare	English, Shona, Ndebele	Christian, traditional beliefs	Zimbabwean dollar	www.zim.gov.zw

*Communauté Financière Africaine franc

Oceania		Area sq km	Area sq miles	Population	Capital	Languages	Religions	Currency	Internet link
AUSTRALIA		7 692 024	2 969 907	19 731 000	Canberra	English, Italian, Greek	Protestant, Roman Catholic, Orthodox	Australian dollar	www.gov.au
FIJI		18 330	7 077	839 000	Suva	English, Fijian, Hindi	Christian, Hindu, Sunni Muslim	Fiji dollar	www.fiji.gov.fj
KIRIBATI		717	277	88 000	Bairiki	Gilbertese, English	Roman Catholic, Protestant	Australian dollar	www.odci.gov/cia/publications/factbook
MARSHALL ISLANDS		181	70	53 000	Delap-Uliga-Djarrit	English, Marshallese	Protestant, Roman Catholic	United States dollar	www.rmiembassyus.org
MICRONESIA, FEDERATED STATES OF		701	271	109 000	Palikir	English, Chuukese, Pohnpeian, local languages	Roman Catholic, Protestant	United States dollar	www.fsmgov.org
NAURU		21	8	13 000	Yaren	Nauruan, English	Protestant, Roman Catholic	Australian dollar	www.un.int/nauru
NEW ZEALAND		270 534	104 454	3 875 000	Wellington	English, Maori	Protestant, Roman Catholic	New Zealand dollar	www.govt.nz
PAPUA NEW GUINEA		462 840	178 704	5 711 000	Port Moresby	English, Tok Pisin (creole), local languages	Protestant, Roman Catholic, traditional beliefs	Kina	www.pngonline.gov.pg
SAMOA		2 831	1 093	178 000	Apia	Samoan, English	Protestant, Roman Catholic	Tala	www.govt.ws
SOLOMON ISLANDS		28 370	10 954	477 000	Honiara	English, creole, local languages	Protestant, Roman Catholic	Solomon Islands dollar	www.commerce.gov.sb
TONGA		748	289	104 000	Nuku'alofa	Tongan, English	Protestant, Roman Catholic	Pa'anga	www.pmo.gov.to
TUVALU		25	10	11 000	Vaiaku	Tuvaluan, English	Protestant	Australian dollar	www.odci.gov/cia/publications/factbook
VANUATU		12 190	4 707	212 000	Port Vila	English, Bislama (creole), French	Protestant, Roman Catholic, traditional beliefs	Vatu	www.vanuatugovernment.gov.vu

North America		Area sq km	Area sq miles	Population	Capital	Languages	Religions	Currency	Internet link
ANTIGUA AND BARBUDA		442	171	73 000	St John's	English, creole	Protestant, Roman Catholic	East Caribbean dollar	www.un.int/antigua
THE BAHAMAS		13 939	5 382	314 000	Nassau	English, creole	Protestant, Roman Catholic	Bahamian dollar	www.bahamas.gov.bs
BARBADOS		430	166	270 000	Bridgetown	English, creole	Protestant, Roman Catholic	Barbados dollar	www.barbados.gov.bb
BELIZE		22 965	8 867	256 000	Belmopan	English, Spanish, Mayan, creole	Roman Catholic, Protestant	Belize dollar	www.belize.gov.bz
CANADA		9 984 670	3 855 103	31 510 000	Ottawa	English, French	Roman Catholic, Protestant, Eastern Orthodox, Jewish	Canadian dollar	canada.gc.ca
COSTA RICA		51 100	19 730	4 173 000	San José	Spanish	Roman Catholic, Protestant	Costa Rican colón	www.casapres.go.cr
CUBA		110 860	42 803	11 300 000	Havana	Spanish	Roman Catholic, Protestant	Cuban peso	www.cubagob.gov.cu
DOMINICA		750	290	79 000	Roseau	English, creole	Roman Catholic, Protestant	East Caribbean dollar	www.dominica.co.uk
DOMINICAN REPUBLIC		48 442	18 704	8 745 000	Santo Domingo	Spanish, creole	Roman Catholic, Protestant	Dominican peso	www.presidencia.gov.do
EL SALVADOR		21 041	8 124	6 515 000	San Salvador	Spanish	Roman Catholic, Protestant	El Salvador colón, United States dollar	www.casapres.gob.sv
GRENADA		378	146	80 000	St George's	English, creole	Roman Catholic, Protestant	East Caribbean dollar	www.grenadaconsulate.org
GUATEMALA		108 890	42 043	12 347 000	Guatemala City	Spanish, Mayan languages	Roman Catholic, Protestant	Quetzal, United States dollar	www.congreso.gob.gt
HAITI		27 750	10 714	8 326 000	Port-au-Prince	French, creole	Roman Catholic, Protestant, Voodoo	Gourde	www.haiti.org
HONDURAS		112 088	43 277	6 941 000	Tegucigalpa	Spanish, Amerindian languages	Roman Catholic, Protestant	Lempira	www.congreso.gob.hn
JAMAICA		10 991	4 244	2 651 000	Kingston	English, creole	Protestant, Roman Catholic	Jamaican dollar	www.jis.gov.jm
MEXICO		1 972 545	761 604	103 457 000	Mexico City	Spanish, Amerindian languages	Roman Catholic, Protestant	Mexican peso	www.presidencia.gob.mx
NICARAGUA		130 000	50 193	5 466 000	Managua	Spanish, Amerindian languages	Roman Catholic, Protestant	Córdoba	www.asamblea.gob.ni
PANAMA		77 082	29 762	3 120 000	Panama City	Spanish, English, Amerindian languages	Roman Catholic, Protestant, Sunni Muslim	Balboa	www.pa
ST KITTS AND NEVIS		261	101	42 000	Basseterre	English, creole	Protestant, Roman Catholic	East Caribbean dollar	www.stkittsnevis.net
ST LUCIA		616	238	149 000	Castries	English, creole	Roman Catholic, Protestant	East Caribbean dollar	www.stlucia.gov.lc
ST VINCENT AND THE GRENADINES		389	150	120 000	Kingstown	English, creole	Protestant, Roman Catholic	East Caribbean dollar	www.odci.gov/cia/publications/factbook
TRINIDAD AND TOBAGO		5 130	1 981	1 303 000	Port of Spain	English, creole, Hindi	Roman Catholic, Hindu, Protestant, Sunni Muslim	Trinidad and Tobago dollar	www.gov.tt
UNITED STATES OF AMERICA		9 826 635	3 794 085	294 043 000	Washington D.C.	English, Spanish	Protestant, Roman Catholic, Sunni Muslim, Jewish	United States dollar	www.firstgov.gov

South America		Area sq km	Area sq miles	Population	Capital	Languages	Religions	Currency	Internet link
ARGENTINA		2 766 889	1 068 302	38 428 000	Buenos Aires	Spanish, Italian, Amerindian languages	Roman Catholic, Protestant	Argentinian peso	www.info.gov.ar
BOLIVIA		1 098 581	424 164	8 808 000	La Paz/Sucre	Spanish, Quechua, Aymara	Roman Catholic, Protestant, Baha'i	Boliviano	www.bolivia.gov.bo
BRAZIL		8 514 879	3 287 613	178 470 000	Brasília	Portuguese	Roman Catholic, Protestant	Real	www.brazil.gov.br
CHILE		756 945	292 258	15 805 000	Santiago	Spanish, Amerindian languages	Roman Catholic, Protestant	Chilean peso	www.gobiernodechile.cl
COLOMBIA		1 141 748	440 831	44 222 000	Bogotá	Spanish, Amerindian languages	Roman Catholic, Protestant	Colombian peso	www.gobiernoenlinea.gov.co
ECUADOR		272 045	105 037	13 003 000	Quito	Spanish, Quechua, other Amerindian languages	Roman Catholic	US dollar	www.ec-gov.net
GUYANA		214 969	83 000	765 000	Georgetown	English, creole, Amerindian languages	Protestant, Hindu, Roman Catholic, Sunni Muslim	Guyana dollar	www.gina.gov.gy
PARAGUAY		406 752	157 048	5 878 000	Asunción	Spanish, Guaraní	Roman Catholic, Protestant	Guaraní	www.presidencia.gov.py
PERU		1 285 216	496 225	27 167 000	Lima	Spanish, Quechua, Aymara	Roman Catholic, Protestant	Sol	www.peru.gob.pe
SURINAME		163 820	63 251	436 000	Paramaribo	Dutch, Surinamese, English, Hindi	Hindu, Roman Catholic, Protestant, Sunni Muslim	Suriname guilder	www.kabinet.sr.org
URUGUAY		176 215	68 037	3 415 000	Montevideo	Spanish	Roman Catholic, Protestant, Jewish	Uruguayan peso	www.presidencia.gub.uy
VENEZUELA		912 050	352 144	25 699 000	Caracas	Spanish, Amerindian languages	Roman Catholic, Protestant	Bolívar	www.gobiernoenlinea.ve

National Statistics

World extremes

Countries				Capitals	
Largest country (area)	**Russian Federation**	17 075 400 sq km	6 592 849 sq miles	Largest national capital (population)	*Tōkyō, Japan*
Smallest country (area)	**Vatican City**	0.5 sq km	0.2 sq miles	Smallest national capital (population)	**Vatican City**
Largest country (population)	**China**	1 289 161 000		Most northerly national capital	**Reykjavík, Iceland**
Smallest country (population)	**Vatican City**	472		Most southerly national capital	**Wellington, New Zealan**
Most densely populated country	**Monaco**	17 000 per sq km	34 000 per sq mile	Highest national capital	**La Paz, Bolivia**
Least densely populated country	**Mongolia**	2 per sq km	4 per sq mile		

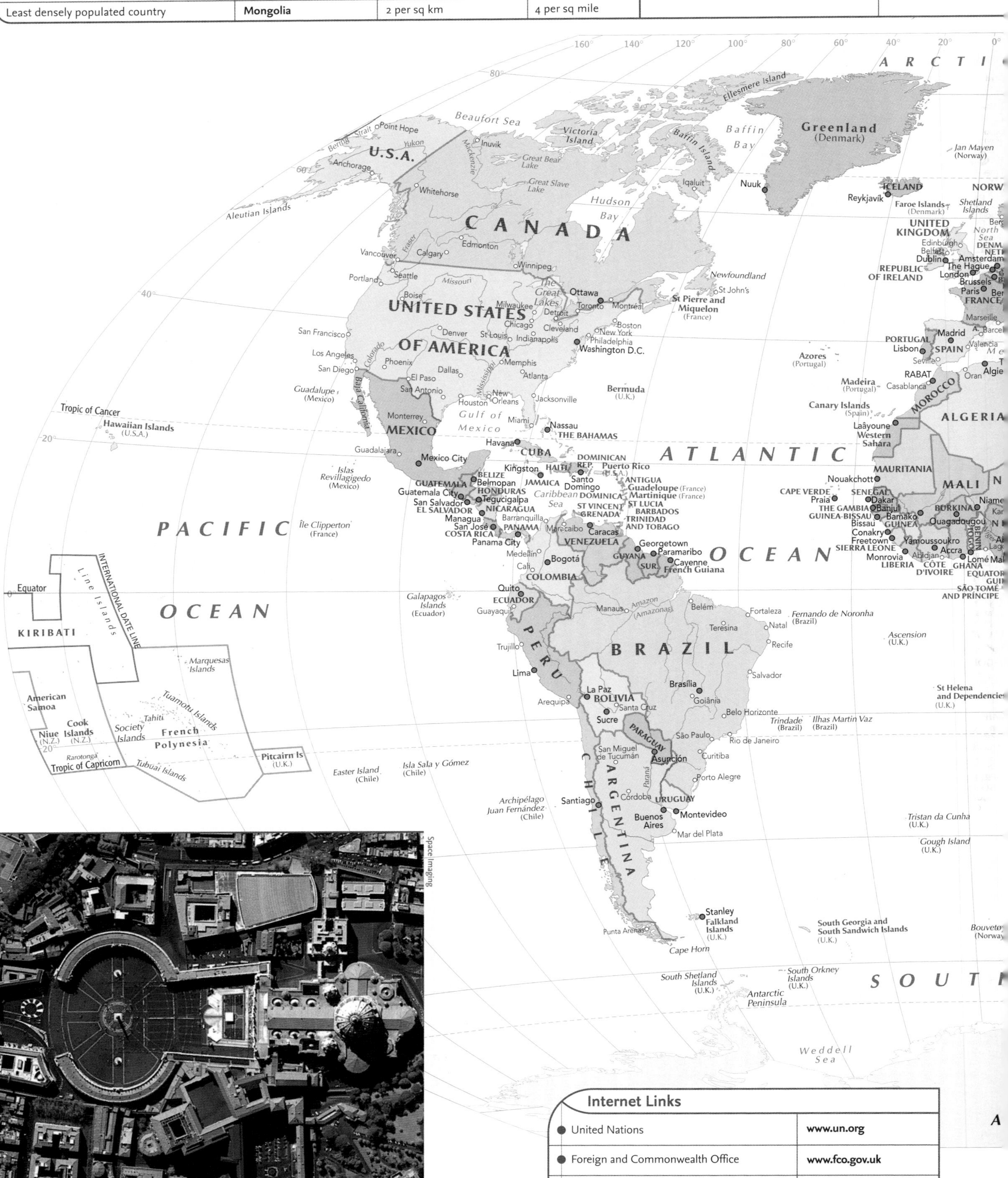

High-resolution satellite image of **Vatican City**, the world's smallest country by both population and area.

Internet Links

United Nations	**www.un.org**
Foreign and Commonwealth Office	**www.fco.gov.uk**
International Boundaries Research Unit	**www.ibru.dur.ac.uk**
Permanent Committee on Geographic Names	**www.pcgn.org.uk**
United States Board on Geographic Names	**geonames.usgs.gov**

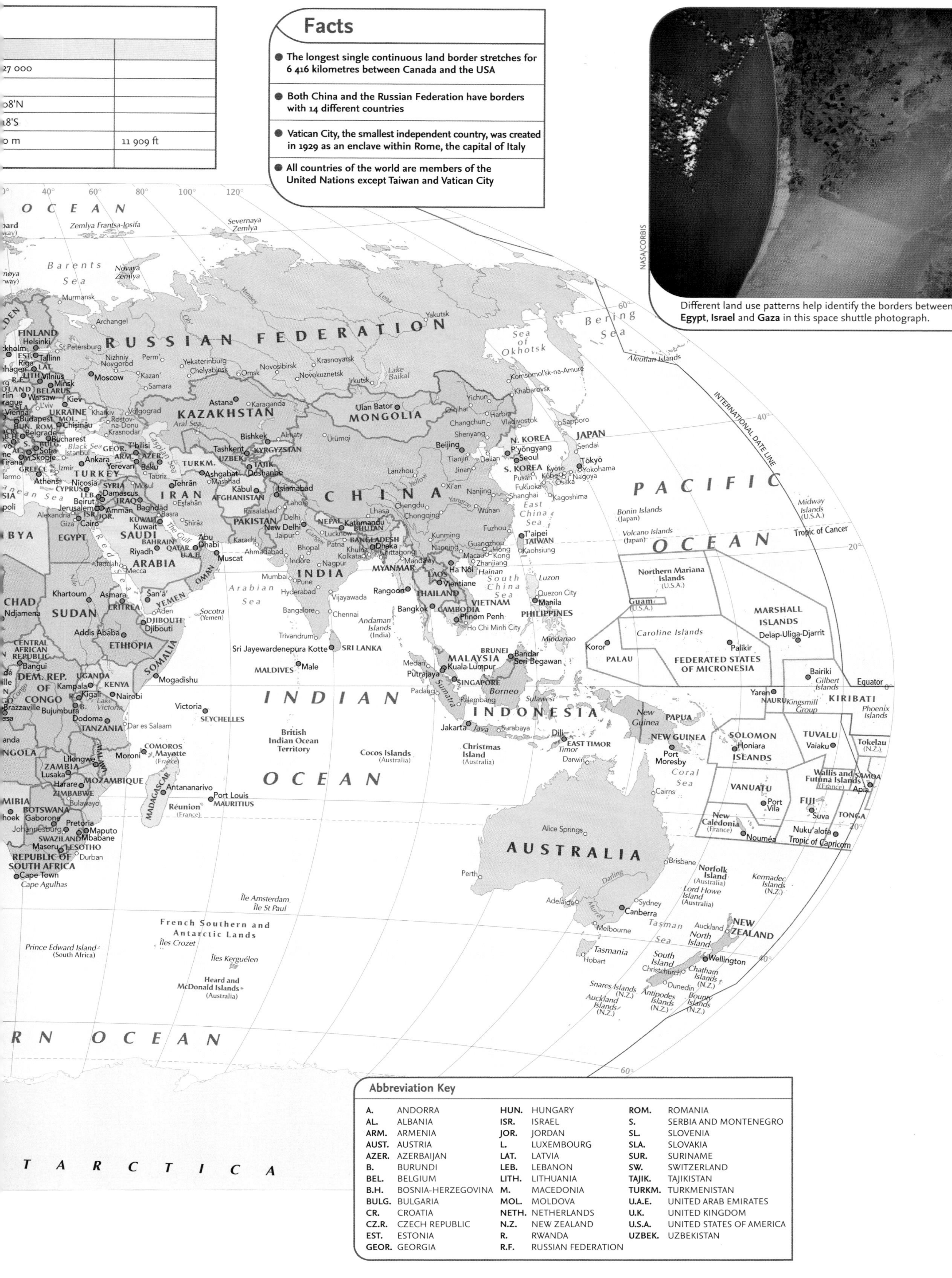

Facts

- The longest single continuous land border stretches for 6 416 kilometres between Canada and the USA
- Both China and the Russian Federation have borders with 14 different countries
- Vatican City, the smallest independent country, was created in 1929 as an enclave within Rome, the capital of Italy
- All countries of the world are members of the United Nations except Taiwan and Vatican City

NASA/CORBIS

Different land use patterns help identify the borders between **Egypt**, **Israel** and **Gaza** in this space shuttle photograph.

Abbreviation Key

A.	ANDORRA	HUN.	HUNGARY	ROM.	ROMANIA
AL.	ALBANIA	ISR.	ISRAEL	S.	SERBIA AND MONTENEGRO
ARM.	ARMENIA	JOR.	JORDAN	SL.	SLOVENIA
AUST.	AUSTRIA	L.	LUXEMBOURG	SLA.	SLOVAKIA
AZER.	AZERBAIJAN	LAT.	LATVIA	SUR.	SURINAME
B.	BURUNDI	LEB.	LEBANON	SW.	SWITZERLAND
BEL.	BELGIUM	LITH.	LITHUANIA	TAJIK.	TAJIKISTAN
B.H.	BOSNIA-HERZEGOVINA	M.	MACEDONIA	TURKM.	TURKMENISTAN
BULG.	BULGARIA	MOL.	MOLDOVA	U.A.E.	UNITED ARAB EMIRATES
CR.	CROATIA	NETH.	NETHERLANDS	U.K.	UNITED KINGDOM
CZ.R.	CZECH REPUBLIC	N.Z.	NEW ZEALAND	U.S.A.	UNITED STATES OF AMERICA
EST.	ESTONIA	R.	RWANDA	UZBEK.	UZBEKISTAN
GEOR.	GEORGIA	R.F.	RUSSIAN FEDERATION		

World Countries

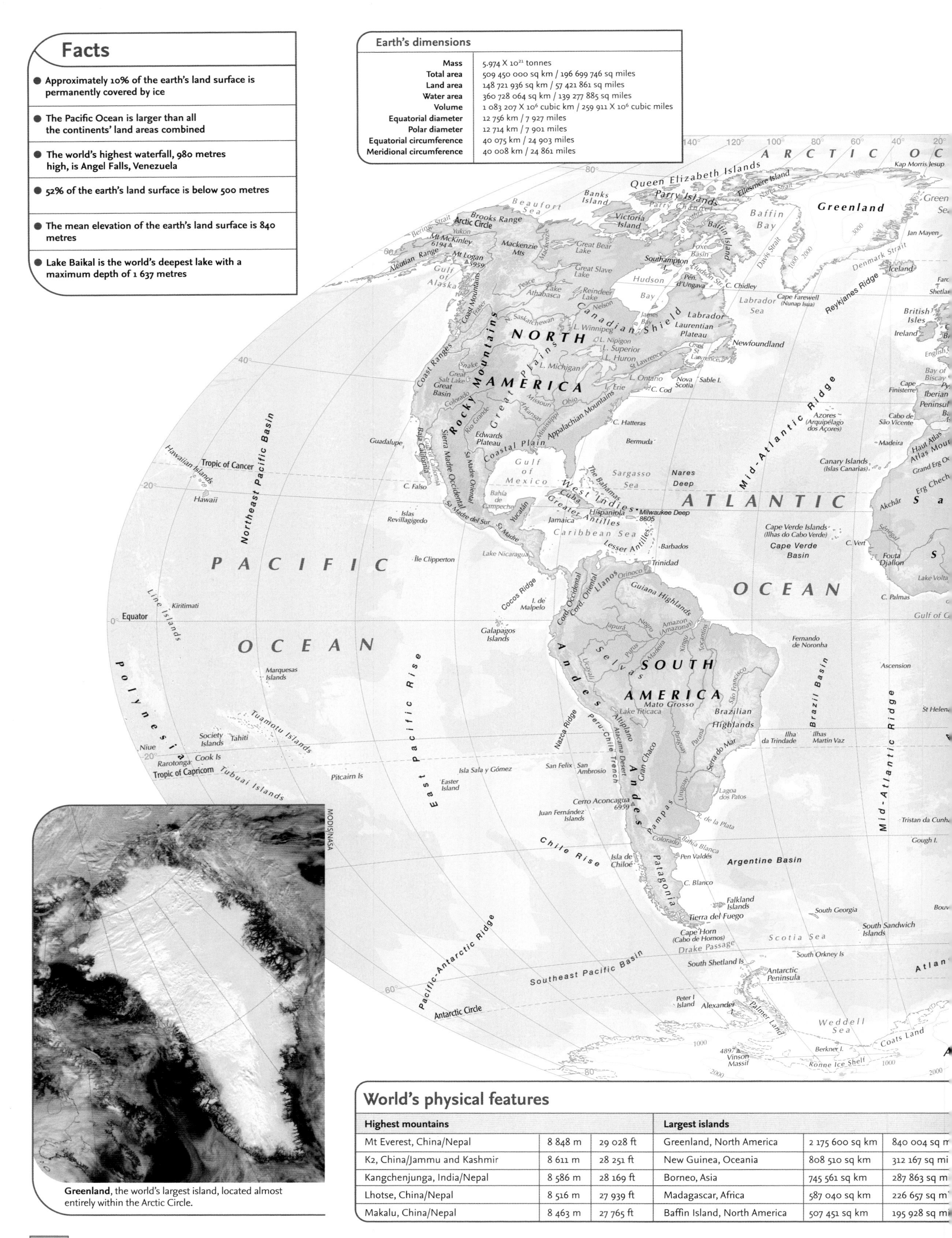

Facts

- Approximately 10% of the earth's land surface is permanently covered by ice

- The Pacific Ocean is larger than all the continents' land areas combined

- The world's highest waterfall, 980 metres high, is Angel Falls, Venezuela

- 52% of the earth's land surface is below 500 metres

- The mean elevation of the earth's land surface is 840 metres

- Lake Baikal is the world's deepest lake with a maximum depth of 1 637 metres

Earth's dimensions

Mass	5.974 X 10²¹ tonnes
Total area	509 450 000 sq km / 196 699 746 sq miles
Land area	148 721 936 sq km / 57 421 861 sq miles
Water area	360 728 064 sq km / 139 277 885 sq miles
Volume	1 083 207 X 10⁶ cubic km / 259 911 X 10⁶ cubic miles
Equatorial diameter	12 756 km / 7 927 miles
Polar diameter	12 714 km / 7 901 miles
Equatorial circumference	40 075 km / 24 903 miles
Meridional circumference	40 008 km / 24 861 miles

Greenland, the world's largest island, located almost entirely within the Arctic Circle.

World's physical features

Highest mountains			Largest islands		
Mt Everest, China/Nepal	8 848 m	29 028 ft	Greenland, North America	2 175 600 sq km	840 004 sq m
K2, China/Jammu and Kashmir	8 611 m	28 251 ft	New Guinea, Oceania	808 510 sq km	312 167 sq mi
Kangchenjunga, India/Nepal	8 586 m	28 169 ft	Borneo, Asia	745 561 sq km	287 863 sq m
Lhotse, China/Nepal	8 516 m	27 939 ft	Madagascar, Africa	587 040 sq km	226 657 sq m
Makalu, China/Nepal	8 463 m	27 765 ft	Baffin Island, North America	507 451 sq km	195 928 sq m

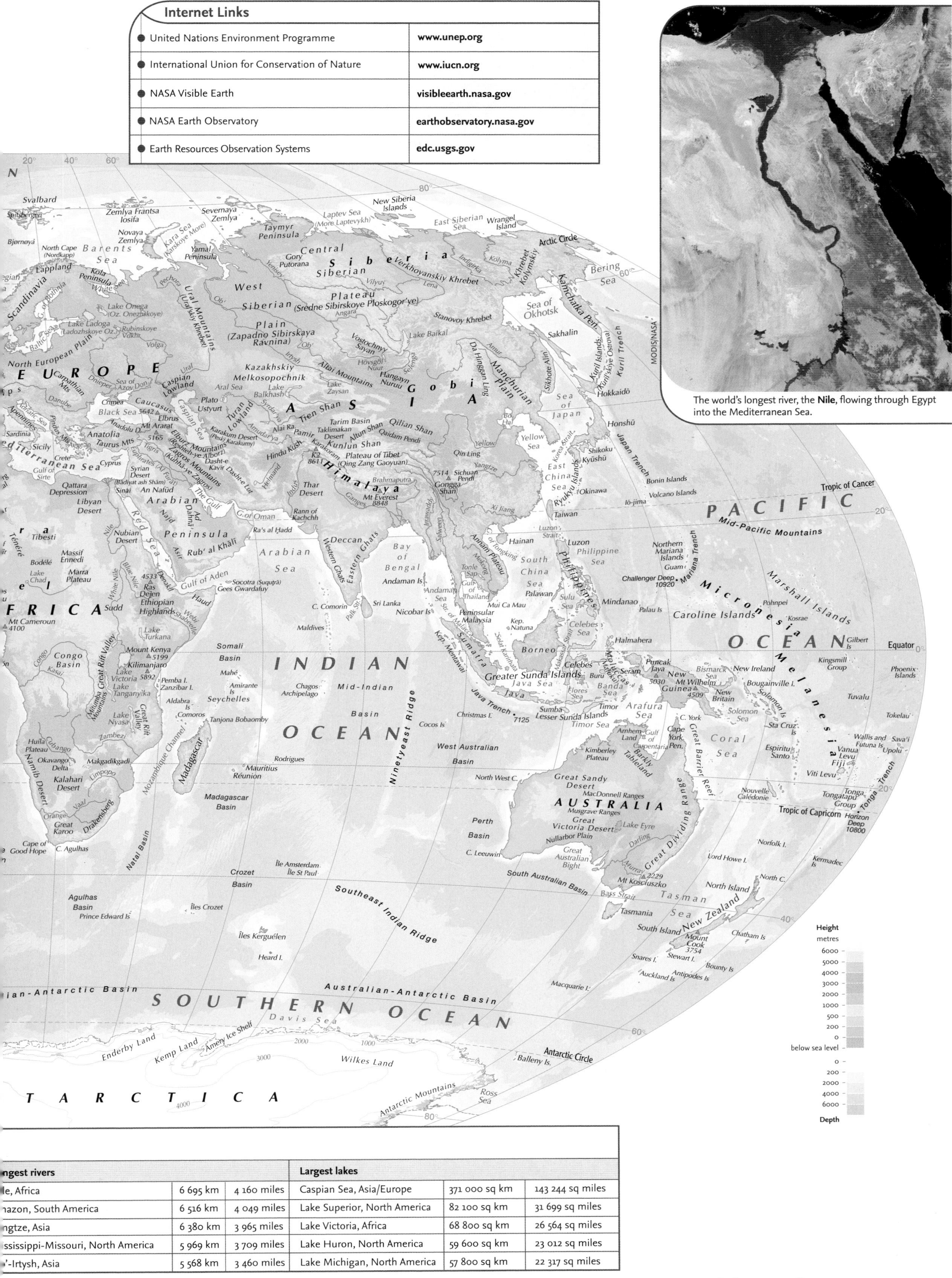

Internet Links	
● United Nations Environment Programme	www.unep.org
● International Union for Conservation of Nature	www.iucn.org
● NASA Visible Earth	visibleearth.nasa.gov
● NASA Earth Observatory	earthobservatory.nasa.gov
● Earth Resources Observation Systems	edc.usgs.gov

MODIS/NASA

The world's longest river, the **Nile**, flowing through Egypt into the Mediterranean Sea.

Height

metres

6000
5000
4000
3000
2000
1000
500
200

below sea level

0

200
2000
4000
6000

Depth

Largest rivers			Largest lakes		
Nile, Africa	6 695 km	4 160 miles	Caspian Sea, Asia/Europe	371 000 sq km	143 244 sq miles
Amazon, South America	6 516 km	4 049 miles	Lake Superior, North America	82 100 sq km	31 699 sq miles
Yangtze, Asia	6 380 km	3 965 miles	Lake Victoria, Africa	68 800 sq km	26 564 sq miles
Mississippi-Missouri, North America	5 969 km	3 709 miles	Lake Huron, North America	59 600 sq km	23 012 sq miles
Ob'-Irtysh, Asia	5 568 km	3 460 miles	Lake Michigan, North America	57 800 sq km	22 317 sq miles

World Landscapes

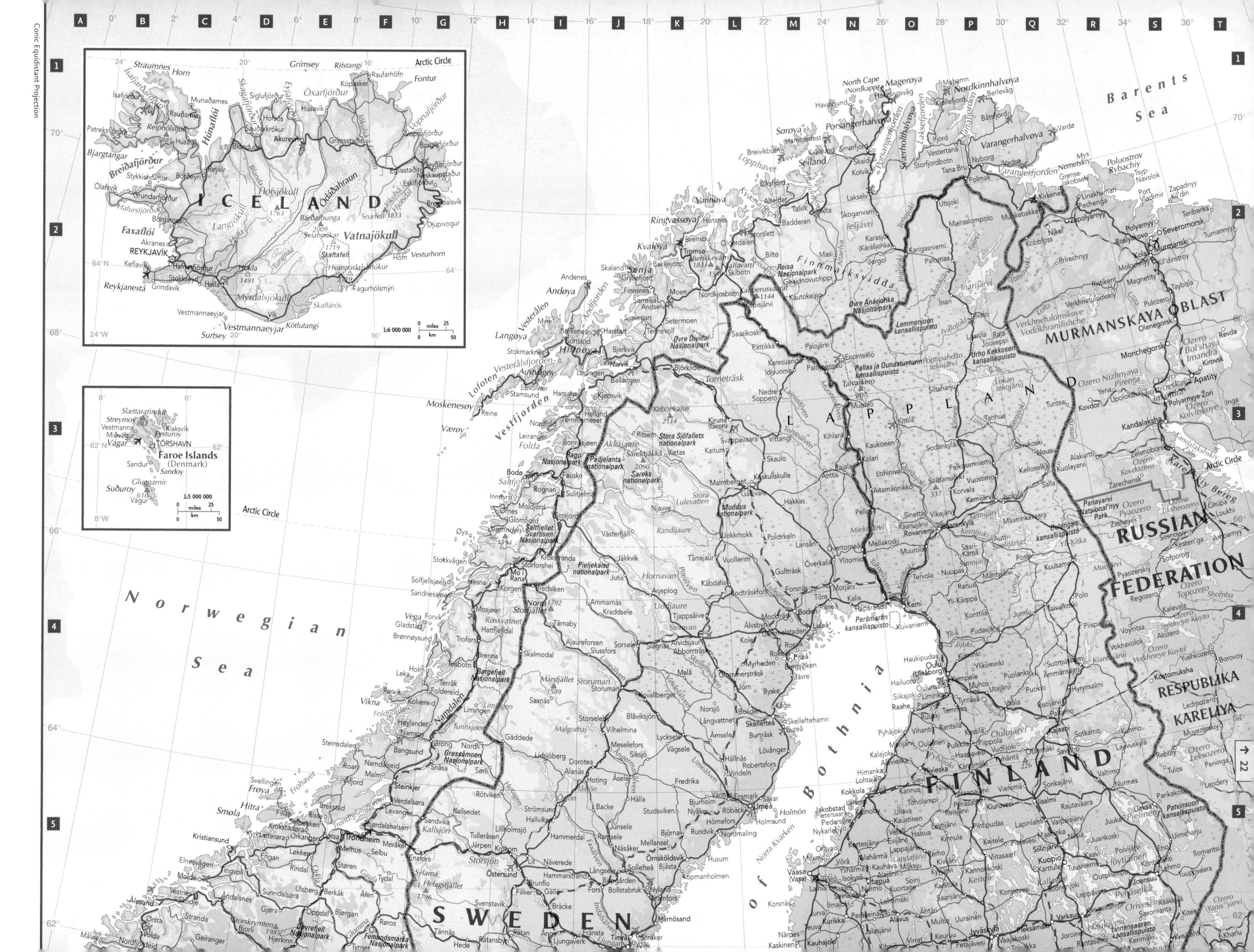

Conic Equidistant Projection

10   1:5 000 000

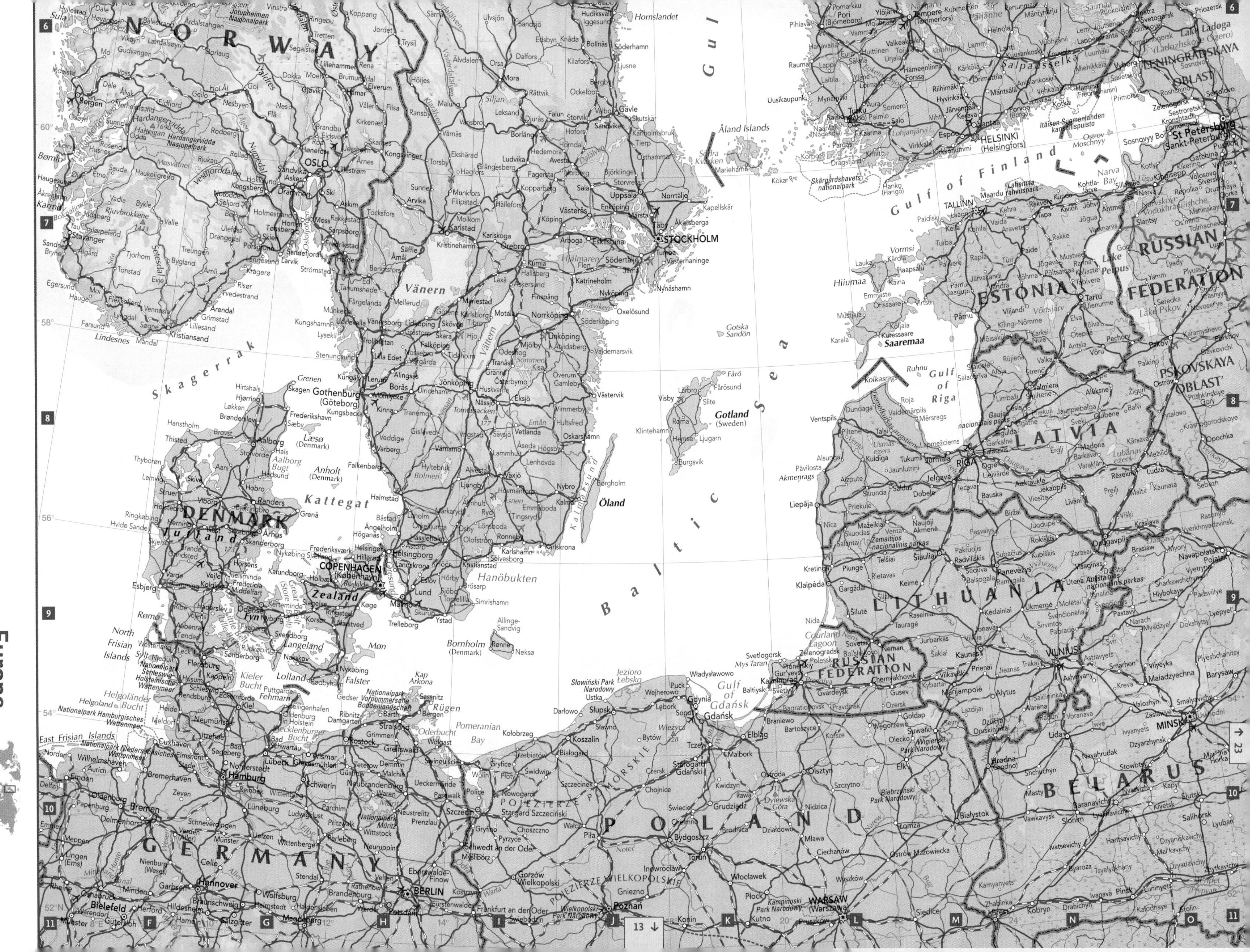

Europe

Scandinavia and the Baltic States

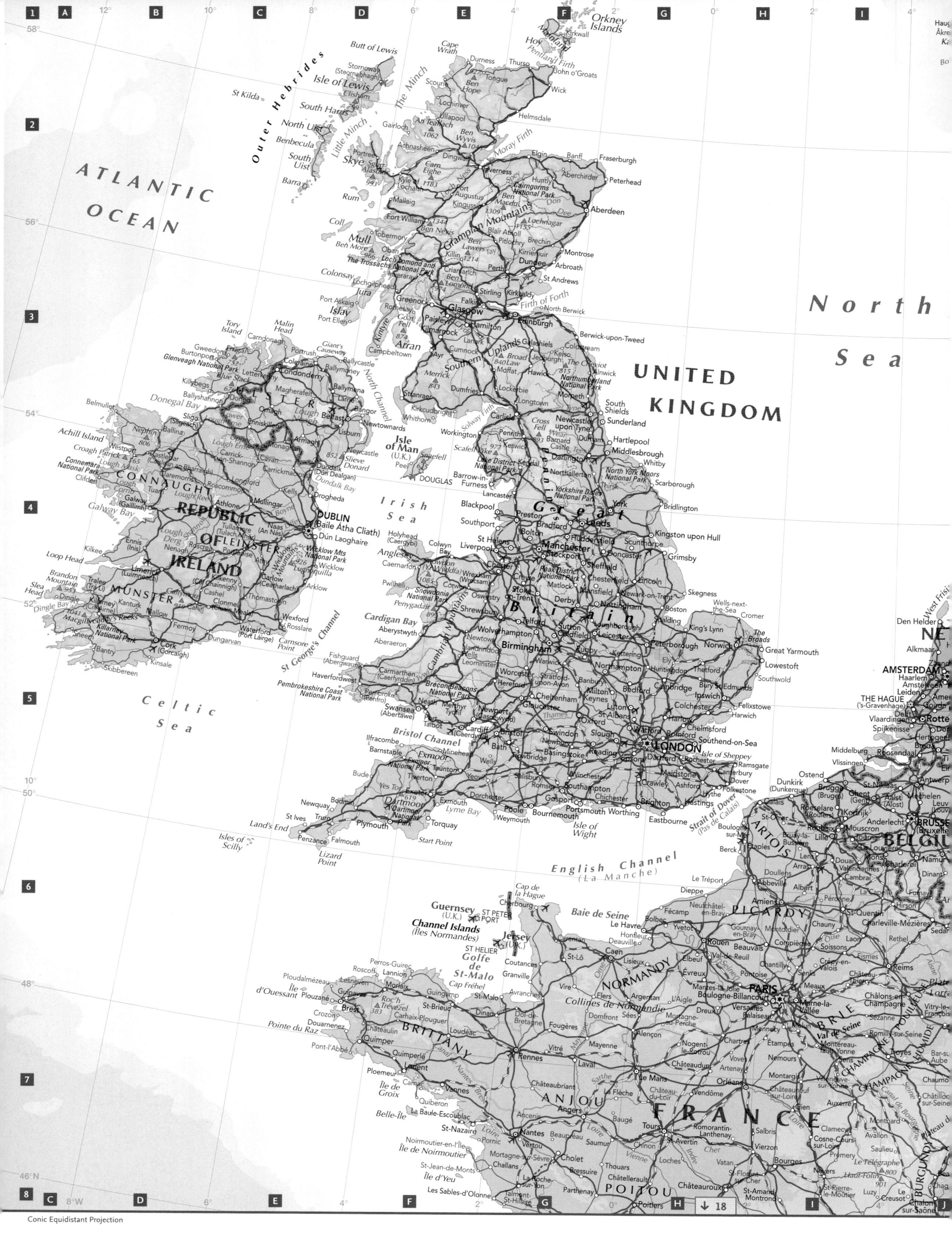
ATLANTIC OCEAN
North Sea
UNITED KINGDOM
Great Britain
REPUBLIC OF IRELAND
FRANCE
Celtic Sea
Irish Sea
English Channel (La Manche)
St George's Channel
Bristol Channel
Cardigan Bay
North Channel
The Minch
Little Minch
Outer Hebrides
Orkney Islands
Isle of Lewis
South Harris
North Uist
Benbecula
South Uist
Barra
Skye
Rum
Coll
Mull
Colonsay
Jura
Islay
Arran
Kintyre
St Kilda
Isle of Man (U.K.)
DOUGLAS
Anglesey
Isles of Scilly
Isle of Wight
Guernsey (U.K.)
Jersey (U.K.)
Channel Islands (Îles Normandes)
ST PETER PORT
ST HELIER
Golfe de St-Malo
Baie de Seine
Strait of Dover (Pas de Calais)
Grampian Mountains
Southern Uplands
Cambrian Mountains
Pennines
Cairngorms National Park
Loch Lomond and The Trossachs National Park
Lake District National Park
Snowdonia National Park
Brecon Beacons National Park
Pembrokeshire Coast National Park
Exmoor National Park
Dartmoor National Park
Peak District National Park
Yorkshire Dales National Park
North York Moors National Park
Northumberland National Park
Killarney National Park
Connemara National Park
Glenveagh National Park
Wicklow Mts National Park
ULSTER
CONNAUGHT
LEINSTER
MUNSTER
NORMANDY
BRITTANY
PICARDY
ARTOIS
ANJOU
POITOU
BRIE
CHAMPAGNE HUMIDE
CHAMPAGNE POUILLEUSE
BURGUNDY
Collines de Normandie
LONDON
DUBLIN (Baile Átha Cliath)
Dún Laoghaire
PARIS
AMSTERDAM
THE HAGUE ('s-Gravenhage)
Edinburgh
Glasgow
Aberdeen
Dundee
Inverness
Perth
Stirling
Belfast
Londonderry
Newcastle upon Tyne
Sunderland
Middlesbrough
Leeds
Bradford
York
Manchester
Liverpool
Sheffield
Kingston upon Hull
Nottingham
Leicester
Birmingham
Coventry
Peterborough
Norwich
Cambridge
Ipswich
Oxford
Reading
Bristol
Cardiff
Swansea
Newport
Plymouth
Exeter
Southampton
Portsmouth
Brighton
Bournemouth
Dover
Cork (Corcaigh)
Limerick (Luimneach)
Galway (Gaillimh)
Waterford (Port Láirge)
Wexford
Sligo (Sligeach)
Rennes
Nantes
Brest
Caen
Rouen
Le Havre
Le Mans
Tours
Orléans
Amiens
Lille
Calais
Boulogne-sur-Mer
Dunkirk (Dunkerque)
Cherbourg
BRUSSELS
Antwerp
Rotterdam
Conic Equidistant Projection
1:5 000 000
0 50 100 150 miles
0 50 100 150 200 250 km

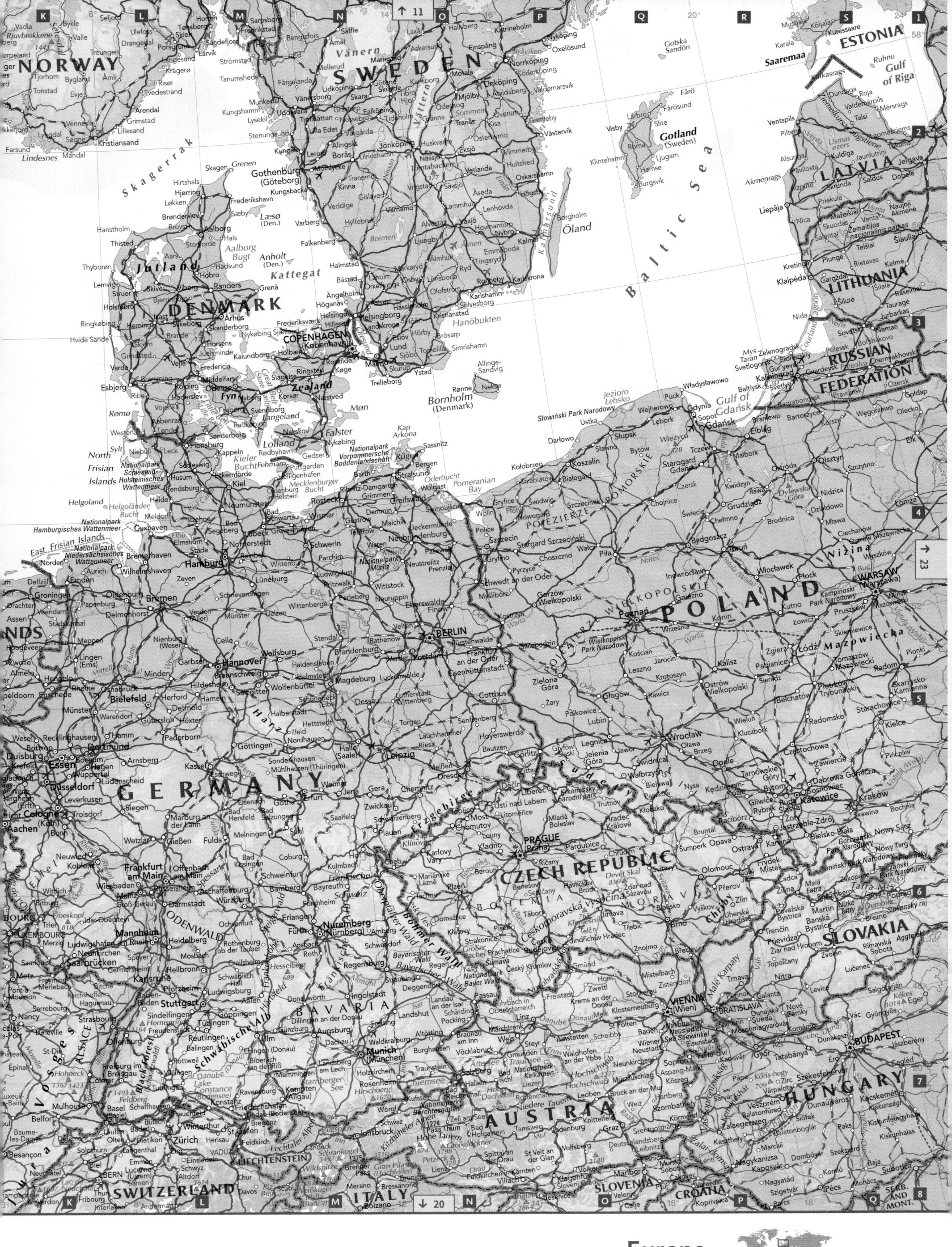

Europe
Northwest Europe

NORWAY
SWEDEN
DENMARK
GERMANY
POLAND
CZECH REPUBLIC
SLOVAKIA
AUSTRIA
HUNGARY
SWITZERLAND
LIECHTENSTEIN
SLOVENIA
CROATIA
ITALY
ESTONIA
LATVIA
LITHUANIA
RUSSIAN FEDERATION
Skagerrak
Kattegat
Baltic Sea
Gulf of Riga
Gulf of Gdańsk
Jutland
Zealand
Fyn
Gotland (Sweden)
Öland
Bornholm (Denmark)
Saaremaa
North Frisian Islands
East Frisian Islands
Helgoland
COPENHAGEN (København)
BERLIN
WARSAW (Warszawa)
PRAGUE (Praha)
VIENNA (Wien)
BRATISLAVA
BUDAPEST
BERN
VADUZ
Gothenburg (Göteborg)
Hamburg
Bremen
Hannover
Leipzig
Dresden
Munich (München)
Nuremberg (Nürnberg)
Frankfurt am Main
Cologne (Köln)
Stuttgart
Zürich
Poznań
Wrocław
Kraków
Gdańsk
Łódź
Szczecin
Bavaria
Bohemia
Harz
Sudety
Black Forest
↑ 11
↓ 20
→ 23

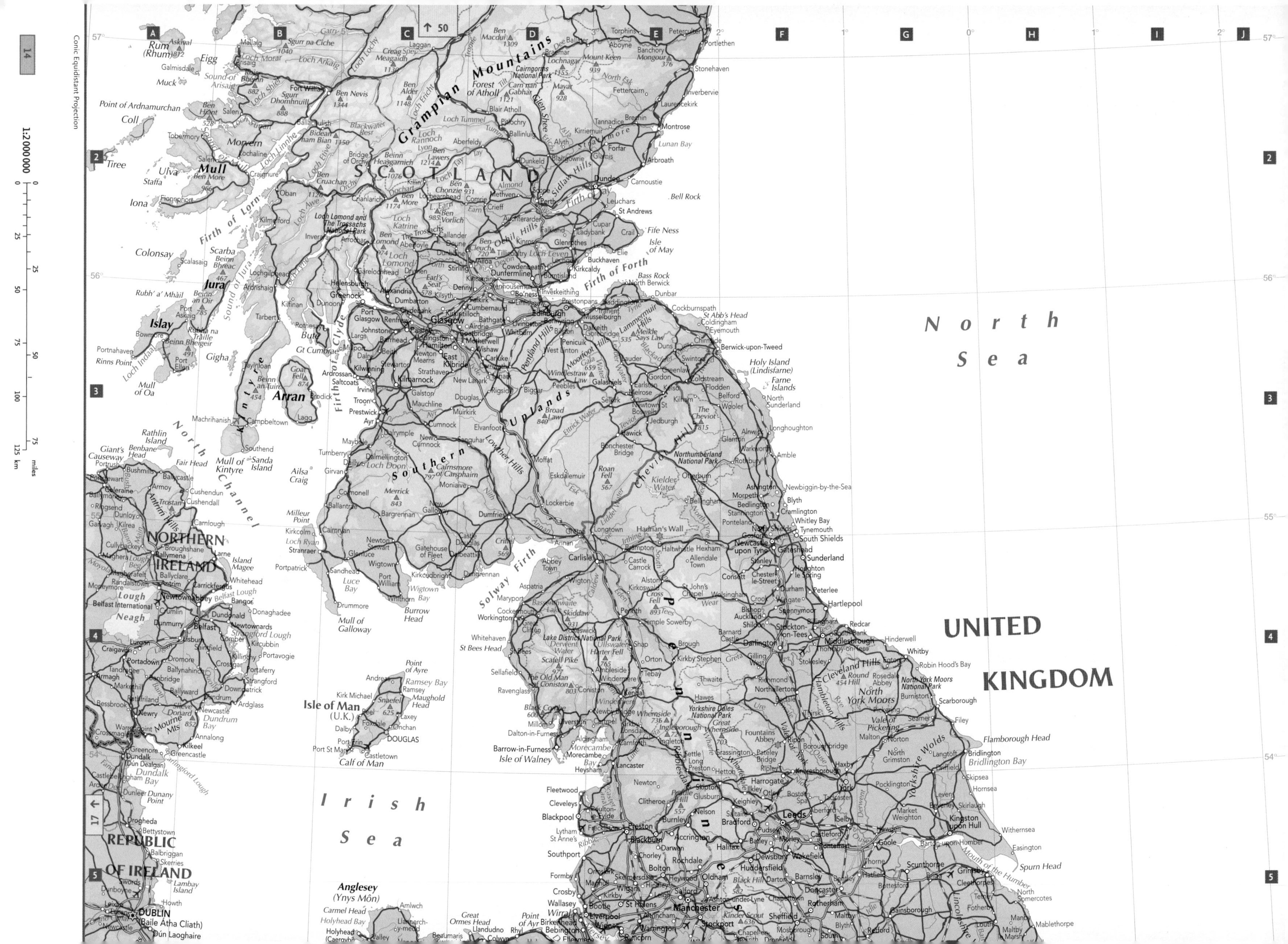
North Sea
Irish Sea
UNITED KINGDOM
SCOTLAND
NORTHERN IRELAND
REPUBLIC OF IRELAND
Grampian Mountains
Southern Uplands
Pennines
Cheviot Hills
North Channel
Firth of Forth
Firth of Clyde
Firth of Lorn
Solway Firth
Isle of Man (U.K.)
DOUGLAS
DUBLIN
Baile Átha Cliath
Edinburgh
Glasgow
Dundee
Newcastle upon Tyne
Sunderland
Middlesbrough
Leeds
Bradford
Manchester
Liverpool
Sheffield
Belfast
Carlisle
Kingston upon Hull
York
Lancaster
Blackpool
Arran
Islay
Jura
Mull
Anglesey (Ynys Môn)
Lough Neagh
Kintyre
Flamborough Head
Spurn Head
Yorkshire Wolds
North York Moors
Lake District National Park
Northumberland National Park
Yorkshire Dales National Park
Conic Equidistant Projection
1:2 000 000
miles
km

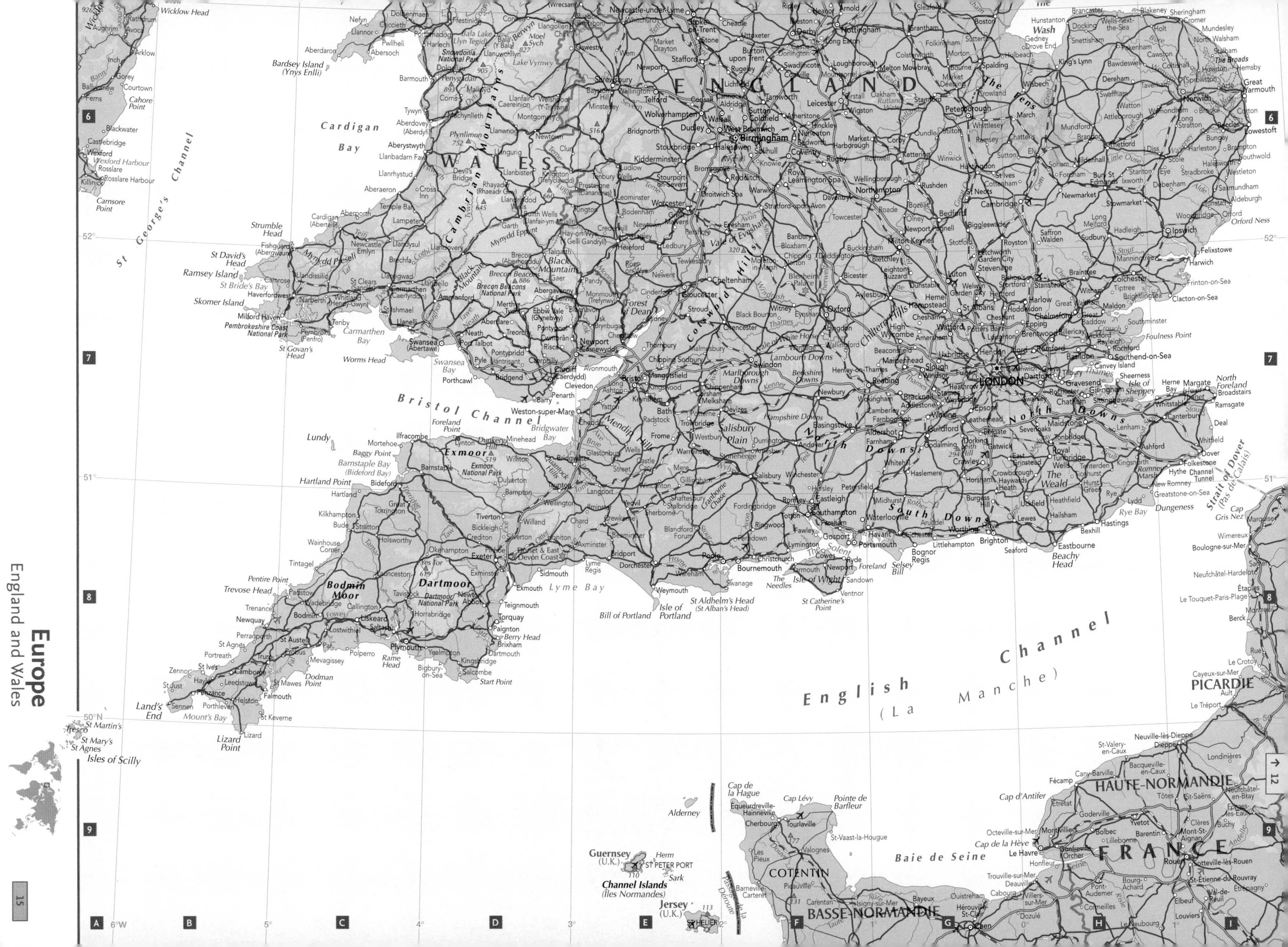

Europe
England and Wales

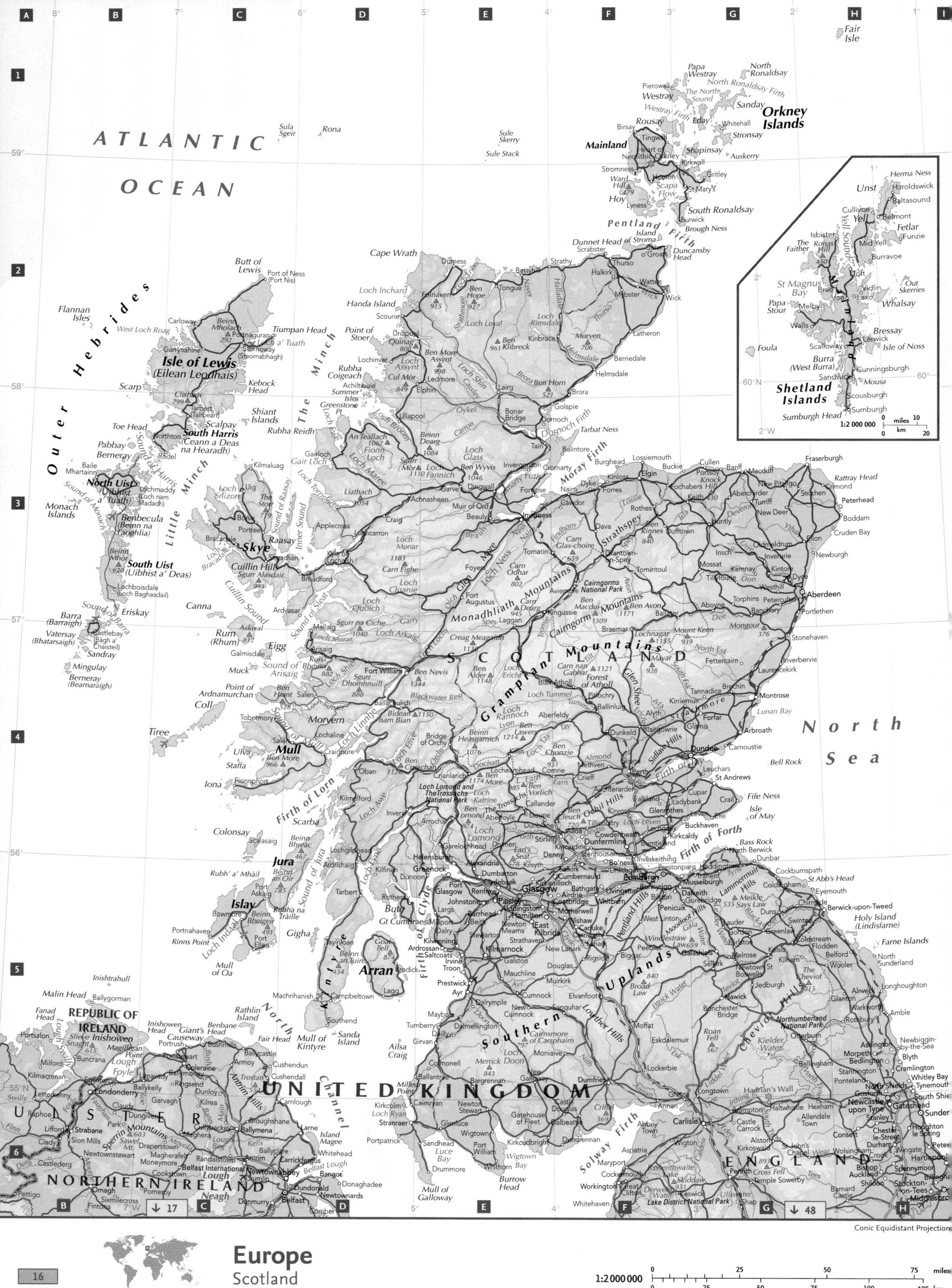

Europe
Scotland

Conic Equidistant Projection

1:2 000 000

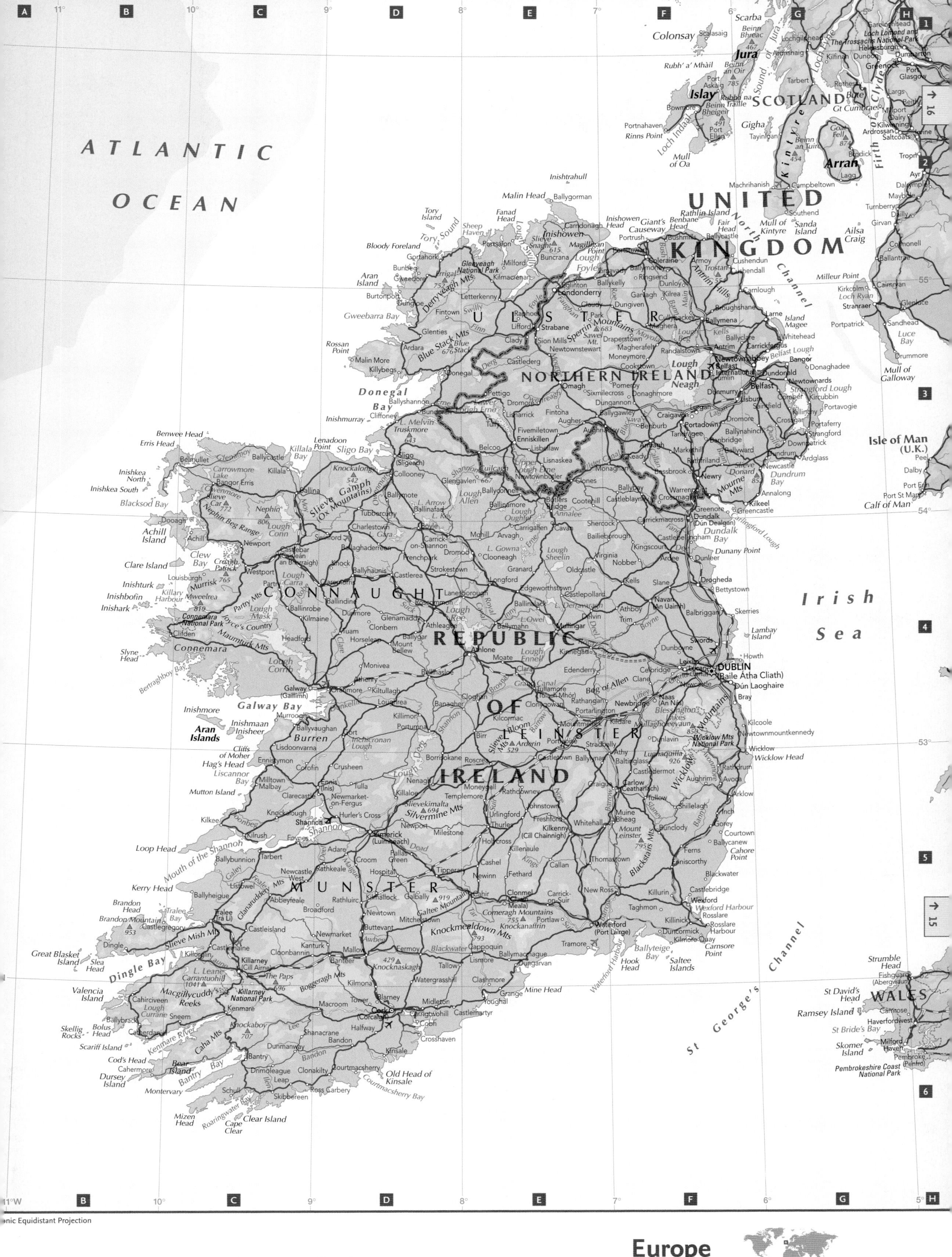

ATLANTIC

OCEAN

SCOTLAND

UNITED

KINGDOM

ULSTER

NORTHERN IRELAND

CONNAUGHT

REPUBLIC

OF

LEINSTER

IRELAND

MUNSTER

DUBLIN
(Baile Átha Cliath)

Irish

Sea

Isle of Man
(U.K.)

WALES

St George's Channel

Conic Equidistant Projection

1:2 000 000

0   25   50   75 miles

0   25   50   75 100 125 km

Europe
Ireland

17

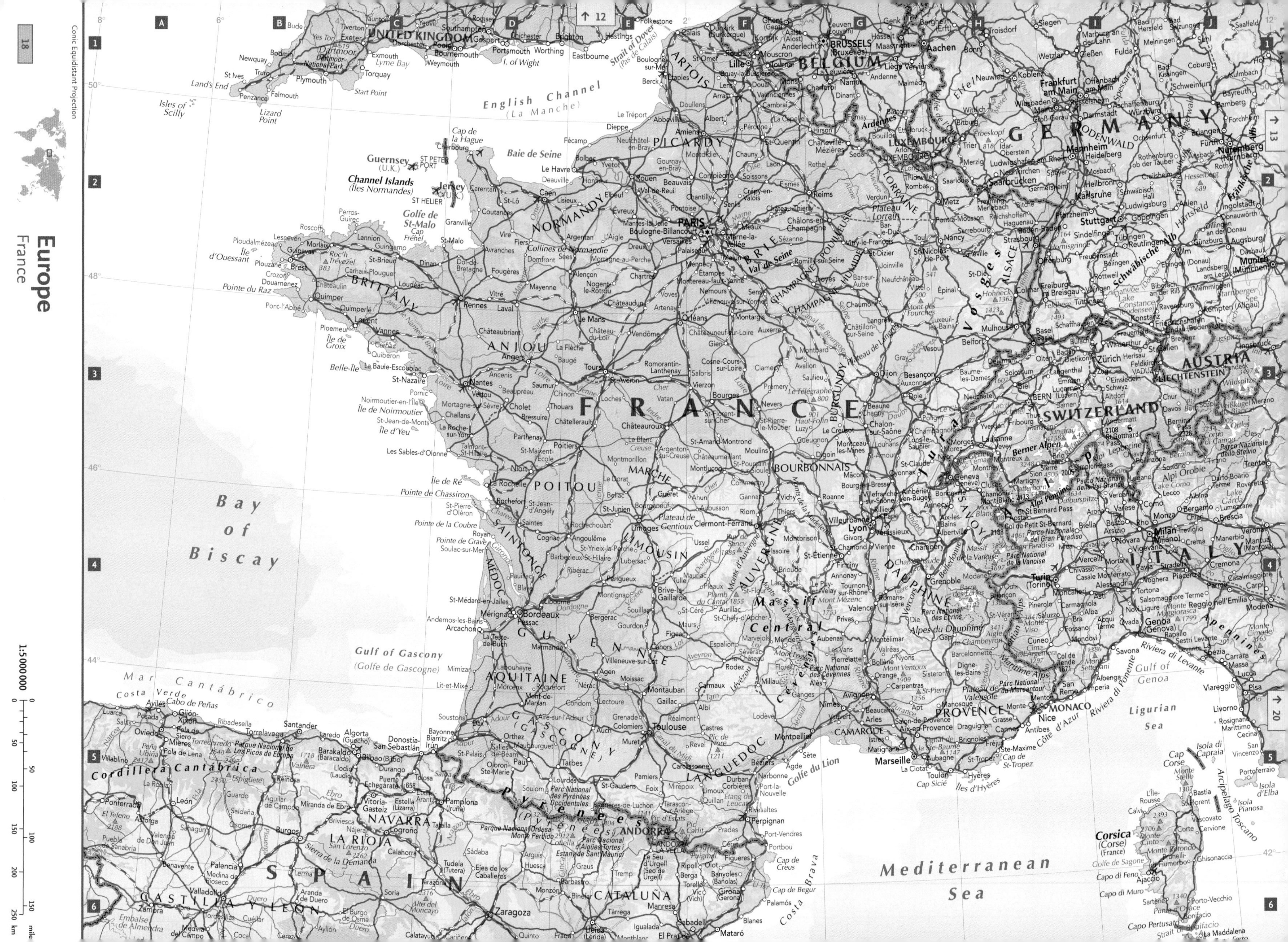

Europe
France

Conic Equidistant Projection

1:5 000 000

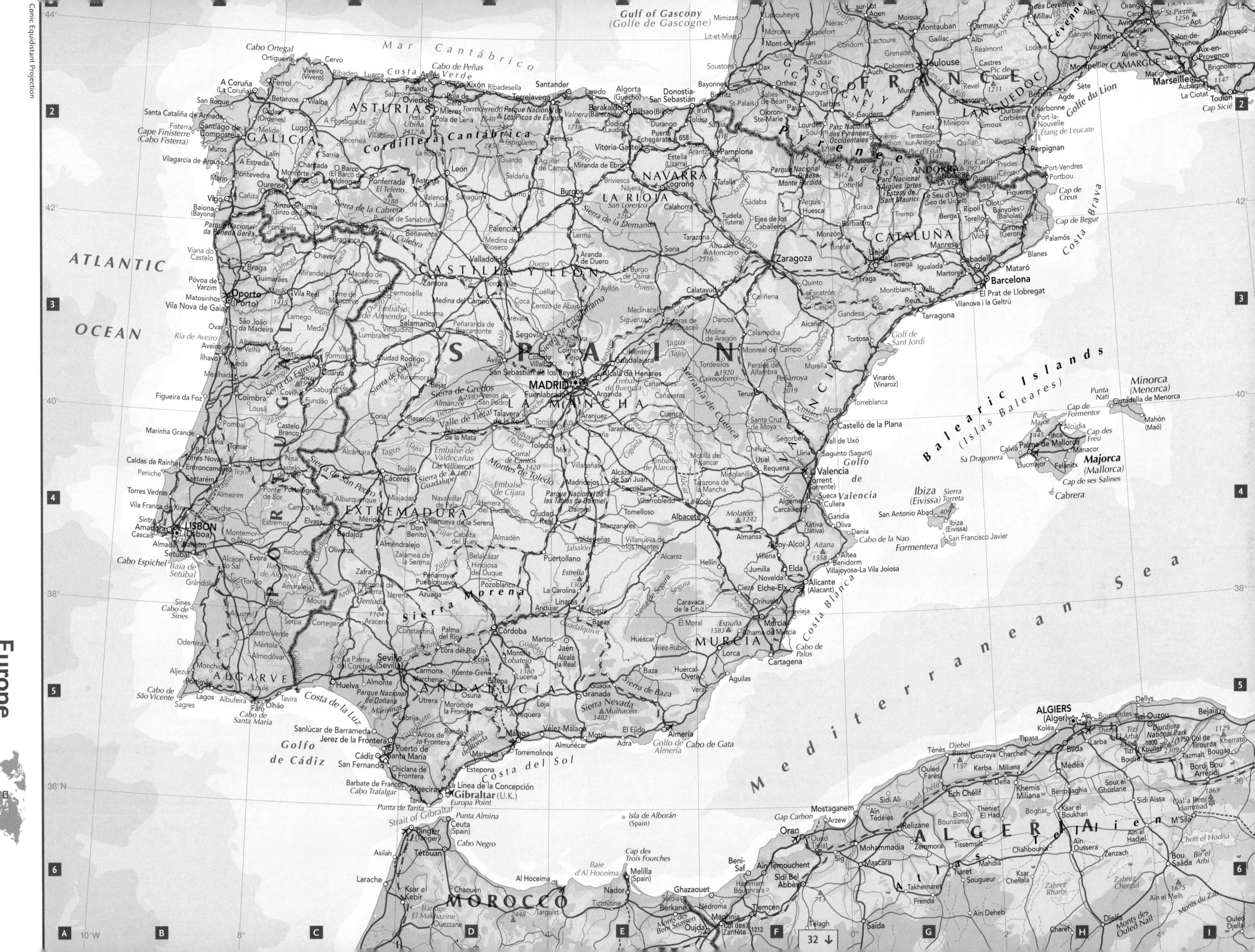

Europe
Spain and Portugal

Conic Equidistant Projection

1:5 000 000

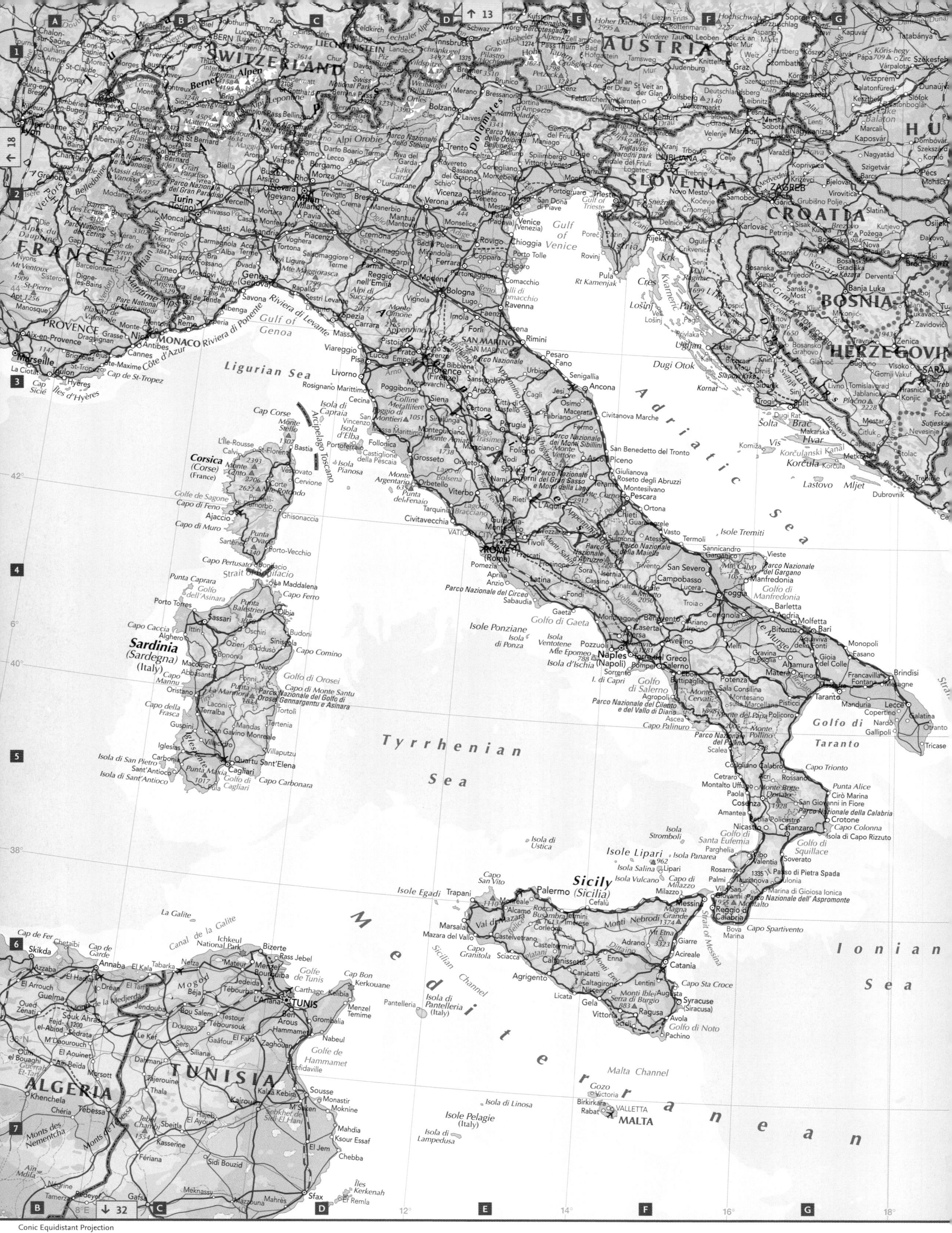

Conic Equidistant Projection

1:5 000 000

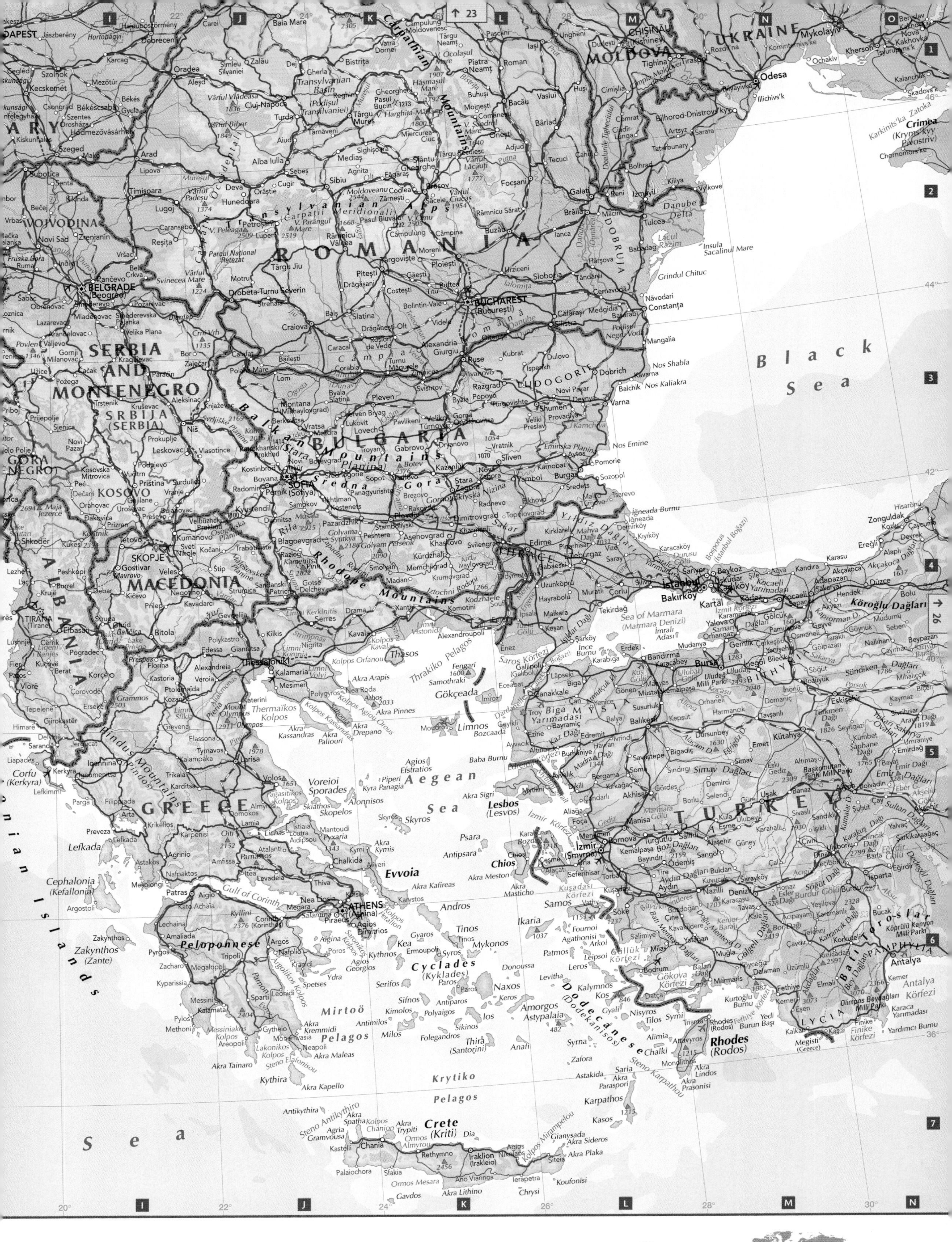

↑ 23
→ 26
UKRAINE
MOLDOVA
ROMANIA
BULGARIA
SERBIA AND MONTENEGRO
SRBIJA (SERBIA)
VOJVODINA
KOSOVO
MACEDONIA
ALBANIA
GREECE
TURKEY
THRACE
DOBRUJA
LUDOGORIE
BITHYNIA
LYCIA
PAMPHYLIA
Black Sea
Aegean Sea
Sea of Marmara (Marmara Denizi)
Ionian Islands
Krytiko Pelagos
Mirtoö Pelagos
Carpathian Mountains
Transylvanian Alps (Carpații Meridionali)
Transylvanian Basin (Podișul Transilvaniei)
Balkan Mountains (Stara Planina)
Rhodope Mountains
Sredna Gora
Pindus Mountains
Danube Delta
Crimea (Kryms'kyy Pivostriv)
Chișinău (Kishinev)
Odesa
Mykolayiv
Kherson
Iași
Cluj-Napoca
Timișoara
Brașov
Galați
Brăila
Constanța
Ploiești
BUCHAREST (București)
Craiova
Pitești
Sibiu
Oradea
Arad
Debrecen
Szeged
BELGRADE (Beograd)
Novi Sad
Niš
Priština
SKOPJE
TIRANA (Tiranë)
Shkodër
Durrës
Vlorë
SOFIA (Sofiya)
Plovdiv
Ruse
Pleven
Varna
Burgas
Stara Zagora
Thessaloniki
Larisa
Volos
Patras
ATHENS (Athina)
Piraeus
Corfu (Kerkyra)
Lefkada
Cephalonia (Kefallonia)
Zakynthos (Zante)
Peloponnese
Evvoia
Lesbos (Lesvos)
Chios
Samos
Ikaria
Cyclades (Kyklades)
Dodecanese (Dodekanisos)
Rhodes (Rodos)
Karpathos
Crete (Kriti)
Chania
Iraklion (Irakleio)
Kythira
Thasos
Limnos
Gökçeada
Edirne
İstanbul
Bursa
İzmir (Smyrna)
Manisa
Balıkesir
Kütahya
Eskişehir
Uşak
Denizli
Aydın
Antalya
Isparta
Çanakkale
Tekirdağ
Zonguldak
Sea

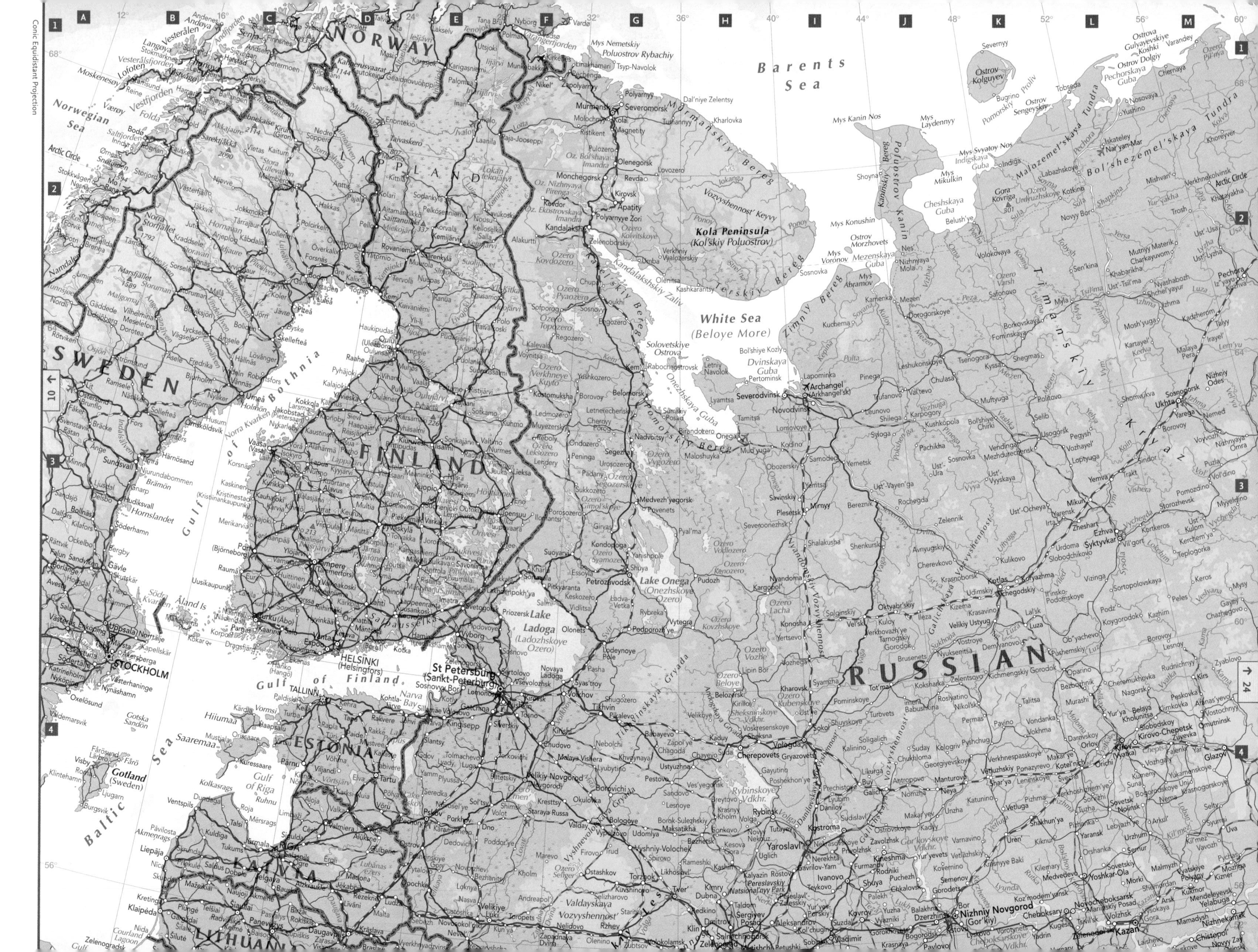

Conic Equidistant Projection

1:7 500 000

| 0 | 100 | 200 | 300 miles |

| 0 | 100 | 200 | 300 | 400 | 500 km |

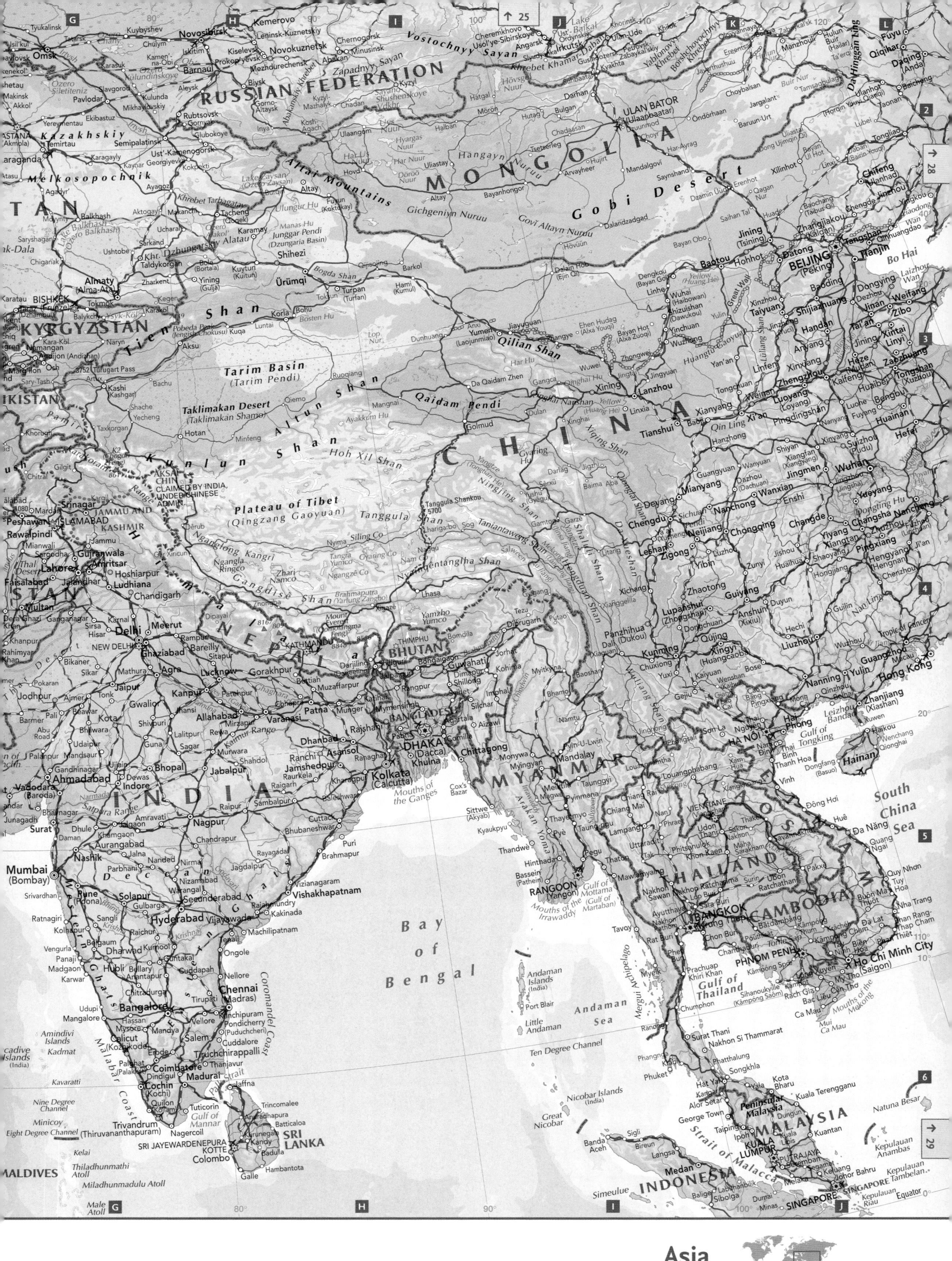

Asia

Central and Southern Asia

27

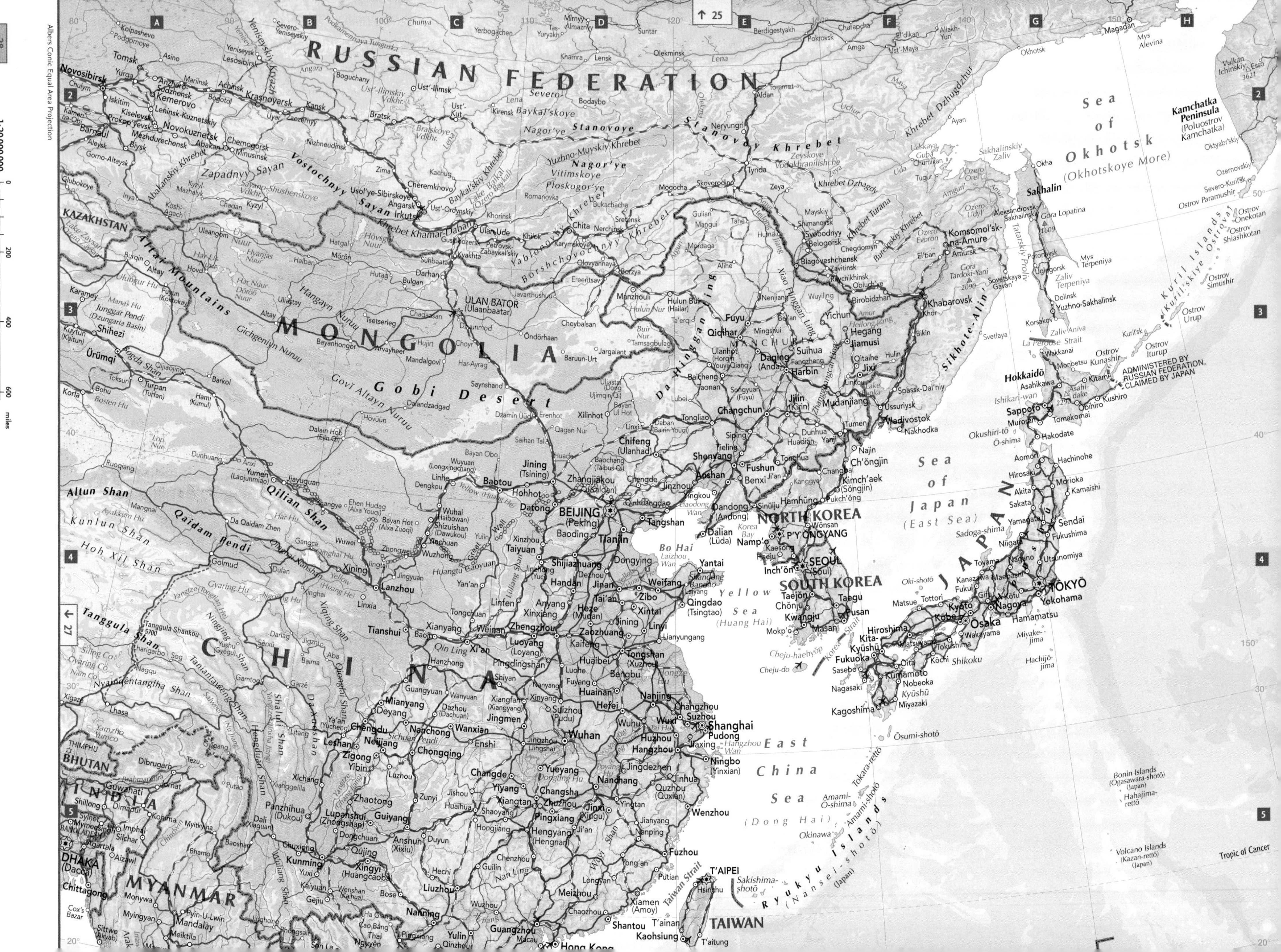

Albers Conic Equal Area Projection

1:20 000 000

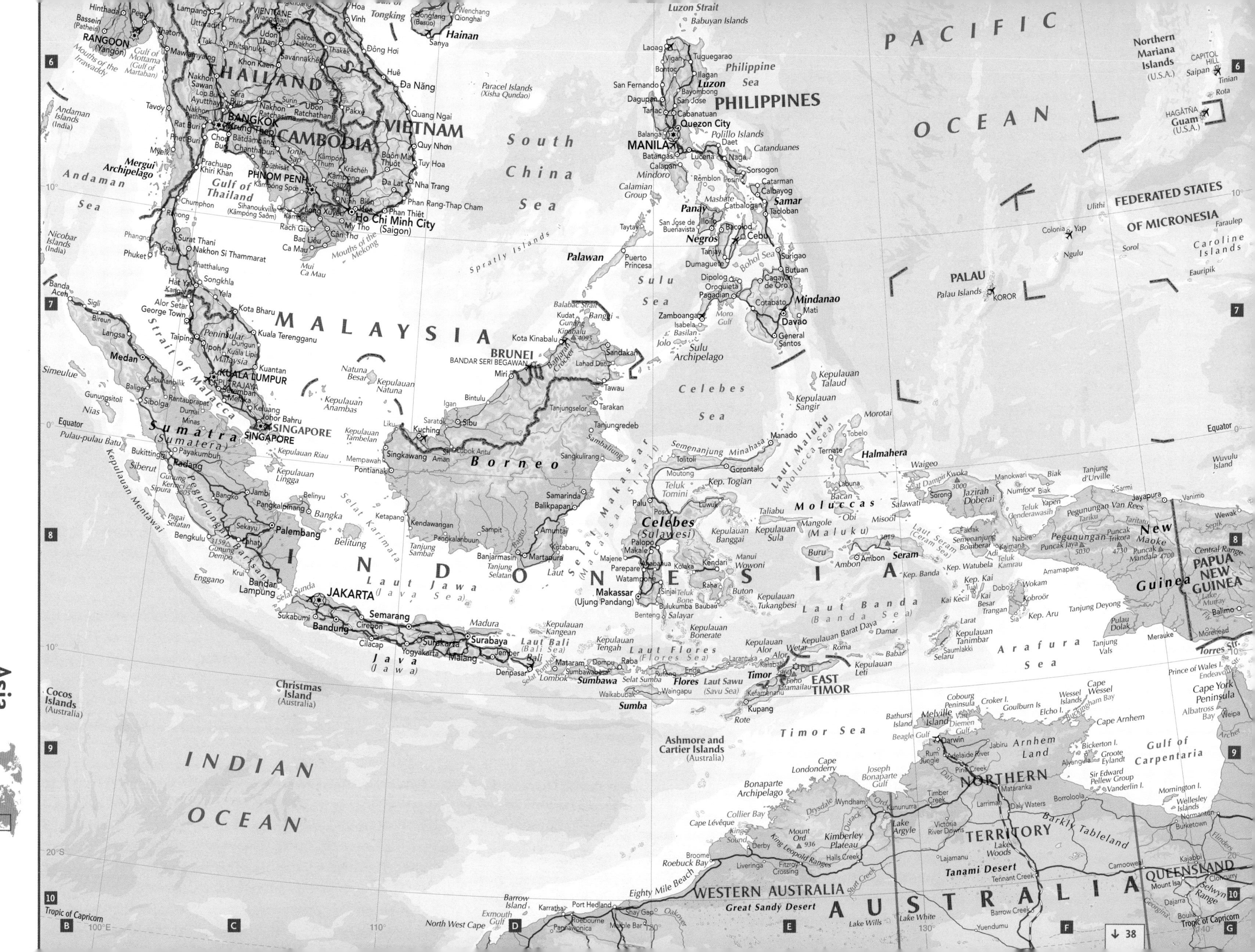

Asia

Eastern and Southeast Asia

PACIFIC OCEAN
PHILIPPINES
MANILA
Quezon City
Luzon
Luzon Strait
Philippine Sea
Mindanao
Palawan
South China Sea
Sulu Sea
Celebes Sea
MALAYSIA
KUALA LUMPUR
SINGAPORE
BRUNEI
BANDAR SERI BEGAWAN
Borneo
INDONESIA
JAKARTA
Sumatra (Sumatera)
Java (Jawa)
Celebes (Sulawesi)
Makassar (Ujung Pandang)
Surabaya
Palembang
Medan
Moluccas (Maluku)
Halmahera
THAILAND
BANGKOK
CAMBODIA
PHNOM PENH
VIETNAM
Ho Chi Minh City (Saigon)
Hainan
RANGOON (Yangon)
Andaman Sea
Strait of Malacca
Gulf of Thailand
INDIAN OCEAN
Timor Sea
Arafura Sea
Laut Banda (Banda Sea)
EAST TIMOR
DILI
PALAU
KOROR
FEDERATED STATES OF MICRONESIA
Caroline Islands
Guam (U.S.A.)
Northern Mariana Islands (U.S.A.)
PAPUA NEW GUINEA
New Guinea
Gulf of Carpentaria
AUSTRALIA
NORTHERN TERRITORY
WESTERN AUSTRALIA
QUEENSLAND
Darwin
Great Sandy Desert
Tanami Desert
Christmas Island (Australia)
Cocos Islands (Australia)
Ashmore and Cartier Islands (Australia)
Equator
Tropic of Capricorn
↓ 38

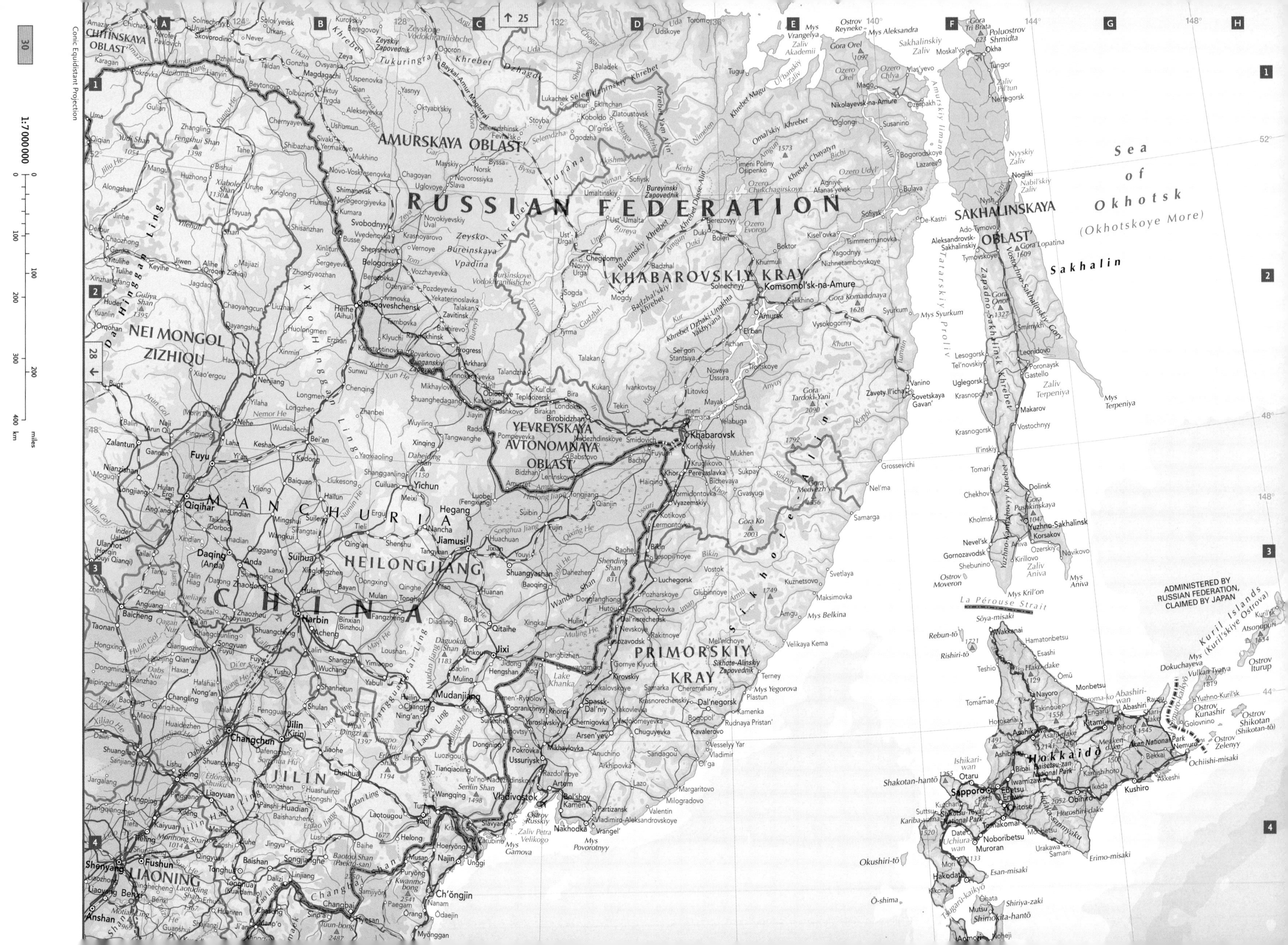

Sea of Okhotsk
(Okhotskoye More)

Sakhalin

SAKHALINSKAYA
OBLAST

ADMINISTERED BY
RUSSIAN FEDERATION.
CLAIMED BY JAPAN

Kuril'skiye Ostrova

La Pérouse Strait

HOKKAIDŌ

Sapporo

RUSSIAN FEDERATION

AMURSKAYA OBLAST

KHABAROVSKIY KRAY

Komsomol'sk-na-Amure

Khabarovsk

YEVREYSKAYA
AVTONOMNAYA
OBLAST

Birobidzhan

PRIMORSKIY
KRAY

MANCHURIA

HEILONGJIANG

Harbin

Qiqihar

Daqing
(Anda)

NEI MONGOL
ZIZHIQU

Da Hinggan Ling

Xiao Hinggan Ling

Jiamusi

Mudanjiang

Vladivostok

JILIN

Jilin

Changchun

CHINA

Chang

LIAONING

Shenyang

Anshan

Conic Equidistant Projection

1:7 000 000

0   100   200   miles
0   100   200   300   400 km

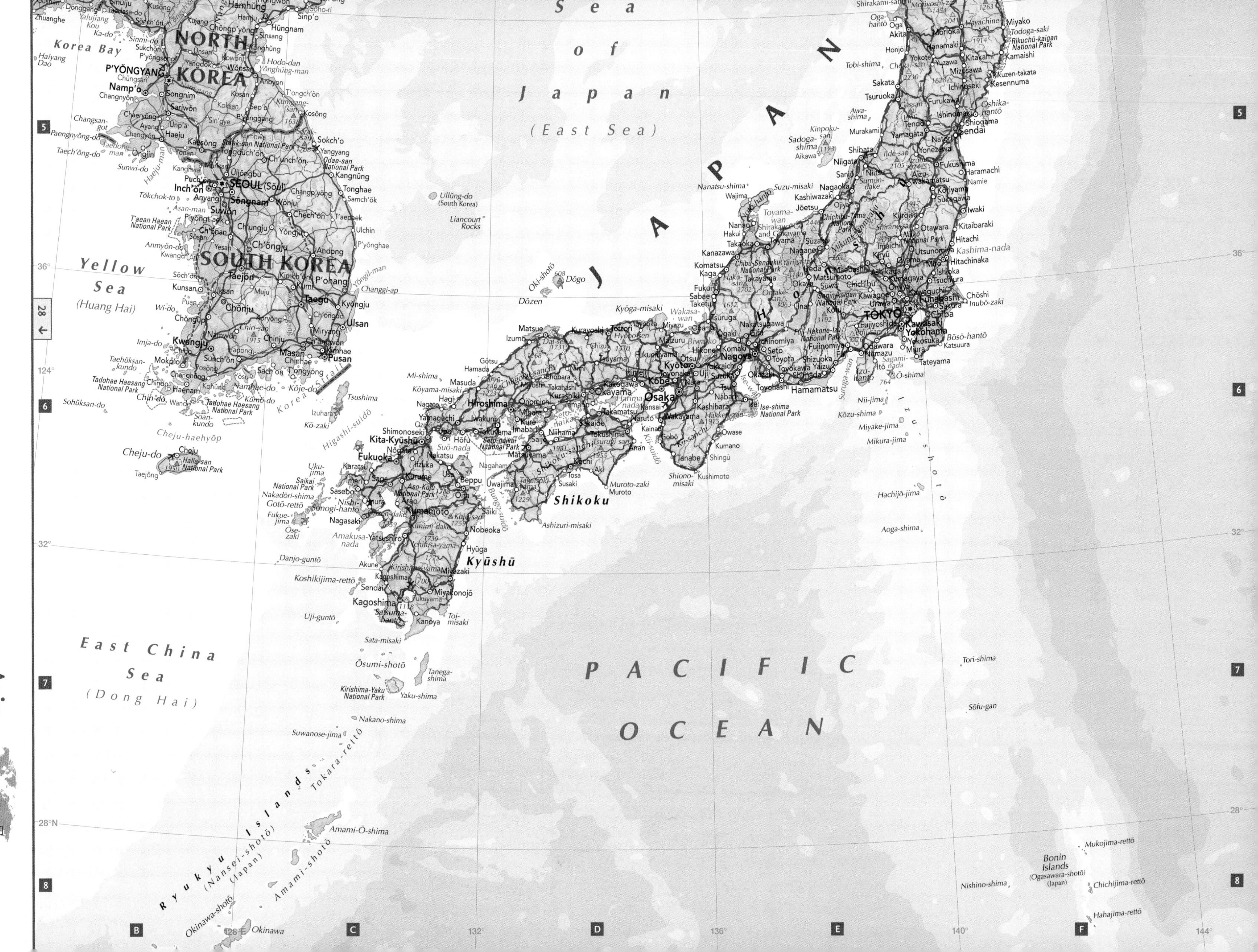
Sea of Japan
(East Sea)
JAPAN
Honshū
PACIFIC OCEAN
East China Sea
(Dong Hai)
Yellow Sea
(Huang Hai)
Korea Bay
Korea Strait
NORTH KOREA
SOUTH KOREA
P'YŎNGYANG
SEOUL (Sŏul)
TŌKYŌ
Ōsaka
Kyōto
Nagoya
Yokohama
Kawasaki
Kōbe
Hiroshima
Okayama
Fukuoka
Kita-Kyūshū
Kumamoto
Sendai
Niigata
Kagoshima
Hamamatsu
Pusan
Taegu
Inch'ŏn
Kwangju
Taejŏn
Ulsan
Shikoku
Kyūshū
Izu-shotō
Bonin Islands
(Ogasawara-shotō)
(Japan)
Ryukyu Islands
(Nansei-shotō)
(Japan)
Tokara-rettō
Amami-shotō
Okinawa-shotō
Okinawa
Cheju-do
Tsushima
Oki-shotō
Sado-shima
Ullŭng-do
(South Korea)
Liancourt Rocks
28 ←

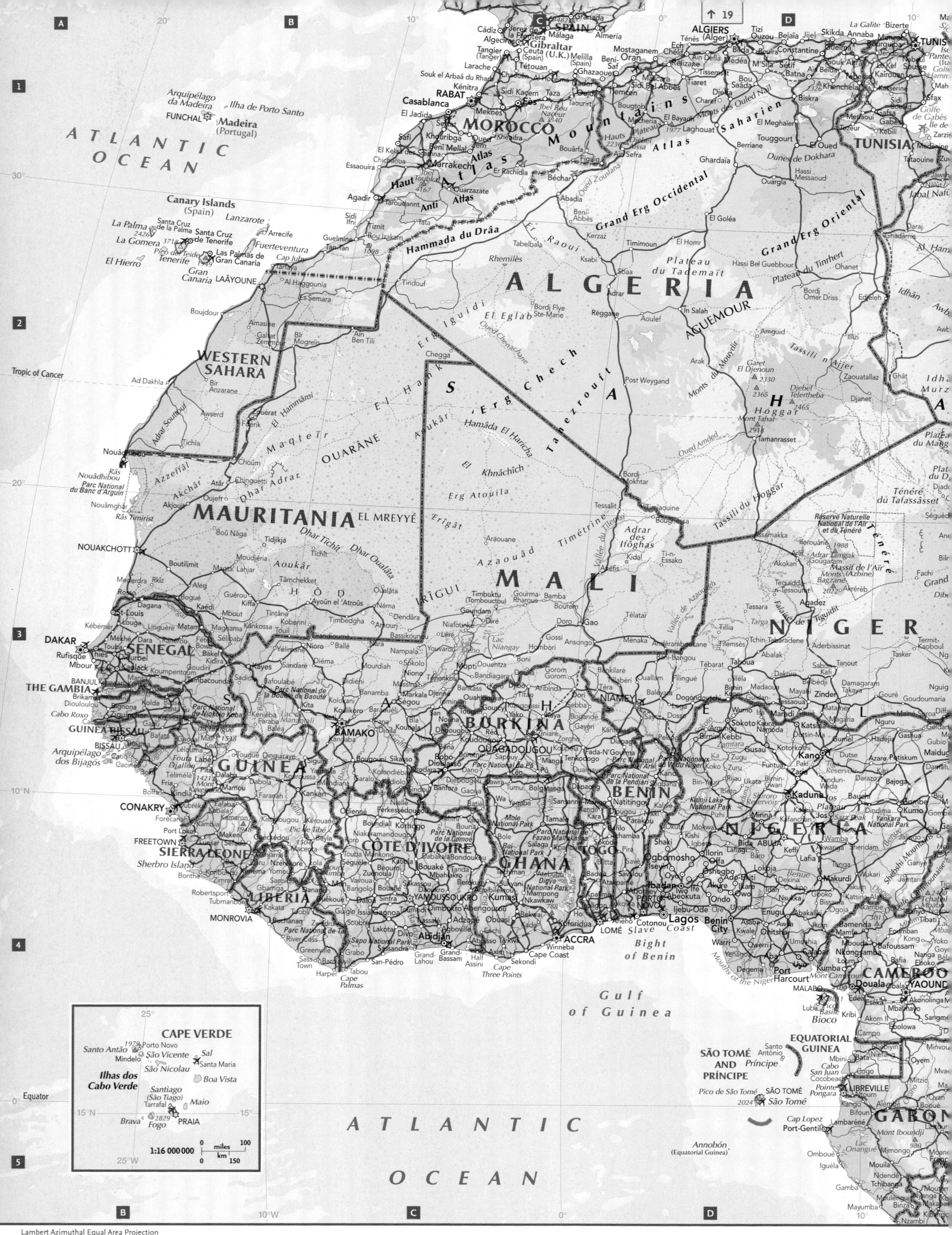

Lambert Azimuthal Equal Area Projection

1:16 000 000

1:16 000 000

Africa
Northern Africa

Mediterranean Sea
Gulf of Sirte (Khalīj Surt)
LIBYA
EGYPT
SUDAN
CHAD
CENTRAL AFRICAN REPUBLIC
DEMOCRATIC REPUBLIC OF CONGO
CONGO
UGANDA
KENYA
TANZANIA
RWANDA
BURUNDI
ETHIOPIA
ERITREA
DJIBOUTI
SOMALIA
YEMEN
SAUDI ARABIA
JORDAN
ISRAEL
LEBANON
SYRIA
IRAQ
IRAN
KUWAIT
TURKEY
GREECE
ITALY
CYPRUS
MALTA
Red Sea
Gulf of Aden
INDIAN OCEAN
Lake Victoria
Lake Nasser
CAIRO (Al Qāhirah)
Alexandria (Al Iskandarīyah)
KHARTOUM
Omdurman
N'DJAMENA
BANGUI
KAMPALA
NAIROBI
KIGALI
BUJUMBURA
ADDIS ABABA (Adis Abeba)
ASMARA
DJIBOUTI
MOGADISHU (Muqdisho)
ŞAN'Ā'
RIYADH (Ar Riyāḑ)
Medina (Al Madīnah)
Mecca (Makkah)
Jeddah (Jiddah)
BAGHDAD
DAMASCUS (Dimashq)
BEIRUT (Beyrouth)
'AMMĀN
JERUSALEM
Tel Aviv-Yafo
NICOSIA (Lefkosia)
ATHENS (Athína)
VALLETTA
KUWAIT (Al Kuwayt)
Benghazi
Port Sudan (Būr Sudan)
Aswān
Libyan Desert
Great Sand Sea
Western Desert
Eastern Desert
Nubian Desert
Tibesti
Darfur
Syrian Desert
An Nafūd
Tropic of Cancer
Equator

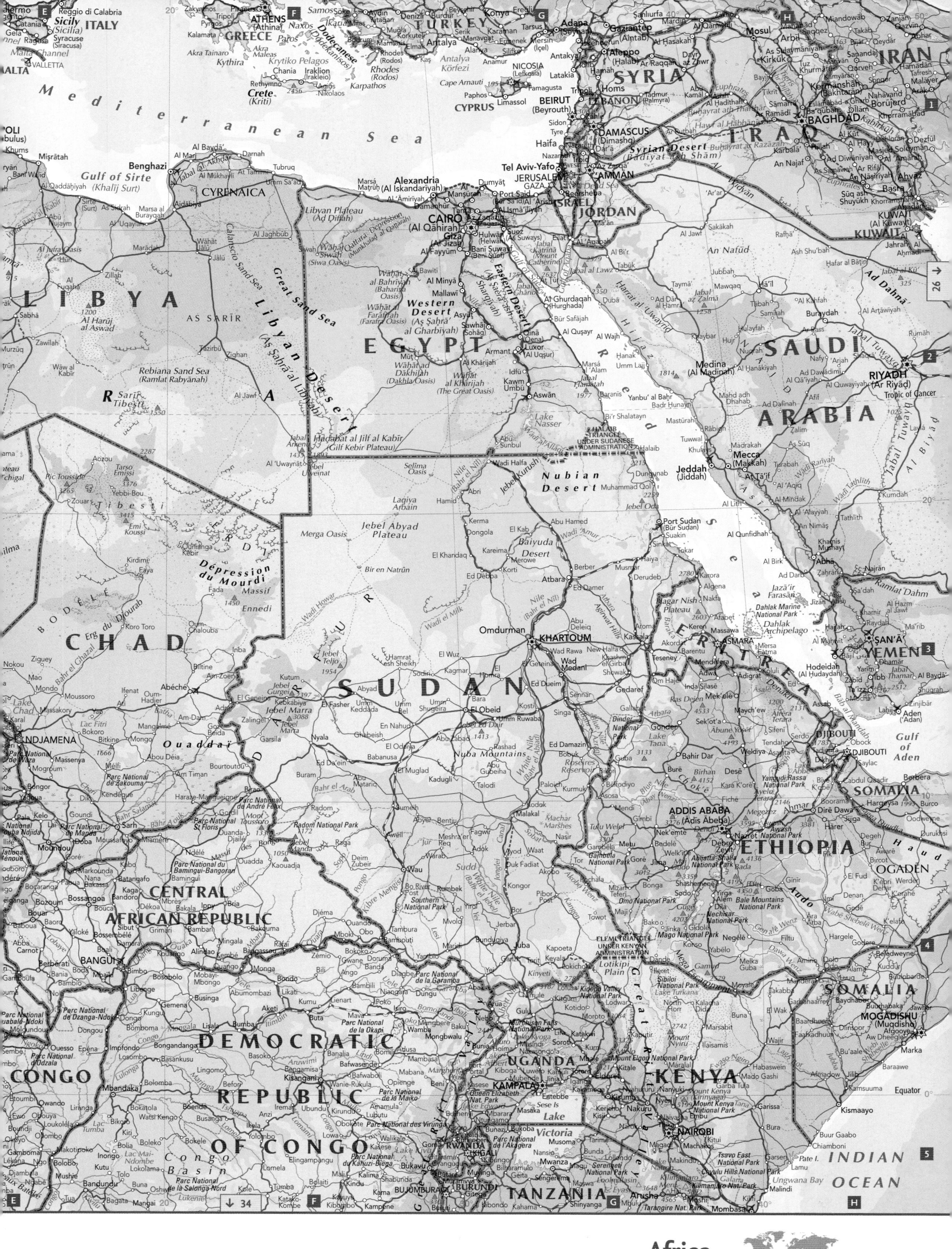

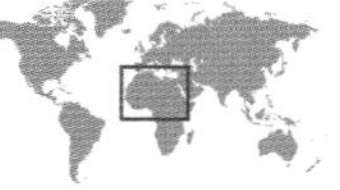

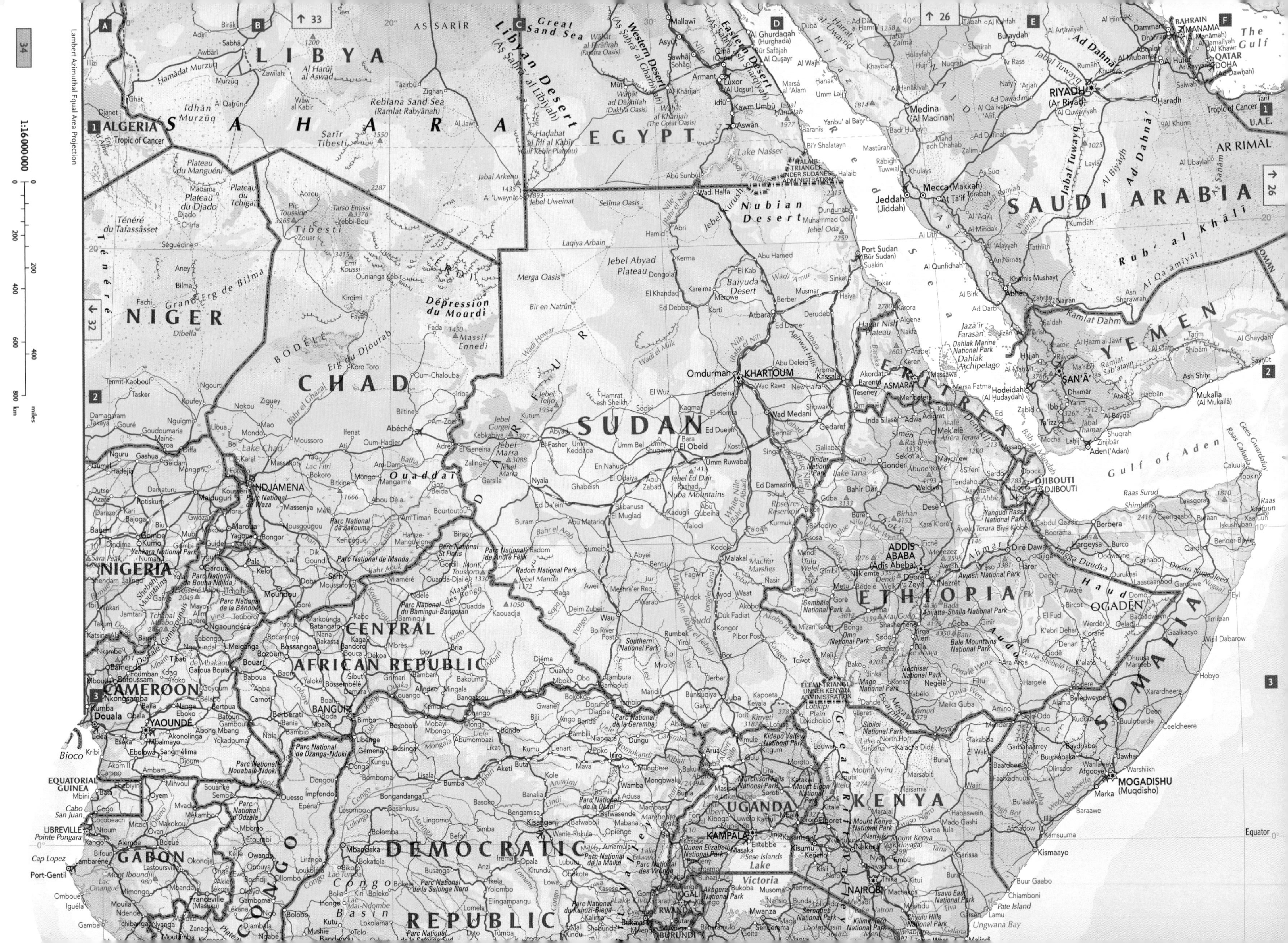

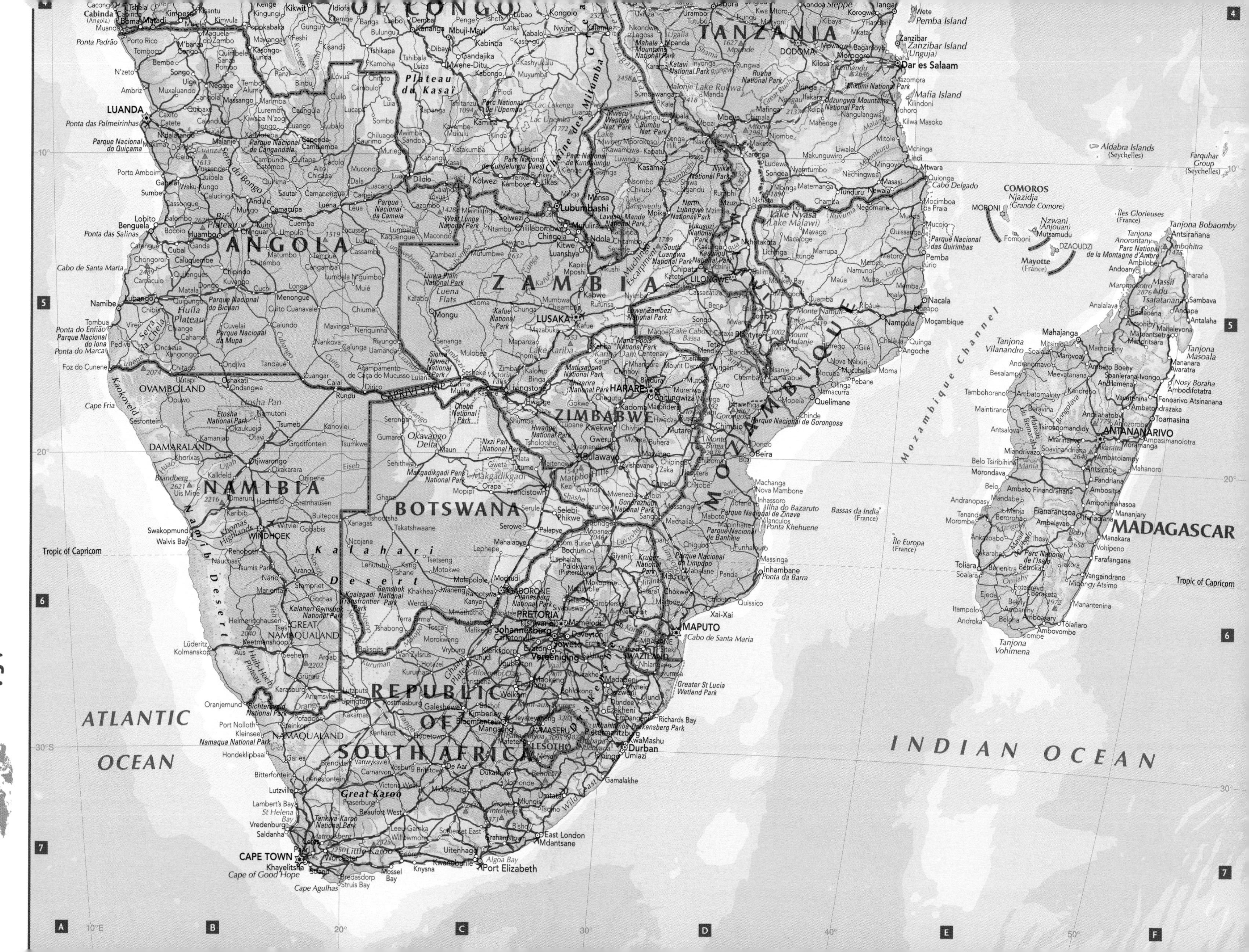

Africa
Central and Southern Africa

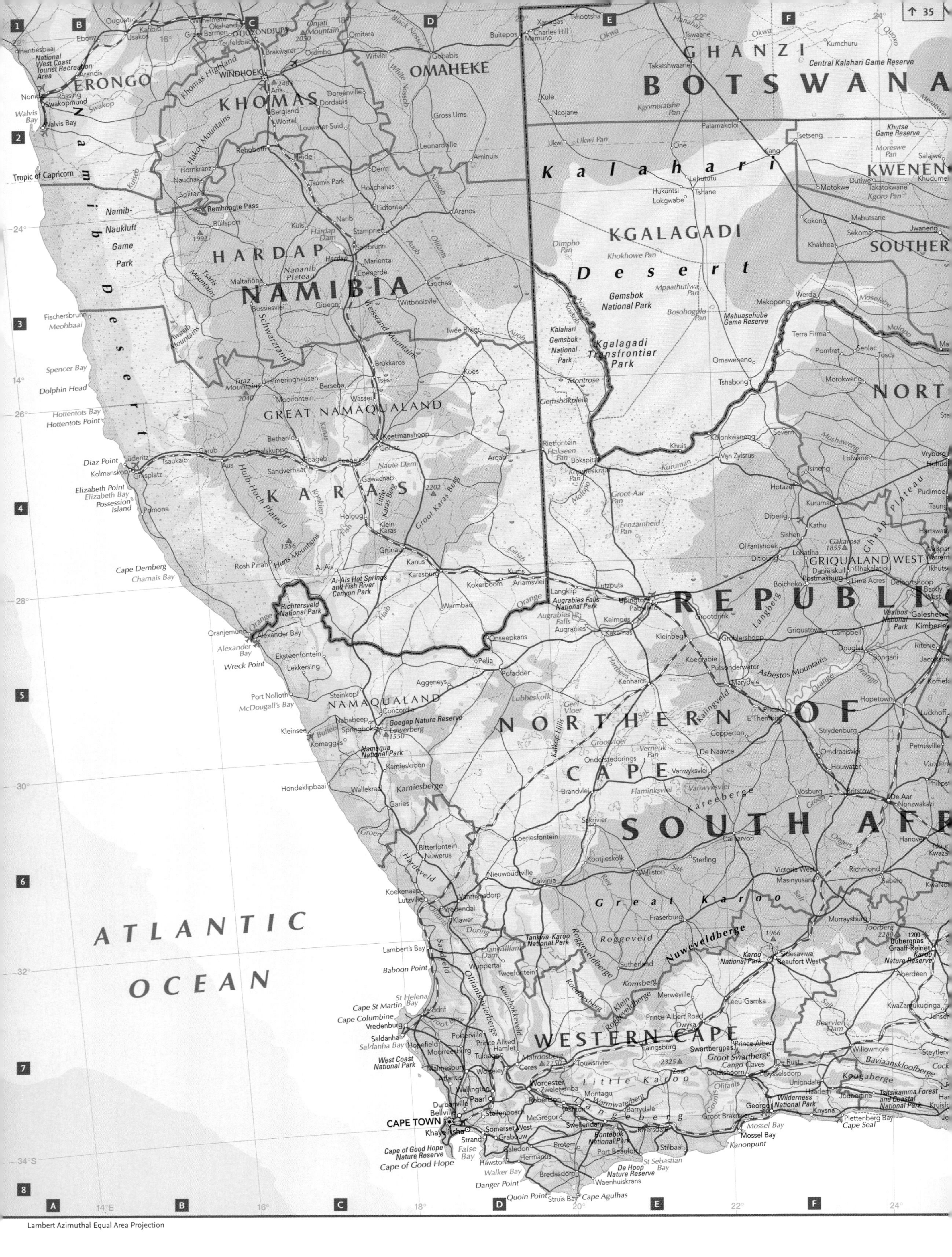

ATLANTIC

OCEAN

NAMIBIA

HARDAP

KHOMAS

ERONGO

KARAS

GREAT NAMAQUALAND

NAMAQUALAND

BOTSWANA

GHANZI

KGALAGADI

K a l a h a r i

D e s e r t

Central Kalahari Game Reserve

KWENEN

SOUTHER

NORT

REPUBLIC

OF

SOUTH AF

NORTHERN

CAPE

GRIQUALAND WEST

WESTERN CAPE

Great Karoo

Little Karoo

OMAHEKE

Windhoek

Walvis Bay

Swakopmund

CAPE TOWN

Tropic of Capricorn

Gemsbok National Park

Kalahari Gemsbok National Park

Kgalagadi Transfrontier Park

Augrabies Falls National Park

Richtersveld National Park

Ai-Ais Hot Springs and Fish River Canyon Park

Namib-Naukluft Game Park

Namaqua National Park

Goegap Nature Reserve

West Coast National Park

Namib Desert

Orange

Lambert Azimuthal Equal Area Projection

1:5 000 000

0 100 200 300 miles
0 100 200 300 400 500 km

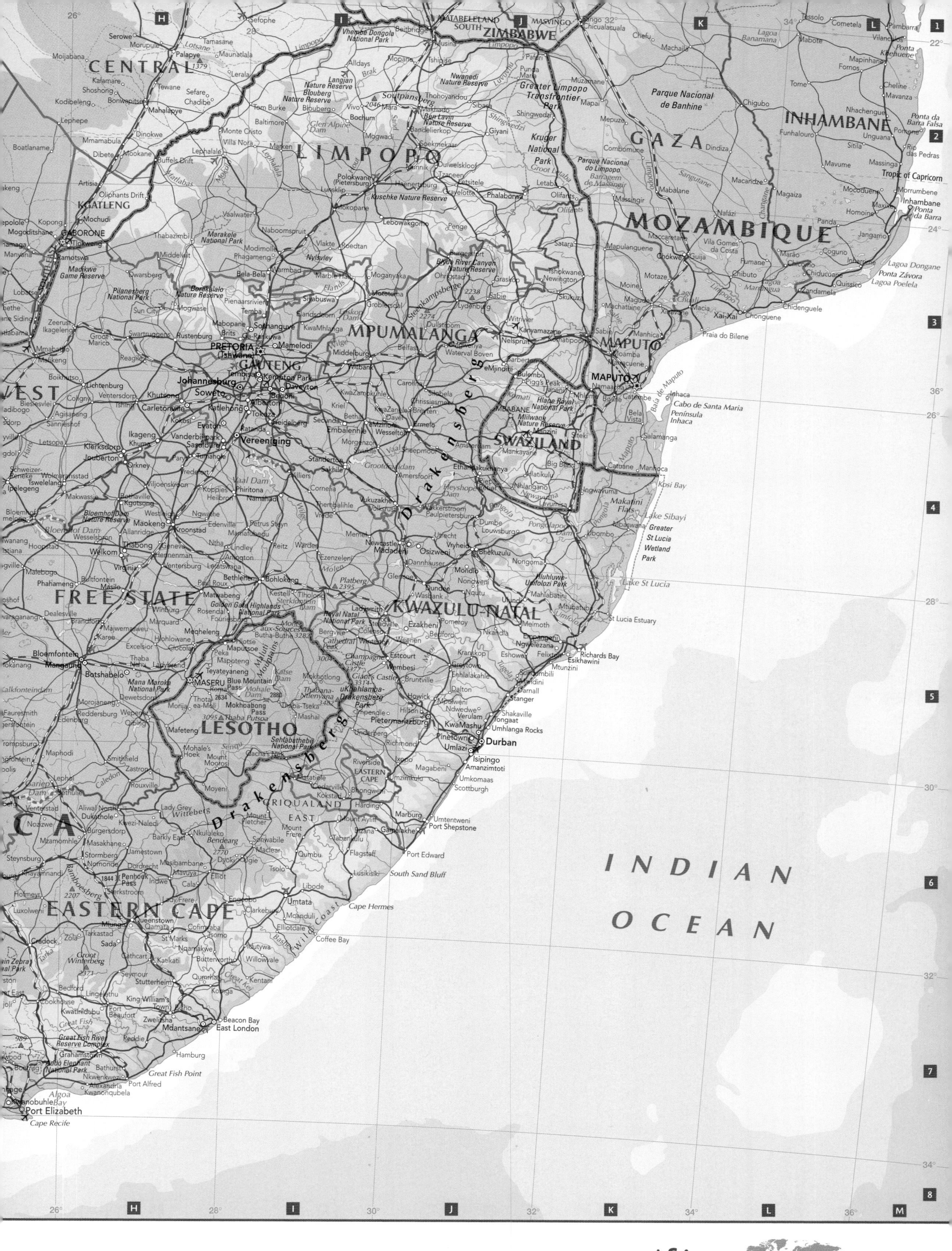

Africa
Republic of South Africa

INDIAN
OCEAN
MOZAMBIQUE
ZIMBABWE
SWAZILAND
LESOTHO
LIMPOPO
MPUMALANGA
GAUTENG
KWAZULU-NATAL
FREE STATE
EASTERN CAPE
GAZA
INHAMBANE
MAPUTO
CENTRAL
KGATLENG
Drakensberg
PRETORIA (Tshwane)
Johannesburg
Soweto
Vereeniging
GABORONE
MBABANE
MASERU
Bloemfontein
Durban
Pietermaritzburg
Richards Bay
East London
Port Elizabeth
Polokwane (Pietersburg)
Nelspruit
Kruger National Park
Greater Limpopo Transfrontier Park
Parque Nacional de Banhine
Parque Nacional do Limpopo
Greater St Lucia Wetland Park
Tropic of Capricorn
Inhambane
Xai-Xai
Cabo de Santa Maria
Península Inhaca
Kosi Bay
Lake St Lucia
St Lucia Estuary
Port Shepstone
Port Edward
Cape Hermes
Coffee Bay
Great Fish Point
Port Alfred
Cape Recife
Algoa Bay

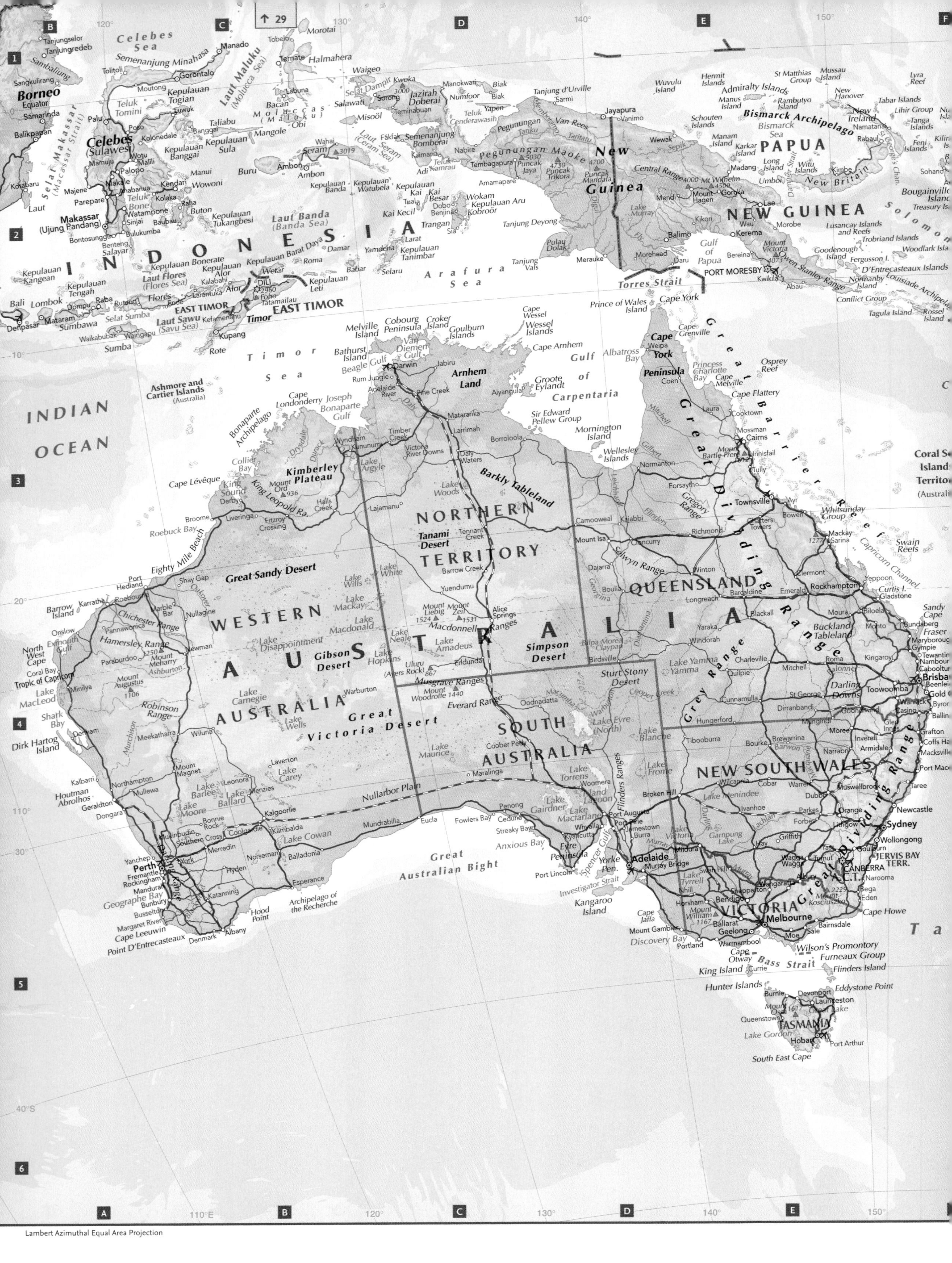

INDONESIA

Borneo
Equator

Celebes Sea

Tanjungselor
Tanjungredeb
Sambaliung
Sangkulirang
Samarinda
Balikpapan

Tolitoli
Semenanjung Minahasa
Manado
Gorontalo
Tobelo
Morotai

Tomini
Luwuk
Teluk Togian

Kolonedale
Kepulauan Banggai
Banggai
Kepulauan Sula

Palu
Poso
Kolaka
Kendari
Wowoni
Buton

Celebes (Sulawesi)

Makassar (Ujung Pandang)

Mamuju
Majene
Parepare
Pinrang
Rappang

Watampone
Bone
Sinjai
Baubau

Bulukumba
Benteng
Selayar
Bontosunggu
Salayar

Laut Maluku (Molucca Sea)

Ternate
Halmahera
Waigeo

Obi
Moluccas (Maluku)

Misool
Salawati
Sorong
Jazirah Doberai

Manokwari
Biak
Numfoor
Biak
Yapen
Teluk Cenderawasih

Kepulauan Banda
Watubela

Laut Seram (Ceram Sea)

Ambon
Ambon
Buru
Wahai
Kepulauan Banda (Banda Sea)

Kai Kecil
Trangan
Kepulauan Aru
Wokam
Kobroor

Laut Banda (Banda Sea)

Kepulauan Tukangbesi
Manui
Raha
Kepulauan Kai
Kai Besar
Dobo

PAPUA

Jayapura
Vanimo
Wewak
Sepik

Pegunungan Maoke
Puncak Jaya
Puncak Trikora
Van Rees
Taritatu
Sarmi

New Guinea

NEW GUINEA

Lae
Morobe

Mendi
Mount Hagen
Goroka
Madang
Wau

Kepulauan Aru
Dolak
Merauke
Morehead
Daru

Gulf of Papua

PORT MORESBY
Kwikila
Abau

Torres Strait

Prince of Wales Island
Cape York

Cape York
Weipa
Coen

York Peninsula

INDIAN OCEAN

Timor Sea

Ashmore and Cartier Islands (Australia)

Melville Island
Bathurst Island
Cobourg Peninsula
Croker Island
Goulburn Islands
Wessel Islands
Cape Wessel

Darwin
Beagle Gulf
Van Diemen Gulf
Jabiru

Cape Arnhem
Gulf of Carpentaria

Arnhem Land

Alyangula
Groote Eylandt
Albatross Bay

Pine Creek
Adelaide River
Rum Jungle

Daly Waters
Mataranka
Larrimah

Borroloola
Sir Edward Pellew Group
Mornington Island
Wellesley Islands

Normanton
Forsayth
Croydon

Cooktown
Mossman
Cairns
Innisfail
Tully

Great Barrier Reef

Cape Flattery
Cape Melville
Princess Charlotte Bay
Osprey Reef

NORTHERN TERRITORY

Tanami Desert
Tennant Creek
Barkly Tableland

Barrow Creek
Yuendumu

Alice Springs
MacDonnell Ranges
Mount Zeil 1531
Mount Liebig 1524

WESTERN AUSTRALIA

Great Sandy Desert
Lake Mackay
Lake Disappointment

Gibson Desert
Lake Macdonald

Lake Amadeus
Lake Neale
Lake Hopkins

Uluru (Ayers Rock) 867

Musgrave Ranges
Mount Woodroffe 1440
Everard Range

Great Victoria Desert

Lake Wells
Lake Carnegie

Warburton
Laverton

SOUTH AUSTRALIA

Simpson Desert
Sturt Stony Desert

Birdsville
Oodnadatta
Coober Pedy

Lake Eyre (North)
Lake Eyre (South)
Lake Blanche

Cooper Creek

Marla
Maralinga

Lake Torrens
Lake Gairdner
Lake Everard

Flinders Ranges

QUEENSLAND

Mount Isa
Cloncurry
Dajarra
Camooweal

Selwyn Range
Julia Creek
Richmond
Hughenden

Townsville
Ayr
Bowen
Whitsunday Group
Mackay 1277
Sarina

Winton
Longreach
Blackall
Barcaldine
Emerald
Clermont

Rockhampton
Gladstone
Curtis I.
Capricorn Channel
Swain Reefs

Boulia
Bedourie
Windorah
Quilpie
Charleville

Roma
Toowoomba
Dalby
Warwick

Brisbane
Gold Coast

Tropic of Capricorn

Buckland Tableland
Sandy Cape
Bundaberg
Fraser Island
Maryborough
Gympie
Kingaroy
Nambour
Caboolture

NEW SOUTH WALES

Broken Hill
Wilcannia
Cobar
Bourke
Brewarrina

Tibooburra
Hungerford
Walgett
Moree
Narrabri

Menindee
Ivanhoe
Hay
Griffith
Forbes
Parkes
Orange
Dubbo
Tamworth
Inverell
Armidale
Glen Innes
Grafton
Coffs Harbour
Casino
Lismore
Byron Bay

Sydney
Wollongong
Newcastle
Gosford
Katoomba
Bathurst
Goulburn

CANBERRA
A.C.T.
JERVIS BAY TERR.

Narooma
Bega
Eden
Cape Howe

Mount Kosciuszko 2229

VICTORIA

Melbourne
Geelong
Ballarat
Bendigo
Shepparton
Mildura
Swan Hill
Echuca

Horsham
Nhill
Mount William 1167

Warrnambool
Portland
Mount Gambier
Discovery Bay
Cape Otway
Cape Howe

Wilson's Promontory
Furneaux Group
Flinders Island
Bass Strait
King Island
Currie

TASMANIA

Burnie
Devonport
Launceston
Queenstown
Mount Ossa 1617
Lake Gordon

Hobart
Port Arthur
South East Cape

Eddystone Point
Hunter Islands

Great Australian Bight

Eucla
Mundrabilla
Nullarbor Plain

Ceduna
Streaky Bay
Anxious Bay
Fowlers Bay
Penong

Eyre Peninsula
Port Lincoln
Investigator Strait
Kangaroo Island
Cape Jaffa

Spencer Gulf
Whyalla
Port Augusta
Port Pirie
Jamestown
Burra

Adelaide
Murray Bridge
Yorke Peninsula
Kyancutta
Kimba

Perth
Fremantle
Rockingham
Mandurah
Bunbury
Busselton
Margaret River
Cape Leeuwin
Point D'Entrecasteaux
Denmark
Albany
Katanning
Hyden
Narrogin

York
Northam
Merredin
Southern Cross
Coolgardie
Kalgoorlie
Norseman
Esperance
Balladonia
Archipelago of the Recherche

Yanchep
Mullewa
Geraldton
Dongara
Houtman Abrolhos
Kalbarri
Northampton

Carnarvon
Shark Bay
Dirk Hartog Island
Denham
Mount Augustus 1106

Onslow
Karratha
Dampier
Roebourne
Port Hedland
Marble Bar
Nullagine

Hamersley Range
Mount Meharry
Mount Bruce
Newman
Paraburdoo
Tom Price
Wiluna
Meekatharra
Mount Magnet
Leonora
Menzies
Leinster

Lake Carey
Lake Wells
Lake Barlee
Lake Moore
Lake Ballard

Chichester Range
Robinson Range

North West Cape
Exmouth Gulf
Coral Bay
Lake MacLeod
Minilya

Broome
Roebuck Bay
Derby
Fitzroy Crossing
Halls Creek
Liveringa
Camballin

King Sound
Cape Lévêque
Collier Bay
Bonaparte Archipelago
King Leopold Ra.
Mount Ord 936

Kimberley Plateau
Kununurra
Wyndham
Lake Argyle
Timber Creek
Victoria River Downs
Lajamanu

Eighty Mile Beach

Cape Londonderry
Joseph Bonaparte Gulf
Cape Domett
Drysdale

Dili
Foho Tatamailau 2960
EAST TIMOR
Timor
Kupang
Kefamenanu
Atambua
Roti

Laut Sawu (Savu Sea)

Laut Flores (Flores Sea)

Flores
Larantuka
Ende
Ruteng
Labuanbajo
Maumere

Bali
Lombok
Sumbawa
Mataram
Denpasar
Dompu
Raba
Bima
Waikabubak
Waingapu
Sumba

Selat Sumba

Arafura Sea

Tanjung Vals
Pulau Dolak

0   200   400   600 miles
0   200   400   600   800   1000 km

Lambert Azimuthal Equal Area Projection

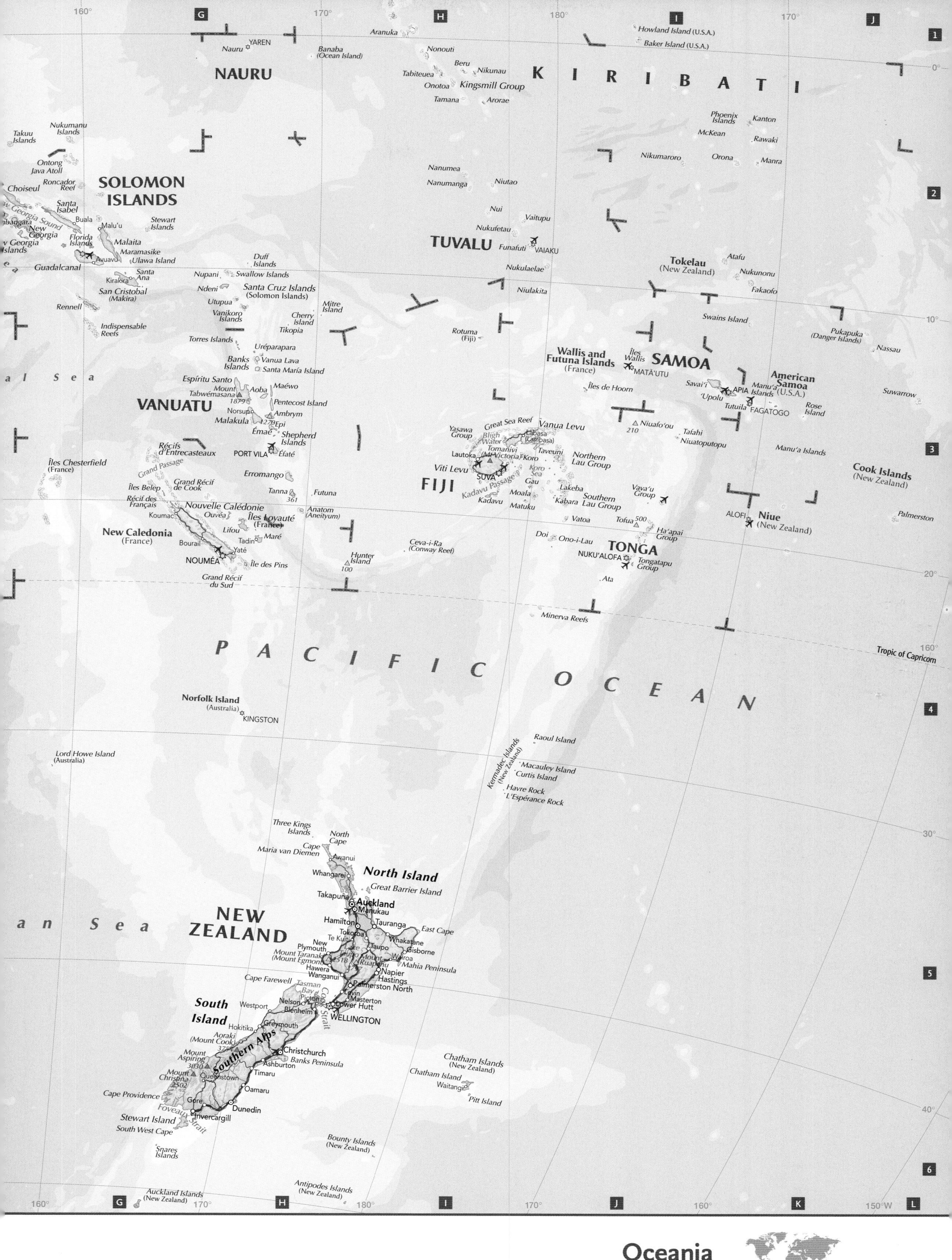

160°   G   170°   H   180°   I   170°   J

1

Howland Island (U.S.A.)
Baker Island (U.S.A.)

Aranuka
Nauru ✡ YAREN
Banaba
(Ocean Island)   Nonouti
Takuu
Islands   Nukumanu
Islands   Beru   Nikunau
Tabiteuea   Onotoa   Kingsmill Group
Tamana   Arorae

NAURU

K I R I B A T I

Phoenix
Islands   Kanton
McKean   Rawaki
Nikumaroro   Orona   Manra

0°

Ontong
Java Atoll   Roncador
Reef
Choiseul
Santa
Isabel
New
Georgia
v Georgia
Islands   Florida
Islands   Stewart
Islands
Malu'u
Malaita
Avuavu   Maramasike
Guadalcanal   Ulawa Island

**SOLOMON
ISLANDS**

Nanumea
Nanumanga   Niutao
Nui
Vaitupu
Nukufetau

TUVALU   Funafuti ✈ VAIAKU

Nukulaelae

Niulakita

Swains Island

Tokelau
(New Zealand)   Atafu
Nukunonu
Fakaofo

Pukapuka
(Danger Islands)   Nassau

2

10°

Rennell
Santa
Ana
San Cristobal
(Makira)
Indispensable
Reefs

Nupani   Swallow Islands
Ndeni
Utupua   Santa Cruz Islands
(Solomon Islands)
Vanikoro
Islands
Torres Islands   Cherry
Island
Tikopia

Duff
Islands
Mitre
Island

Rotuma
(Fiji)

Wallis and
Futuna Islands
(France)   Îles
Wallis

Îles de Hoorn
MATA'UTU ✈

SAMOA
Savai'i
'Upolu   APIA ✈
Manu'a
Islands
Tutuila   FAGATOGO   **American
Samoa**
(U.S.A.)

Rose
Island

Suwarrow

3

al Sea

Uréparapara
Banks
Islands   Vanua Lava
Santa María Island

Espíritu Santo
Tabwémasana
1879▲   Aoba   Maéwo
Norsup   Pentecost Island
Ambrym

VANUATU   Malakula   1270▲   Epi
Émaé   Shepherd
Islands
Récifs
d'Entrecasteaux   PORT VILA ✈   Éfaté

Îles Chesterfield
(France)   Grand Passage   Erromango

Grand Récif
de Cook   Tanna ▲
361   Futuna

Northern
Lau Group

Great Sea Reef   Vanua Levu
Yasawa
Group   Bligh
Water   Labasa
(Lambasa)
Tomanivi
Lautoka   ▲Victoria   Taveuni
1322   Koro
Viti Levu   Koro
Sea   Gau
SUVA ✈   Ovalau   Lakeba
FIJI   Kadavu Passage   Moala   Southern
Kadavu   Lau Group
Matuku   Kabara

Niuafo'ou
210△   Tafahi
Niuatoputapu

Vava'u
Group   ✈

Manu'a Islands

Cook Islands
(New Zealand)

Îles Belep
Récif des
Français   Îles Belep
Koumac   Nouvelle Calédonie   Îles Loyauté
Ouvéa   (France)
Lifou
Bourail   Tadin
Yaté   Maré

New Caledonia
(France)   NOUMÉA   Île des Pins

Anatom
(Aneityum)   Ceva-i-Ra
(Conway Reef)

Vatoa
Tofua 500△

Doi   Ono-i-Lau
NUKU'ALOFA ✈   Ha'apai
Group
TONGA   Tongatapu
Group
Ata   ALOFI ✈   **Niue**
(New Zealand)

Palmerston

Grand Récif
du Sud

Hunter
Island
100

20°

P A C I F I C   O C E A N

Minerva Reefs

Tropic of Capricorn   160°

4

Norfolk Island
(Australia)
KINGSTON

Lord Howe Island
(Australia)

Raoul Island
Kermadec Islands
(New Zealand)   Macauley Island
Curtis Island
Havre Rock
L'Espérance Rock

30°

Three Kings
Islands
Maria van Diemen   North
Cape
Cape
Whangarei   Awanui

North Island

an Sea   Takapuna   Great Barrier Island
Auckland
Manukau
Hamilton   Tauranga
Tokoroa   East Cape
Te Kuiti   Whakatane
**NEW
ZEALAND**   New
Plymouth   Taupo   Whakatane
Gisborne
Mount Taranaki
(Mount Egmont)   Mount   Wairoa
▲2518   ▲Ruapehu   Mahia Peninsula
Hawera   Napier
Wanganui   Hastings
Cape Farewell   Levin   Palmerston North
Tasman
Bay   Picton   Masterton
South   Nelson   Lower Hutt
Island   Westport   Blenheim   **WELLINGTON**
Hokitika   Greymouth
Aoraki
(Mount Cook)   Banks Peninsula
Mount   ▲3754   **Christchurch**
Aspiring   Ashburton
▲3033   Timaru
Mount Christina   Southern Alps
▲2502   Queenstown   Oamaru
Cape Providence   Gore   Dunedin
Invercargill
Stewart Island
South West Cape   Foveaux Strait

Chatham Islands
(New Zealand)
Chatham Island
Waitangi

Pitt Island

5

40°

Auckland Islands
(New Zealand)

Antipodes Islands
(New Zealand)

Bounty Islands
(New Zealand)

Snares
Islands

6

160°   G   170°   H   180°   I   170°   J   160°   K   150°W   L

Oceania
Australia, New Zealand and Southwest Pacific

39

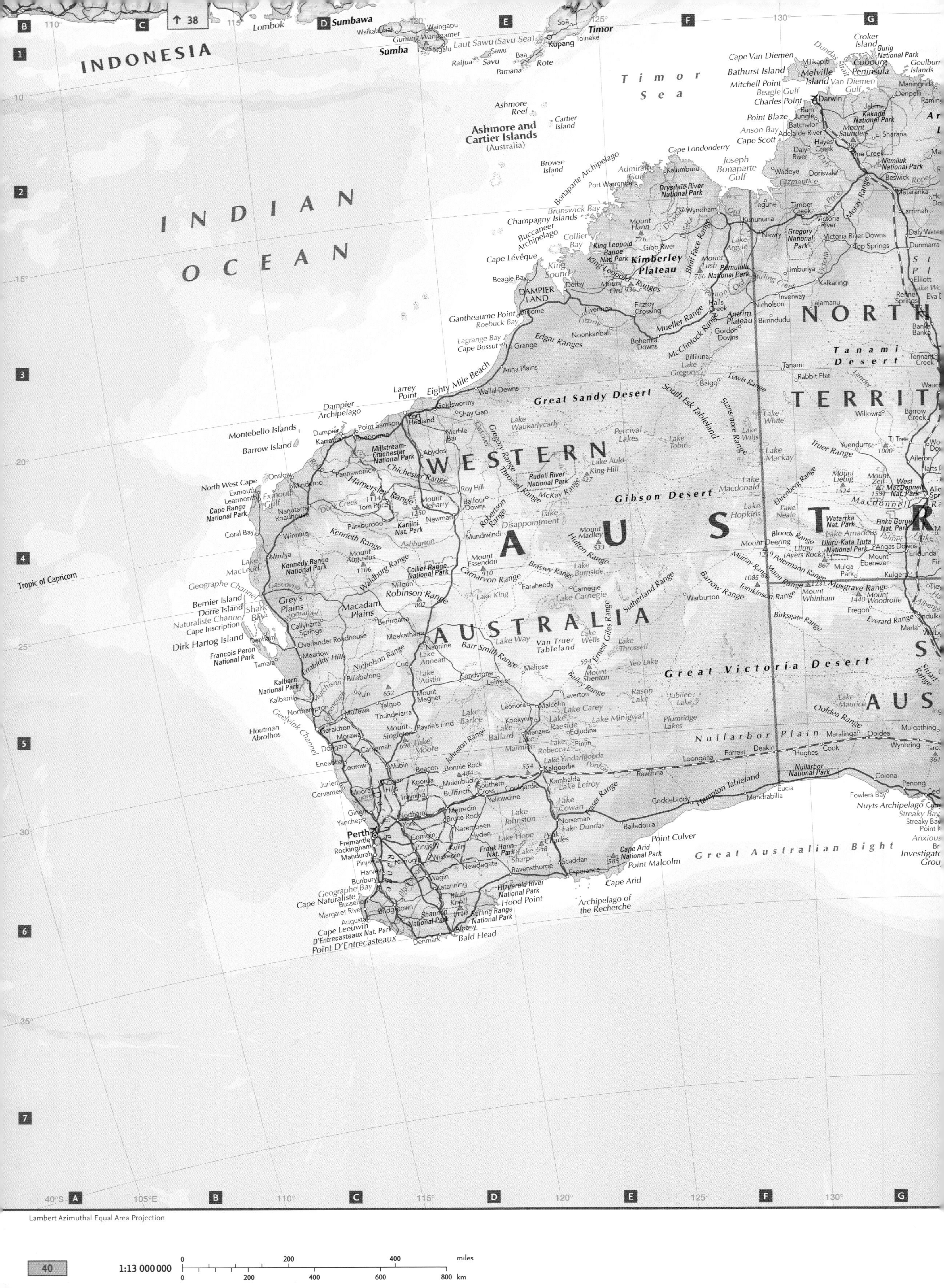

INDONESIA

INDIAN

OCEAN

Timor
Sea

Ashmore
Reef

Ashmore and
Cartier Islands
(Australia)

WESTERN

AUSTRALIA

A U S T R A L I A

Great Sandy Desert

Gibson Desert

Great Victoria Desert

Nullarbor Plain

Great Australian Bight

NORTH
TERRIT

Kimberley
Plateau

DAMPIER
LAND

Perth

Tropic of Capricorn

Lambert Azimuthal Equal Area Projection

1:13 000 000

200   400   miles

200   400   600   800 km

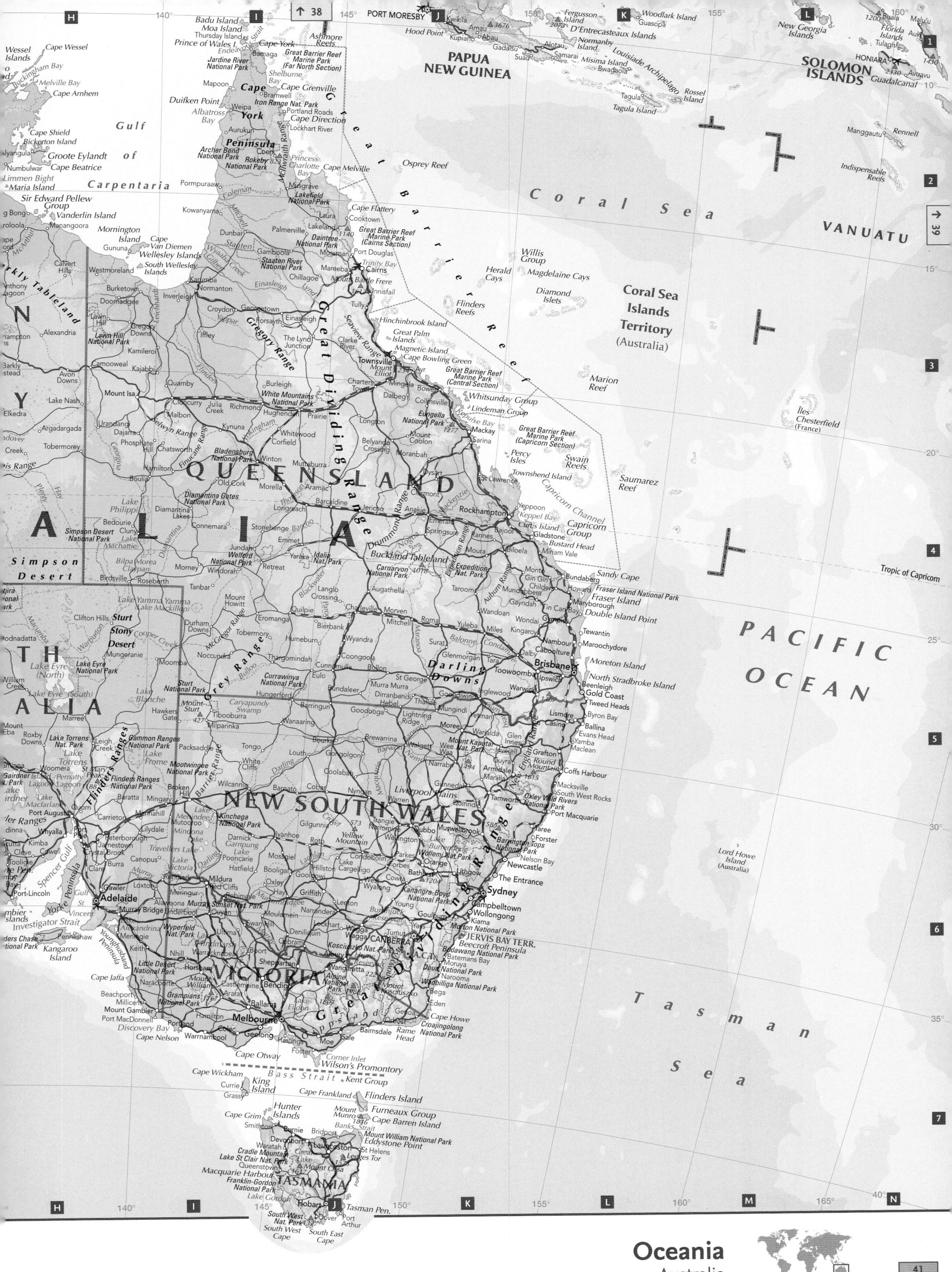

PAPUA NEW GUINEA

SOLOMON ISLANDS

HONIARA

Gulf

of

Carpentaria

Cape York
Peninsula

Great Barrier Reef Marine Park (Far North Section)

Coral Sea

VANUATU

Coral Sea Islands Territory (Australia)

Great Barrier Reef Marine Park (Cairns Section)

QUEENSLAND

Cairns

Townsville

Great Barrier Reef Marine Park (Central Section)

Îles Chesterfield (France)

Great Barrier Reef Marine Park (Capricorn Section)

Tropic of Capricorn

Rockhampton

Simpson Desert

Brisbane

Gold Coast

PACIFIC OCEAN

NEW SOUTH WALES

Lord Howe Island (Australia)

Newcastle

Sydney
Wollongong

CANBERRA
A.C.T.

JERVIS BAY TERR.

VICTORIA

Adelaide

Melbourne
Geelong

Tasman Sea

Bass Strait

King Island

Flinders Island

TASMANIA

Hobart

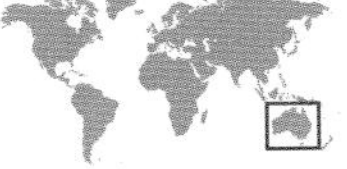

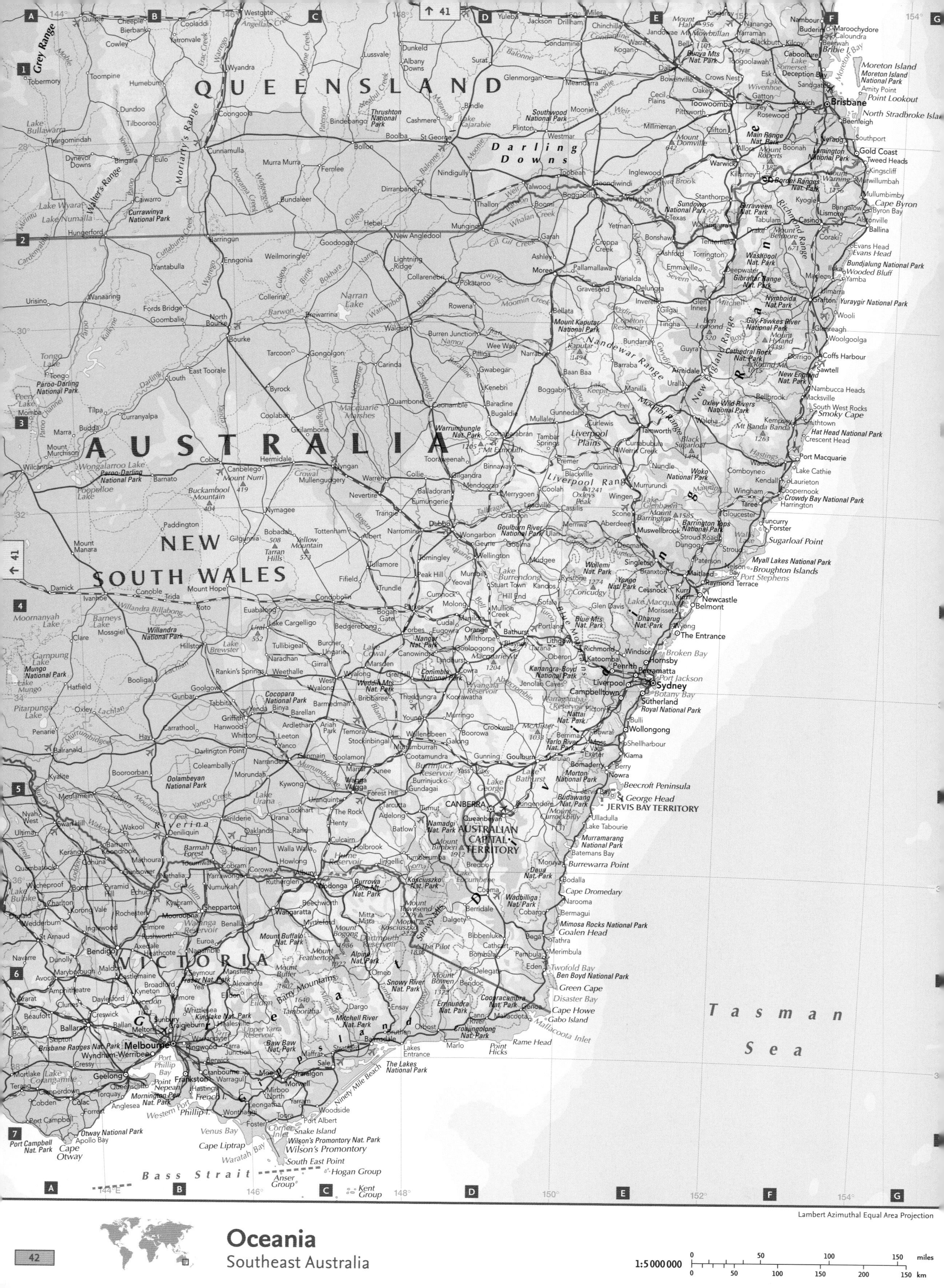

Oceania
Southeast Australia

1 : 5 000 000

Lambert Azimuthal Equal Area Projection

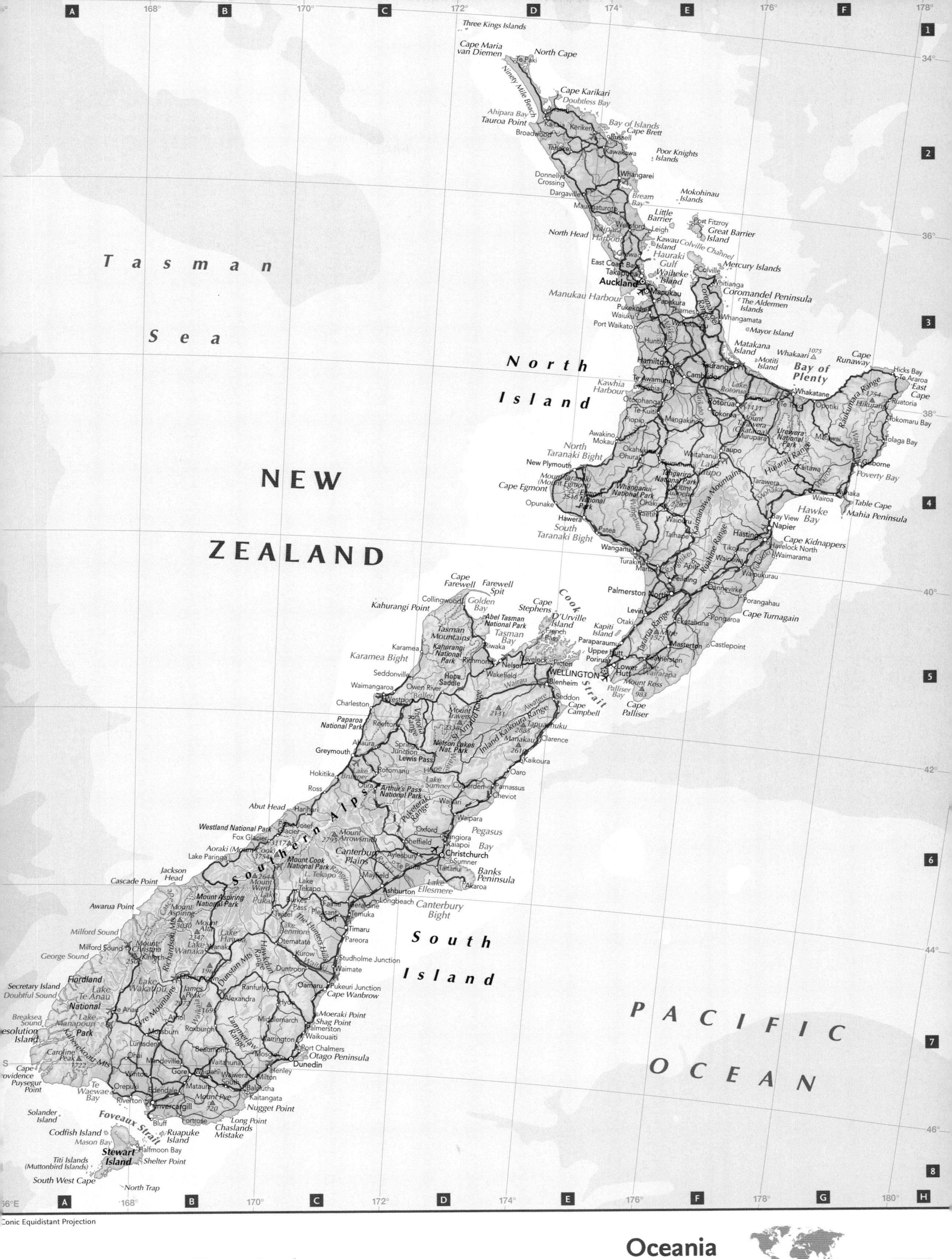

T a s m a n

S e a

NEW

ZEALAND

North

Island

Three Kings Islands

Cape Maria
van Diemen
North Cape
Te Paki
Cape Karikari
Ninety Mile Beach
Doubtless Bay
Ahipara Bay
Tauroa Point
Broadwood
Kaitaia
Kerikeri
Bay of Islands
Cape Brett
Russell
Kawakawa
Poor Knights
Islands
Whangarei
Donnellys
Crossing
Dargaville
Maungaturoto
Bream
Bay
Mokohinau
Islands
North Head
Warkworth
Leigh
Port Fitzroy
Great Barrier
Island
Little
Barrier
Island
Kawau
Island
Colville Channel
Helensville
Whangaparaoa
East Coast Bays
Takapuna
Hauraki
Gulf
Waiheke
Island
Colville
Mercury Islands
Auckland
Manukau
Papakura
Whitianga
Coromandel Peninsula
The Aldermen
Islands
Manukau Harbour
Pukekohe
Thames
Whangamata
Waiuku
Port Waikato
Mayor Island
Huntly
Matakana
Island
Motiti
Island
Whakaari
1075
Cape
Runaway
Hicks Bay
Hamilton
Tauranga
Te Araroa
Te Awamutu
Cambridge
Lake
Rotorua
Whakatane
Raukumara Range
1754
East
Cape
Ruatoria
Kawhia
Harbour
Kihikihi
Rotorua
Te Puke
Opotiki
Tokomaru Bay
Otorohanga
Te Kuiti
Tokoroa
Mangakino
Murupara
Urewera
National
Park
Matawai
Tolaga Bay
Awakino
Mokau
Okahu
Ohura
Whitianga
Taupo
Whakatane
Gisborne
Poverty Bay
North
Taranaki Bight
New Plymouth
Mount Taranaki
(Mount Egmont)
2516
Egmont
National
Park
Whanganui
National
Park
Tongariro
National
Park
Turangi
Mount
Tongariro
1968
Mount
Ruapehu
2797
Kaweka Range
Kaimanawa Mountains
Huiarau Range
Waikaremoana
Wairoa
Mahia Peninsula
Table Cape
Cape Egmont
Opunake
Hawera
Patea
South
Taranaki Bight
Wanganui
Raetihi
Ohakune
Taihape
Waiouru
Kaitieke
Marton
Ruahine Range
Hawke
Bay
Napier
Bay View
Hastings
Havelock North
Waimarama
Cape Kidnappers
Palmerston North
Feilding
Dannevirke
Porangahau
Cape Turnagain
Levin
Ekatahuna
Pongaroa
Cape
Farewell
Farewell
Spit
Golden
Bay
Collingwood
Kahurangi Point
Cape
Stephens
D'Urville
Island
French
Pass
Cook
Strait
Paraparaumu
Kapiti
Island
Upper
Hutt
Waikanae
Otaki
Tararua Range
1571
Masterton
Castlepoint
Tasman
Mountains
Abel Tasman
National Park
Tasman
Bay
Riwaka
Motueka
Kahurangi
National
Park
Karamea
Richmond
Nelson
Havelock
Picton
WELLINGTON
Lower
Hutt
Porirua
Mount Ross
983
Martinborough
Palliser
Bay
Cape
Palliser
Karamea Bight
Seddonville
Waimangaroa
Westport
Charleston
Owen River
Wakefield
Wairau
Blenheim
Seddon
Awatere
Cape
Campbell
Paparoa
National Park
Reefton
Hope
Saddle
Owen
Junction
Lewis Pass
Springs
Junction
Mount
Travers
2338
St Arnaud Range
Nelson Lakes
Nat. Park
2131
Inland Kaikoura Range
2885
Tapuaenuku
2610
Clarence
Manakau
Greymouth
Hokitika
Ross
Brunner
Otira
Rotomanu
Arthur's Pass
National Park
Hope
Lake
Sumner
Culverden
Parnassus
Cheviot
Kaikoura
Puketeraki
Range
Southern Alps
Harihari
Abut Head
Waitaha
Waipara
Pegasus
Bay
Westland National Park
Franz Josef
Glacier
Fox Glacier
Mount
2795
Arrowsmith
Oxford
Rangiora
Kaiapoi
Sheffield
Christchurch
Sumner
Banks
Peninsula
Akaroa
Jackson
Head
Cascade Point
Aoraki (Mount
Cook)
3754
Mount Cook
National Park
3030
Canterbury
Plains
Rakaia
Aylesbury
Te Pirita
Mayfield
Awarua Point
Mount
Aspiring
National Park
Mount
Ward
2644
Mount
Aspiring
3030
Lake
Tekapo
Lake
Pukaki
Lake
Ohau
Geraldine
Temuka
Ashburton
Lake
Ellesmere
Longbeach
Canterbury
Bight
Milford Sound
Mount
Christina
2474
Mount
Aspiring
Lake
Wanaka
Lake
Hawea
2347
Richardson Mts
Hunters Hills
Pleasant
Point
Timaru
Pareora
George Sound
Secretary Island
Doubtful Sound
Fiordland
Lake
Te Anau
National
Park
Lake
Manapouri
Te Anau
Kingston
The
Hunters Hills
Studholme Junction
Waimate
South
Island
PACIFIC
OCEAN
Breaksea
Sound
Resolution
Island
Eyre Mountains
Mount
Nicholas
Lake
Wakatipu
James Peak
2231
Dunstan Mts
Tarras
Pukeuri Junction
Cape Wanbrow
Oamaru
Moeraki Point
Shag Point
Palmerston
Cape
Providence
Puysegur
Point
Caroline
Peak
1722
Mavora
Lakes
Athol
Garston
Bannockburn
Alexandra
Hyde
Middlemarch
Waikouaiti
Port Chalmers
Otago Peninsula
Solander
Island
Te Waewae
Bay
Tuatapere
Orepuki
Winton
Lumsden
Mandeville
Riversdale
Raes Junction
Roxburgh
Beaumont
Lawrence
Milton
Dunedin
Mount Pye
720
Nugget Point
Foveaux Strait
Riverton
Invercargill
Bluff
Gore
Mataura
Edendale
Wyndham
Waikawa
Kaitangata
Balclutha
Long Point
Chaslands
Mistake
Codfish Island
Mason Bay
Halfmoon Bay
Ruapuke
Island
Shelter Point
Stewart
Island
Titi Islands
(Muttonbird Islands)
South West Cape
North Trap

Conic Equidistant Projection

1:5 250 000

0 50 100 150 miles

0 50 100 150 200 250 km

Oceania
New Zealand

43

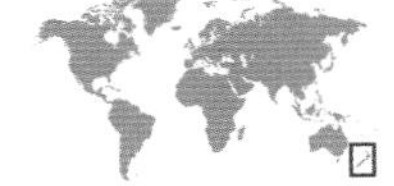

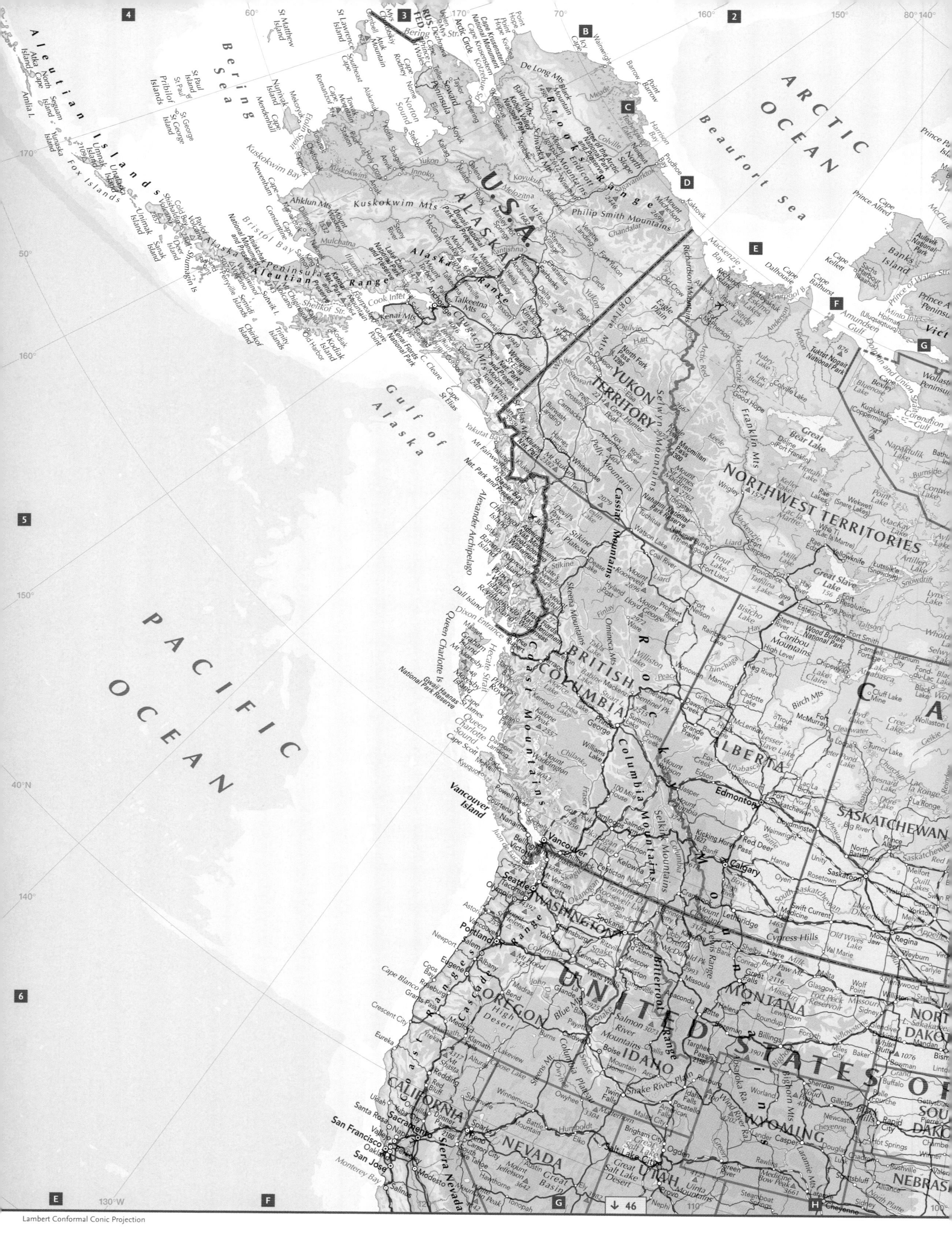

Lambert Conformal Conic Projection

1:16 000 000

| 0 | 200 | 400 | miles |

| 0 | 200 | 400 | 600 | 800 | km |

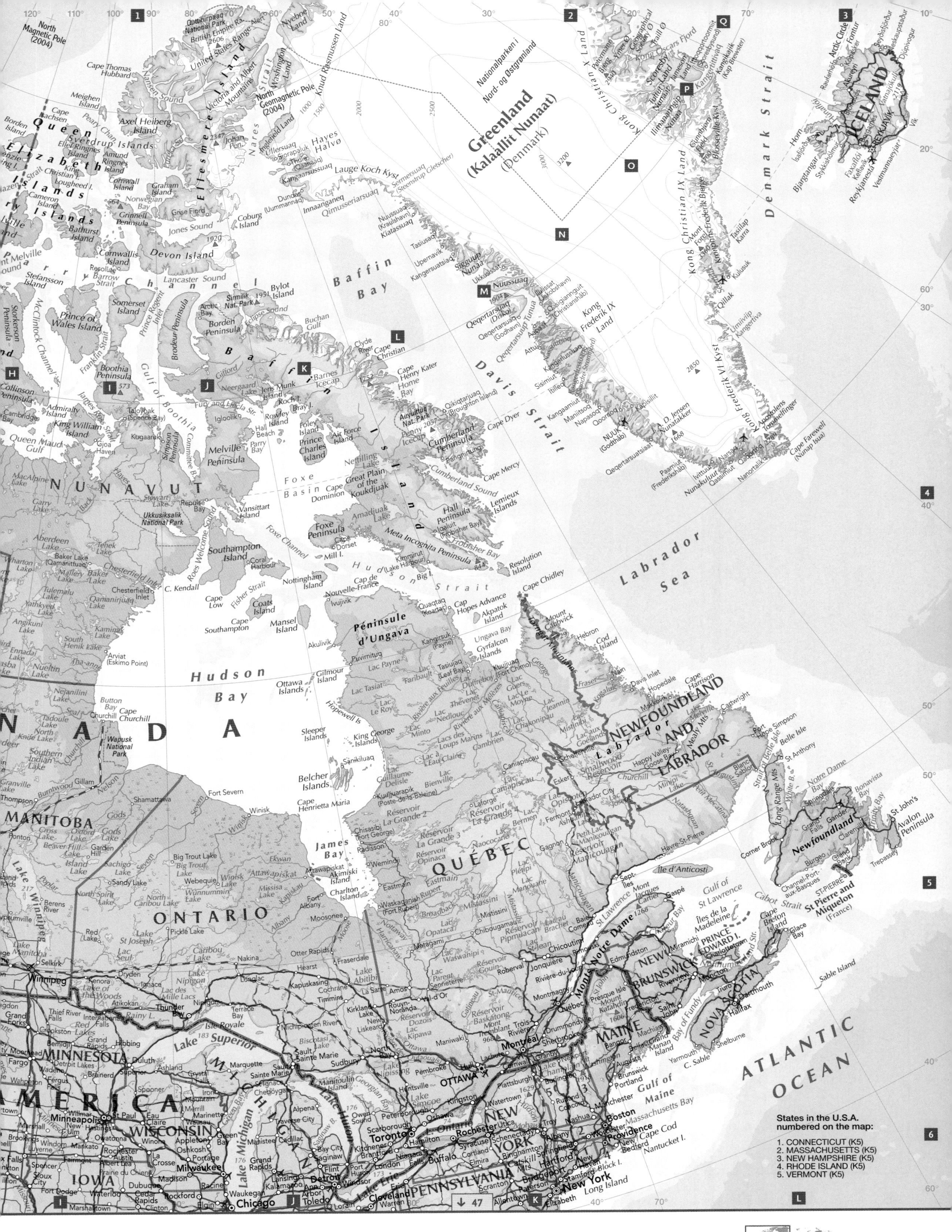

North America
Canada

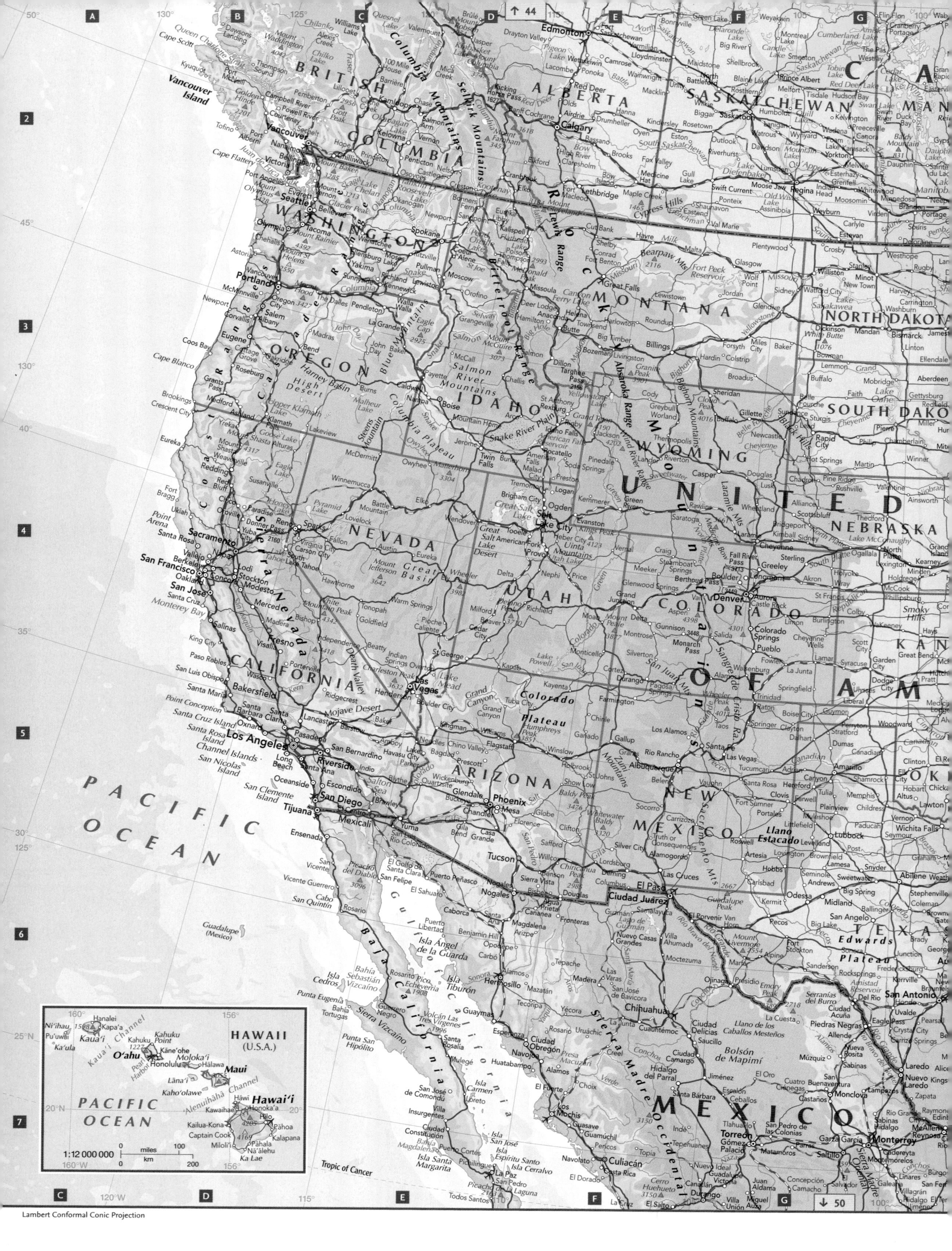

Lambert Conformal Conic Projection

1:12 000 000

| 0 | 100 | 200 | 300 | 400 | miles |

| 0 | 100 | 200 | 300 | 400 | 500 | 600 | 700 | km |

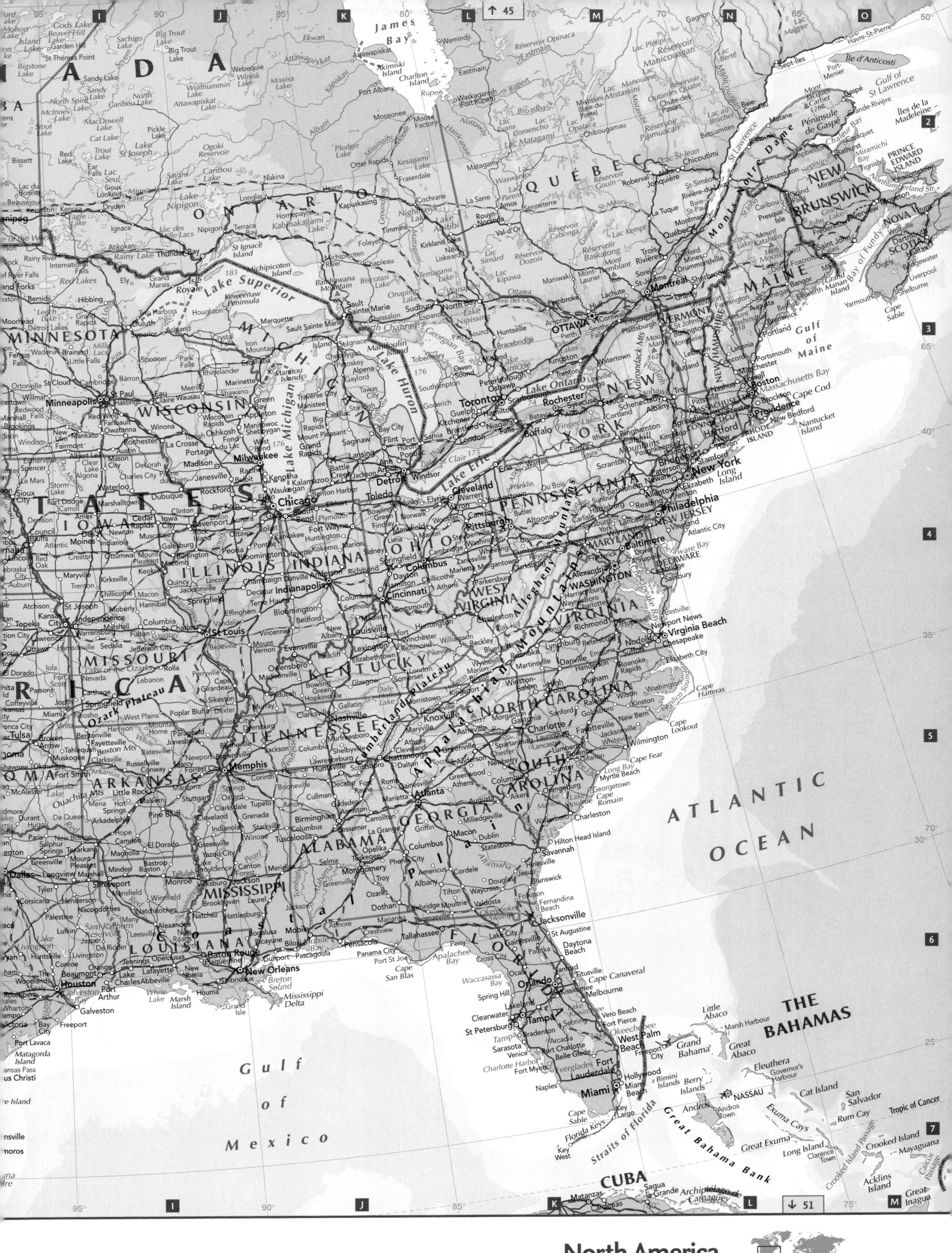

North America
United States of America

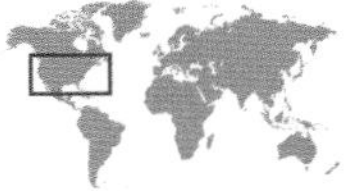

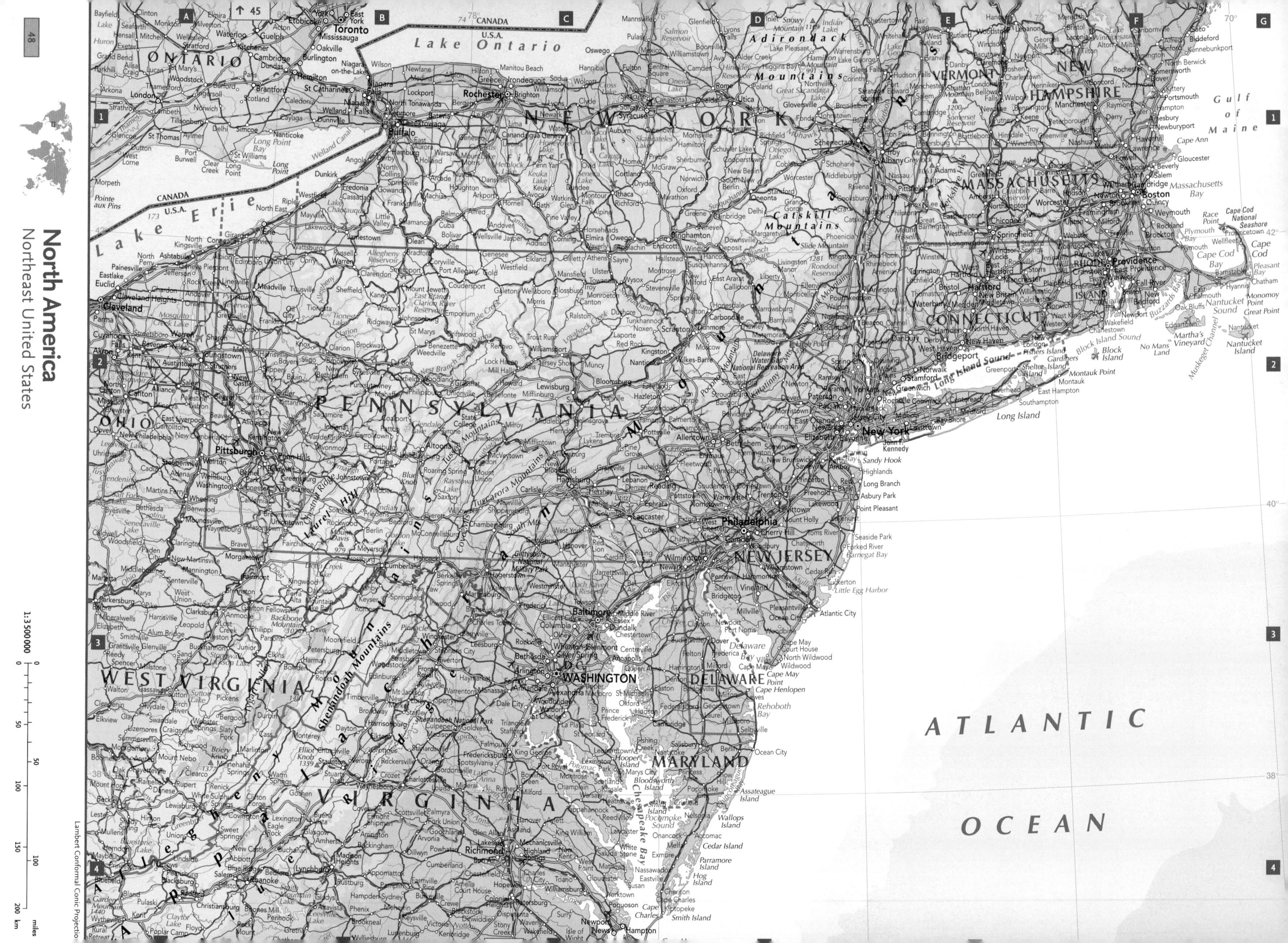

North America

Northeast United States

Lambert Conformal Conic Projection

1 : 3 500 000

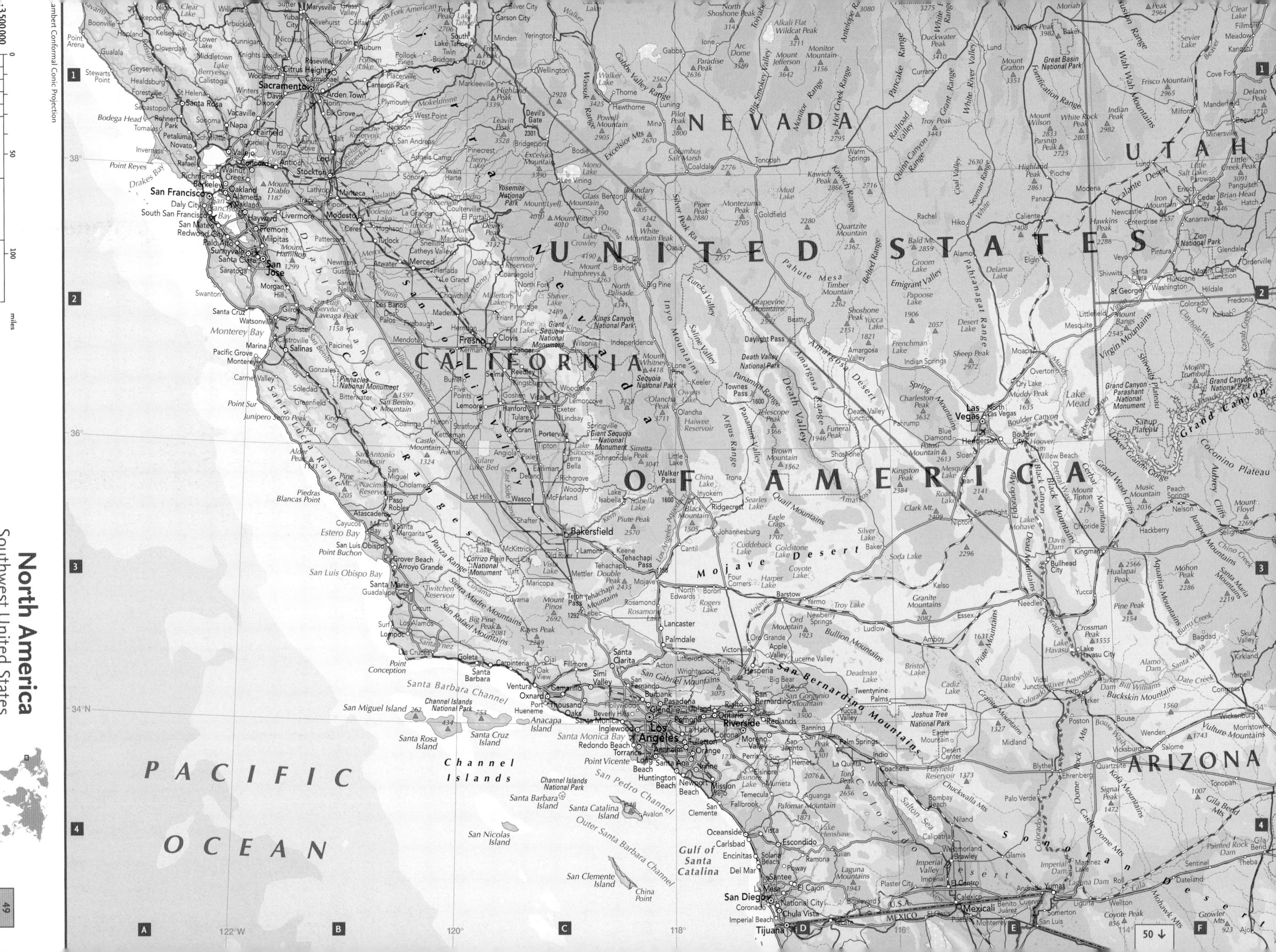

North America
Southwest United States

Lambert Conformal Conic Projection

1 : 3 500 000

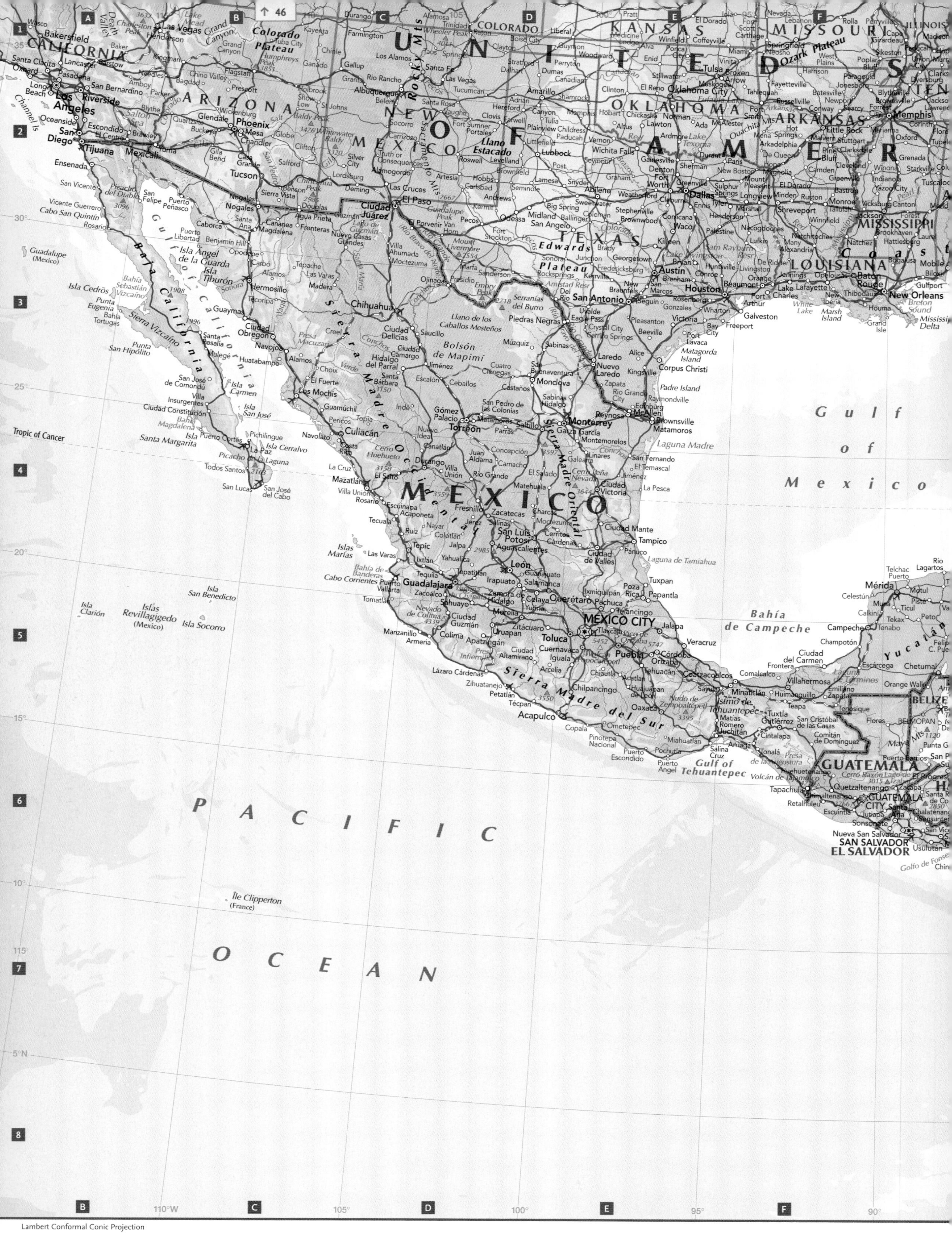

Lambert Conformal Conic Projection

50

1:14 000 000

0   200   400   miles

0   200   400   600   800 km

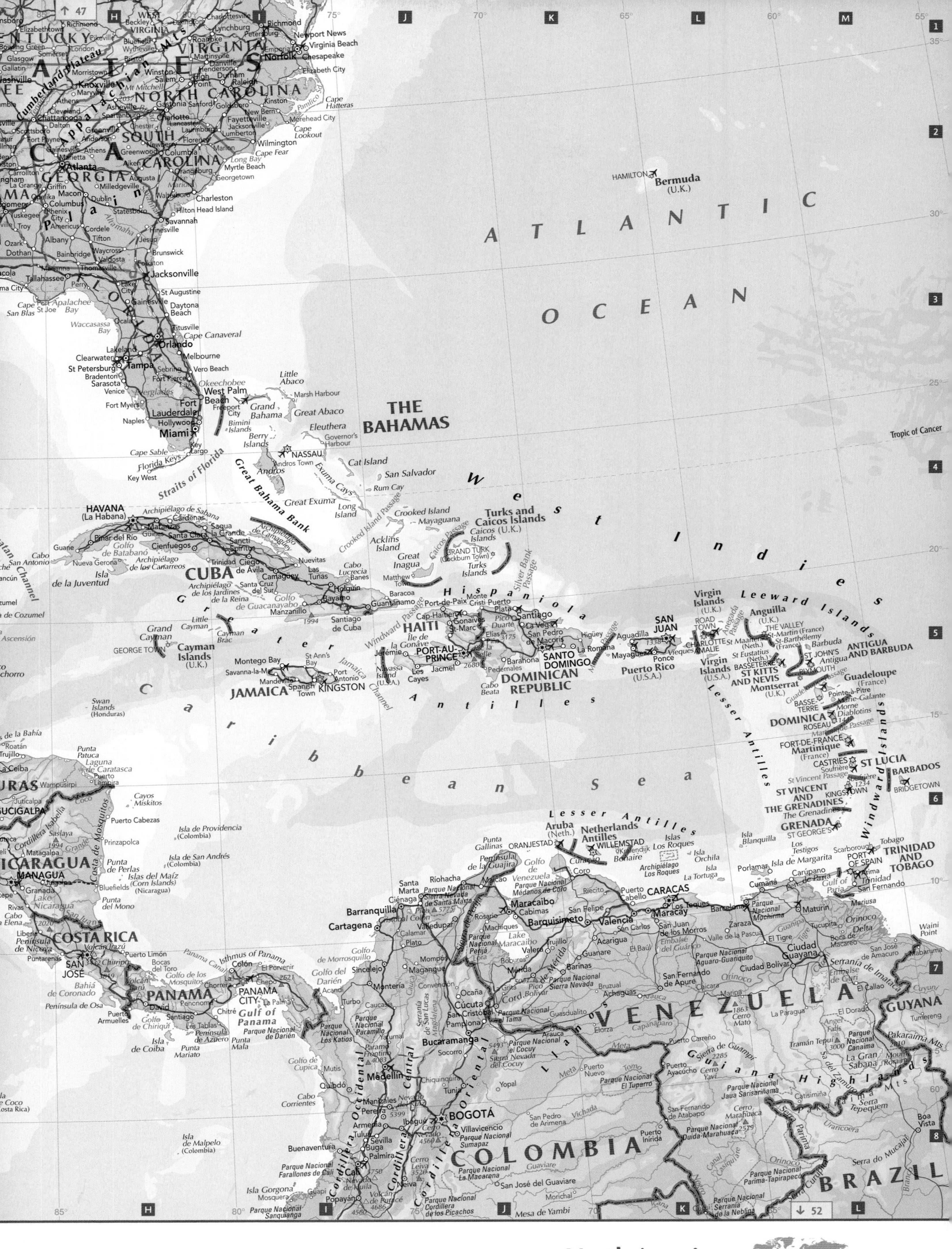

ATLANTIC

OCEAN

HAMILTON • Bermuda
(U.K.)

Tropic of Cancer

THE
BAHAMAS

NASSAU

Cat Island

San Salvador

Rum Cay

Crooked Island

Mayaguana

Acklins
Island

Great
Inagua

Matthew
Town

West

Indies

Turks and
Caicos Islands
Caicos (U.K.)
Islands

GRAND TURK
(Cockburn Town)

Turks
Islands

Silver Bank
Passage

Hispaniola

Virgin
Islands
(U.K.)

Leeward Islands

Anguilla
(U.K.)
THE VALLEY
St-Martin (France)
St-Barthélemy
(France)

ANTIGUA
AND BARBUDA

Barbuda

SAN JUAN

CHARLOTTE
AMALIE
Virgin
Islands
(U.S.A.)

St Maarten
(Neth.)
St Eustatius
(Neth.)

BASSETERRE
ST KITTS
AND NEVIS

ROAD
TOWN

Ponce

Puerto Rico
(U.S.A.)

BASSE-
TERRE

Montserrat
(U.K.)

PLYMOUTH

Antigua

ST JOHN'S

Guadeloupe
(France)

Pointe-à-Pitre

Marie-Galante

CUBA

HAVANA
(La Habana)

HAITI

PORT-AU-
PRINCE

DOMINICAN
REPUBLIC

SANTO
DOMINGO

Morne
Diablotins

DOMINICA

ROSEAU

FORT-DE-FRANCE
Martinique
(France)

CASTRIES

ST LUCIA

Soufrière

BARBADOS

BRIDGETOWN

ST VINCENT
AND
THE GRENADINES

KINGSTOWN

The Grenadines

GRENADA
ST GEORGE'S

JAMAICA

KINGSTON

Cayman
Islands
(U.K.)

Grand
Cayman

GEORGE TOWN

Montego Bay

Greater

Antilles

Caribbean

Sea

Lesser

Antilles

Lesser Antilles

Aruba
(Neth.)

ORANJESTAD

Netherlands
Antilles

WILLEMSTAD

Curaçao
Bonaire

Islas
Los Roques

Tobago

TRINIDAD
AND
TOBAGO

PORT
OF SPAIN

Isla de Margarita

HONDURAS

Swan
Islands
(Honduras)

Isla de
Providencia
(Colombia)

Isla de San Andrés
(Colombia)

Islas del Maíz
(Corn Islands)
(Nicaragua)

NICARAGUA

MANAGUA

Lake
Nicaragua

COSTA
RICA

SAN
JOSÉ

PANAMA

PANAMA
CITY

COLOMBIA

Cartagena

Barranquilla

Santa
Marta

MARACAIBO

Lake
Maracaibo

CARACAS

Barquisimeto

Valencia

Maracay

VENEZUELA

Ciudad
Bolívar

Ciudad
Guayana

Orinoco

GUYANA

BOGOTÁ

Medellín

Cali

BRAZIL

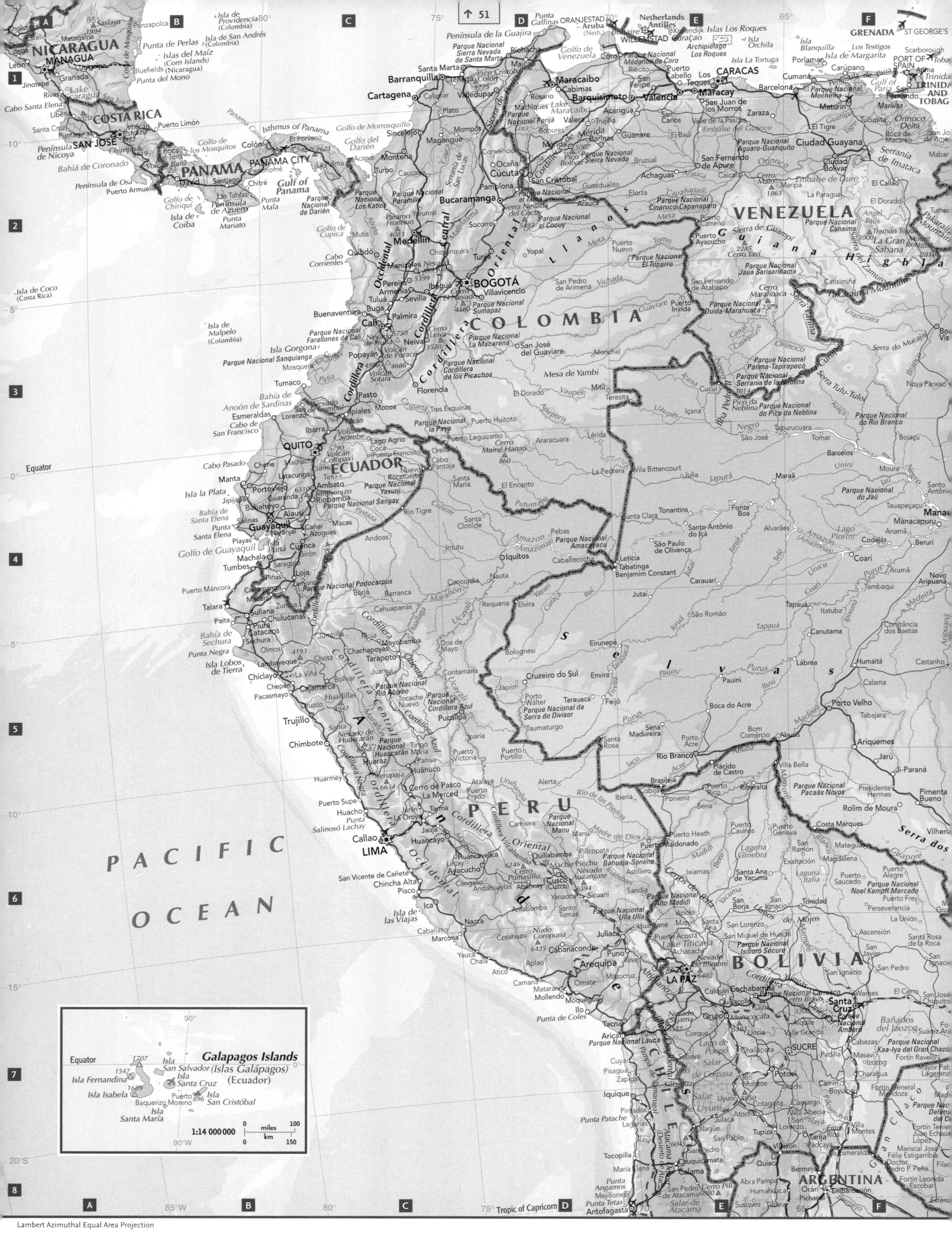

PACIFIC

OCEAN

Galapagos Islands
San Salvador (Islas Galápagos)
(Ecuador)

Equator
Isla Fernandina
Isla Isabela
Isla
Santa María
Santa Cruz
Puerto
Baquerizo Moreno
Isla
San Cristóbal

1:14 000 000

miles 100
km 150

90° 90°W

NICARAGUA
MANAGUA
COSTA RICA
SAN JOSÉ
PANAMA
PANAMA CITY

COLOMBIA
BOGOTÁ
Medellín
Cali
QUITO
ECUADOR
Guayaquil

VENEZUELA
CARACAS
Maracaibo
Valencia

GRENADA

PERU
LIMA
Callao

BOLIVIA
LA PAZ
SUCRE
Santa Cruz

CHILE

ARGENTINA

Lambert Azimuthal Equal Area Projection

1:14 000 000

miles
200   400

km
200   400   600   800

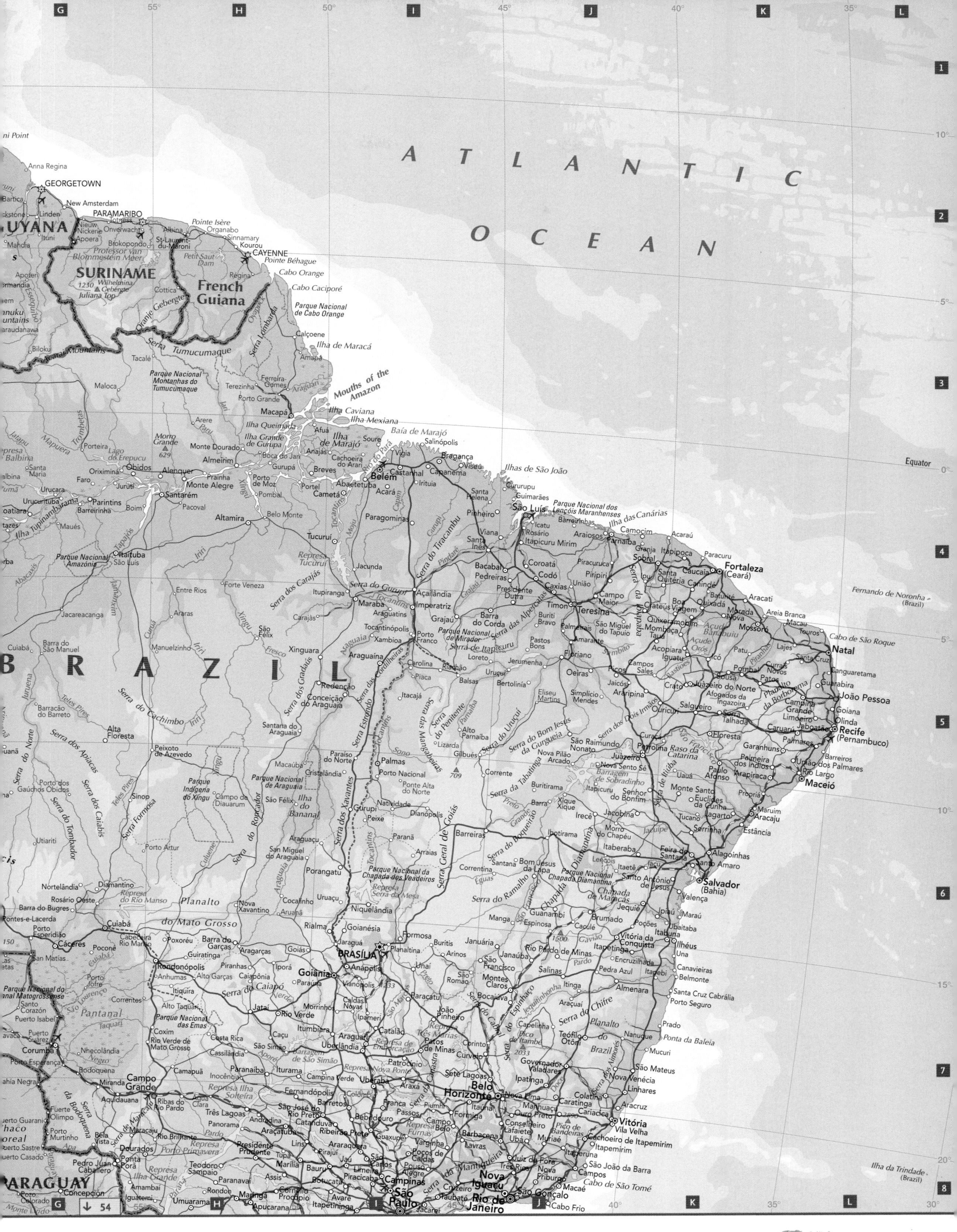
ATLANTIC
OCEAN
BRAZIL
SURINAME
French Guiana
GUYANA
PARAGUAY
GEORGETOWN
PARAMARIBO
CAYENNE
BRASÍLIA
Equator
Mouths of the Amazon
Ilha de Marajó
Baía de Marajó
Ilha Caviana
Ilha Mexiana
Ilha de Maracá
Ilhas de São João
Cabo Orange
Cabo Caciporé
Pointe Béhague
Pointe Isère
Parque Nacional de Cabo Orange
Parque Nacional Montanhas do Tumucumaque
Serra Tumucumaque
Serra Lombarda
Parque Nacional dos Lençóis Maranhenses
Ilha das Canárias
Fernando de Noronha (Brazil)
Cabo de São Roque
Ilha da Trindade (Brazil)
Cabo de São Tomé
Cabo Frio
Planalto do Mato Grosso
Pantanal
Serra do Cachimbo
Serra dos Carajás
Serra do Roncador
Serra Geral de Goiás
Serra do Espinhaço
Chapada Diamantina
Serra da Mantiqueira
Planalto do Brazil
Serra da Borborema
Parque Nacional da Chapada dos Veadeiros
Parque Nacional da Chapada Diamantina
Parque Nacional das Emas
Parque Indígena do Xingu
Represa de Sobradinho
Represa Tucuruí
Represa de Furnas
Ilha do Bananal
Macapá
Belém
São Luís
Fortaleza (Ceará)
Natal
João Pessoa
Recife (Pernambuco)
Maceió
Aracaju
Salvador (Bahia)
Teresina
Palmas
Goiânia
Cuiabá
Campo Grande
Belo Horizonte
Vitória
Rio de Janeiro
São Paulo
Campinas
Nova Iguaçu
São Gonçalo
Santarém
Imperatriz
Marabá
Altamira
Itaituba
Juàzeiro
Petrolina
Feira de Santana
Vitória da Conquista
Uberlândia
Montes Claros
Juiz de Fora
Ribeirão Preto
Corumbá
Rondonópolis
Londrina
Maringá
Caruaru
Campina Grande
Mossoró
Ilhéus
Juàzeiro do Norte

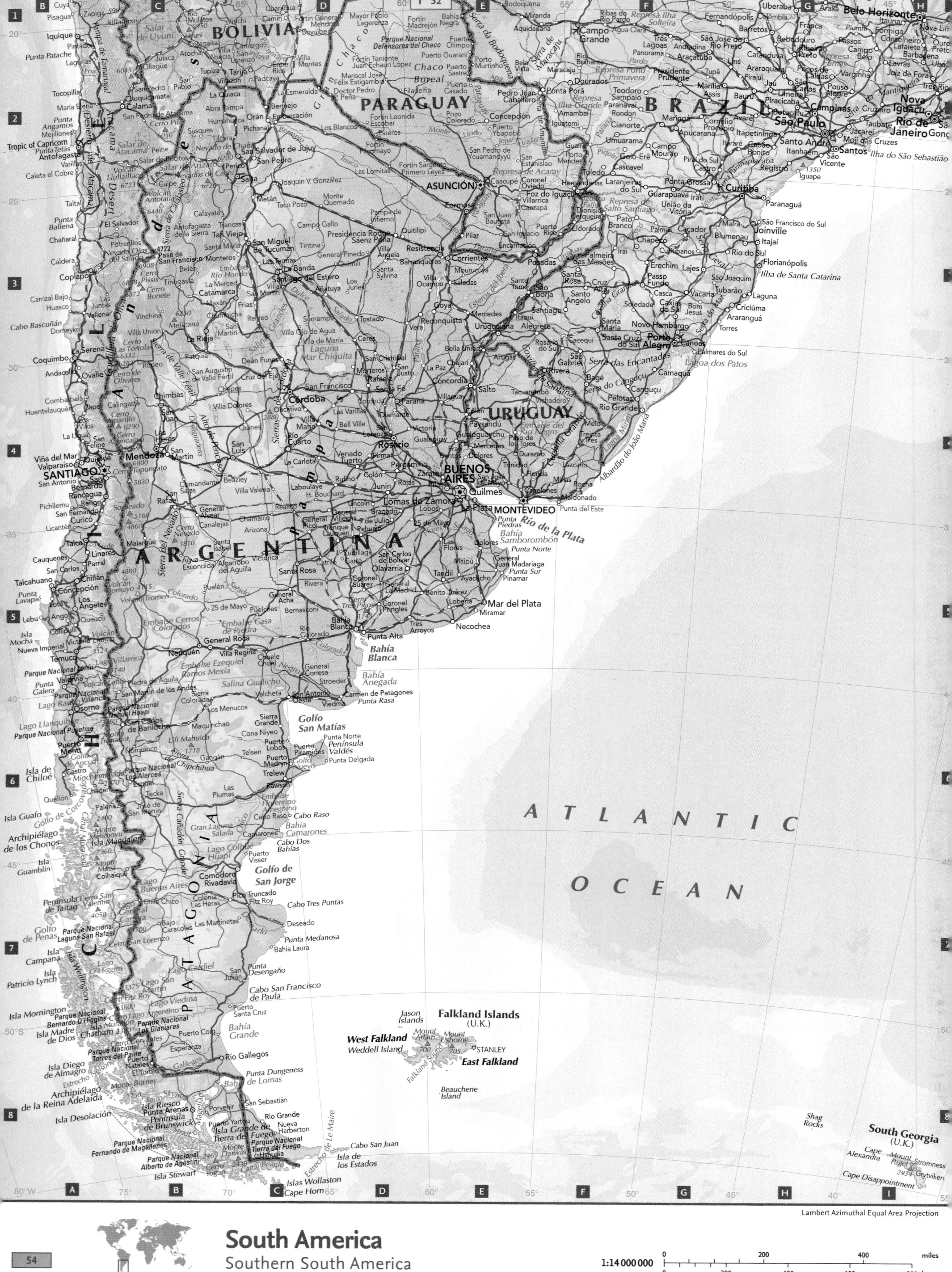

South America
Southern South America

1:14 000 000

Lambert Azimuthal Equal Area Projection

MATO
GROSSO

TOCANTINS

BAHIA

GOIAS

DISTRITO
FEDERAL

BRASÍLIA

B R A Z I L

MINAS GERAIS

ESPÍRITO SANTO

Belo
Horizonte

Vitória

SÃO PAULO

RIO DE JANEIRO

Nova
Iguaçu

Rio de
Janeiro

São Paulo

Santos

PARANÁ

Curitiba

SANTA
CATARINA

Florianópolis

RIO GRANDE
DO SUL

Porto Alegre

A T L A N T I C

O C E A N

Tropic of Capricorn

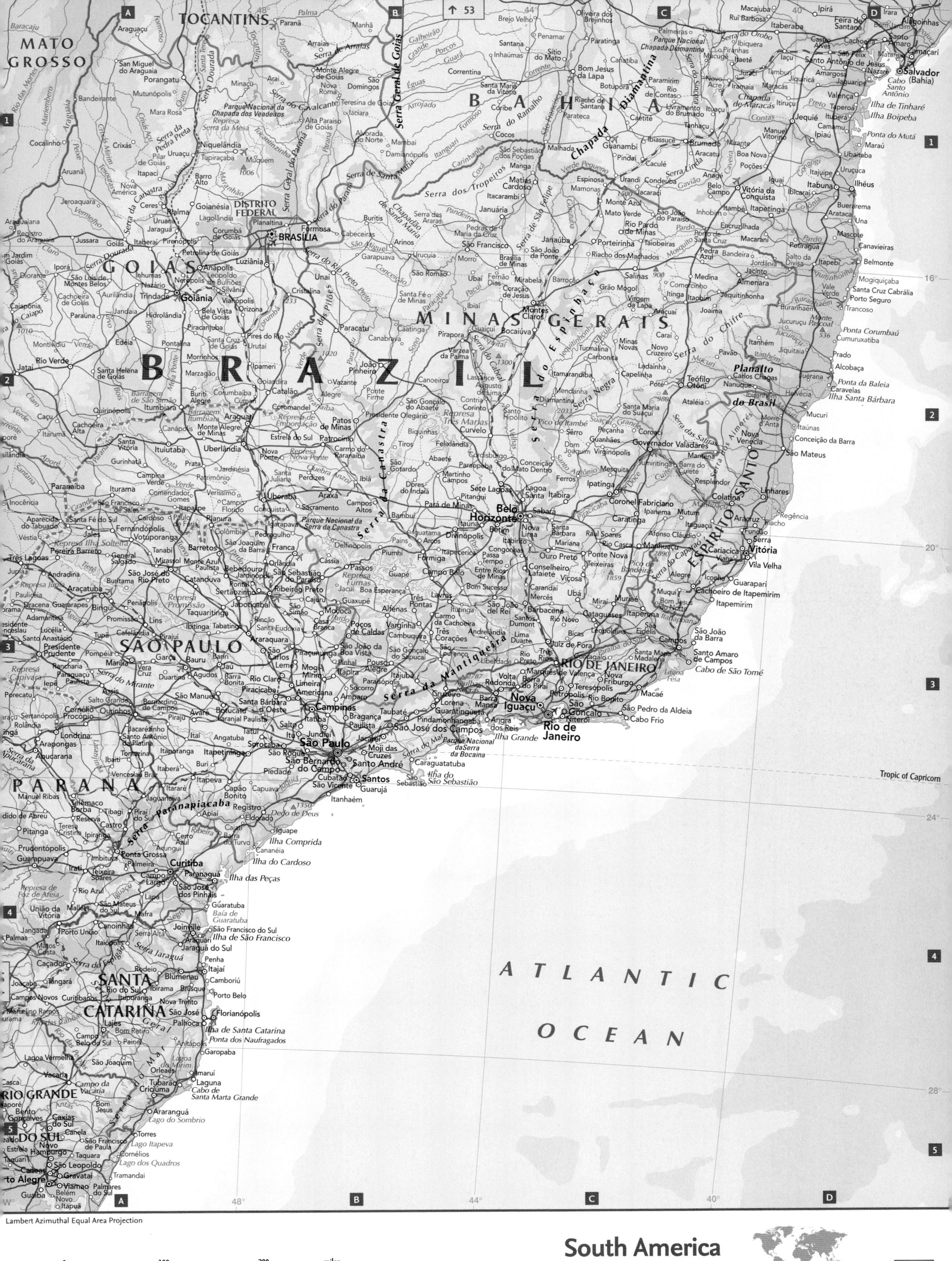

Lambert Azimuthal Equal Area Projection

South America
Southeast Brazil

1:7 000 000

| 0 | 100 | 200 | miles |
| 0 | 100 | 200 | 300 | 400 | km |

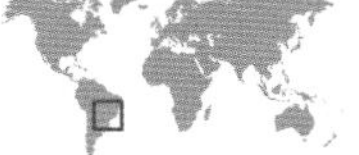

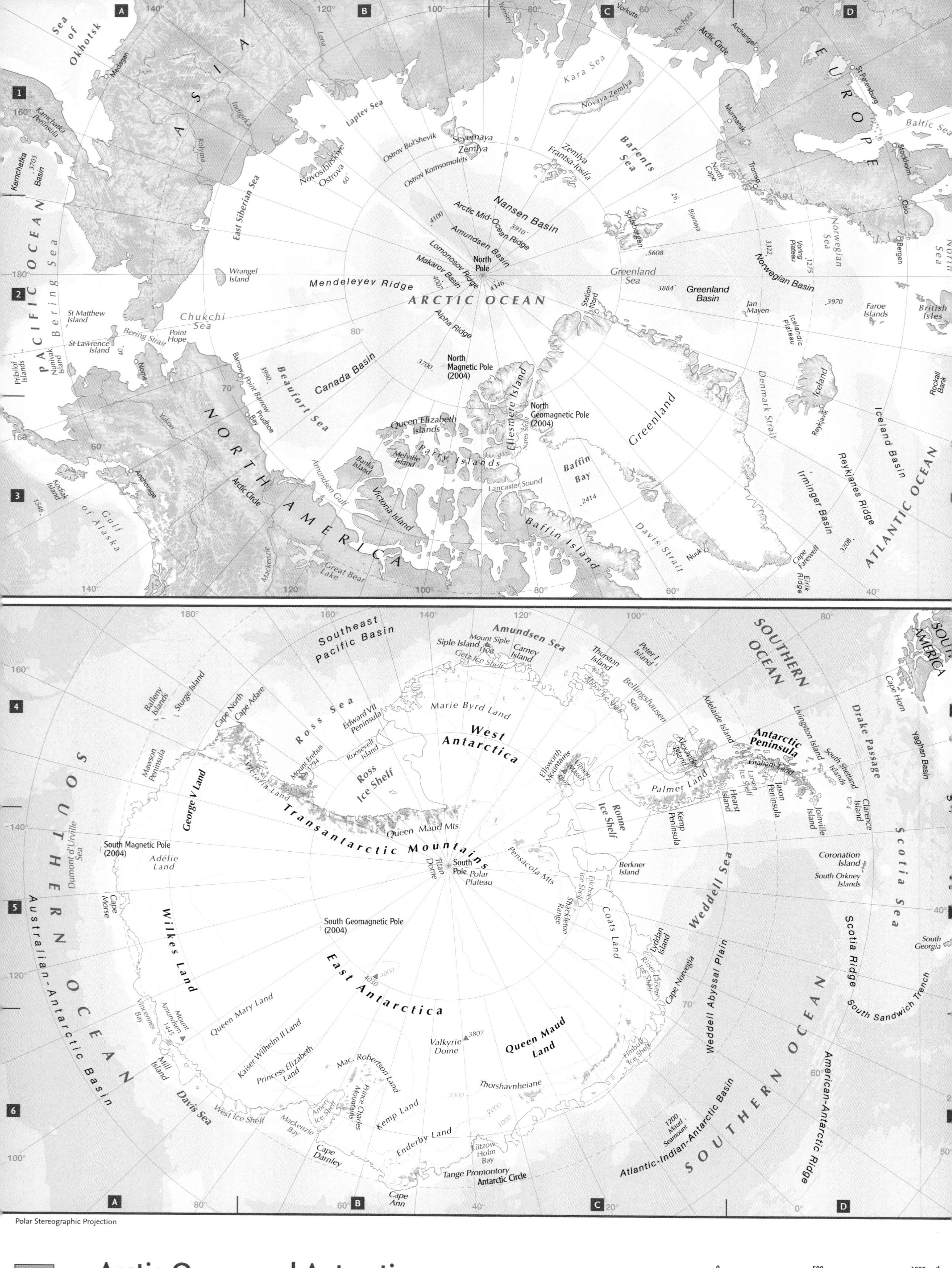

Arctic Ocean and Antarctica

Polar Stereographic Projection

1:35 000 000

| | 0 | 500 | 1000 miles |
| 0 | 500 | 1000 | 1500 km |

Index

The index includes the most significant names on the maps in the atlas. The names are generally indexed to the largest scale map on which they appear. For large physical features this will be the largest scale map on which they appear in their entirety or in the majority. Names can be located using the grid reference letters and numbers around the edges of the map. Names located on insets have a symbol □.

Abbreviations used to describe features in the index:

admin. dist. administrative district
admin. div. administrative division
admin. reg. administrative region
aut. reg. autonomous region
aut. rep. autonomous republic
b. bay
c. cape
depr. depression
des. desert
esc. escarpment
est. estuary
for. forest
g. gulf
hd. headland
i. island
imp. lake impermanent lake
is islands
l. lake
lag. lagoon
mt. mountain
mts mountains
pen. peninsula
plat. plateau
pref. prefecture
prov. province
pt point
r. river
r. mouth river mouth
reg. region
resr. reservoir
salt l. salt lake
sea chan. sea channel
terr. territory
vol. volcano

1

9 de Julio 54D5
25 de Mayo 54D5

A

Aabenraa 11F9
Aachen 13K5
Aalborg 11F8
Aalborg Bugt *b.* 11G8
Aalen 13M6
Aalst 12J5
Aars 11F8
Asiaat 45M3
Aba 32D4
Ābādān 33H1
Ābādeh 26E3
Abadla 32C1
Abaeté 55B2
Abaetetuba 53I4
Abakaliki 32D4
Abakan 24K4
Abakanskiy Khrebet *mts* 24J4
Abancay 52D6
Abarqū 26E3
Abashiri 30G3
Abbeville 18E1
Abbeville 47I6
Abéché 33F3
Abengourou 32C4
Abeokuta 32D4
Aberdare 15D7
Aberdeen 16G3
Aberdeen 42E4
Aberdeen 46H2
Abergavenny 15D7
Aberystwyth 15C6
Abhā 34E2
Abhar 33H1
Abidjan 32C4
Abilene 46H5
Abingdon 15F7
Abinsk 23H7
Abitibi, Lake 45J5
Aboisso 32C4
Abomey 32D4
Abong Mbang 32E4
Aboyne 16G3
Abqaiq 34E1
Abrantes 19B4
Absaroka Range *mts* 46E3
Abū 'Arīsh 34E2
Abu Dhabi 26E4
Abu Hamed 33G3
Abuja 32D4
Abū Kamāl 33H1
Abu Road 27G4
Açailândia 53I5
Acaponeta 50C4
Acapulco 50E5
Acará 53I4
Acaraú 53J4
Acarigua 52E2
Acatlan 50E5
Accra 32C4
Accrington 14E5
Achaguas 52E2
Acheng 30B3
Achinsk 24K4
Acıpayam 21M6
Acireale 20F6
Acklins Island 47M7
Acle 15I6
Aconcagua, Cerro *mt.* 54B4
Acopiara 53K5
A Coruña 19B2
Acqui Terme 20C2
Acri 20G5
Ada 47H5
Adamantina 55A3
Adams 48E1
Adana 33G1
Adapazarı 21N4
Ad Dafinah 34E1
Ad Dahnā' *des.* 34E1
Ad Dakhla 32B2
Ad Dār al Ḩamrā' 34D1
Ad Darb 34E2
Ad Dawādimī 34E1
Addis Ababa 34D3
Ad Dīwānīyah 33H1
Addlestone 15G7
Adelaide 41H6
Aden 34E2
Aden, Gulf of 34E2
Adīgrat 34D2
Adīrī 33E2
Adirondack Mountains 48D1
Adjud 21L1
Admiralty Gulf 40F2
Admiralty Islands 38E2
Ado-Ekiti 32D4
Adrano 20F6
Adrar 32C2
Adrian 46G4
Adriatic Sea 20E2
Ādwa 34D2
Adzopé 32C4
Aegean Sea 21K5
A Estrada 19B2
Afanas'yevo 22L4
Afghanistan *country* 26F3
Afgooye 34E3
Afogados da Ingazoira 53K5
Afonso Cláudio 55C3
Afuá 53H4
Afyon 21N5
Agadez 32D3
Agadir 32C1
Agadyr' 27G2
Agara 23I8
Agartala 27I4
Agboville 32C4
Ağcabädi 23J8
Agde 18F5
Agen 18E4
Agios Dimitrios 21J6
Agios Nikolaos 21K7
Agnibilékrou 32C4
Agrinia 21K2
Agra 27G4
Ağrı 26D3
Agrigento 20E6
Agrinio 21I5
Aguadilla 51K5
Agua Prieta 46F5
Aguascalientes 50D4
Agudos 55A3
Águilas 19F5
Agulhas, Cape 36E8
Ahar 26D3
Ahmadabad 27G4
Ahmar *mts* 34E3
Ahtme 11O7
Ahväz 33H1
Aigio 21J5
Aiken 47K5
Aïn Beïda 20B7
Aïn Defla 19H5
Aïn Deheb 19G6
Aïn el Hadjel 19H6
Aïn Oussera 19H6
Aïn Sefra 32C1
Aïn Taya 19H5
Aïn Tédélès 19G6
Aïn Temouchent 19F6
Airdrie 16F5
Aitutaki 1J1
Aix-en-Provence 18G5
Aix-les-Bains 18G4
Aizawl 27I4
Aizkraukle 11N8
Aizu-wakamatsu 31E5
Ajaccio 18I6
Ajdābiyā 33F1
Ajmer 27G4
Akçakoca 21N4
Akchâr *reg.* 32B3
Åkersberga 11K7
Aketi 34C3
Akhali Ap'oni 23I8
Akhḑar, Al Jabal al *mts* 33F1
Akhisar 21L5
Akhtubinsk 23J6
Akhty 23J8
Aki 31D6
Akita 31F5
Akjoujt 32B3
Akkajaure *l.* 10J3
Akkol' 27G1
Akkuş 23H8
Akom II 32E4
Akonolinga 32E4
Akordat 33G3
Akranes 10□2
Åkrehamn 11D7
Akron 48A2
Aksay 23H7
Akşehir 21N5
Aksu 27H2
Aksubayevo 23K5
Aktau 26E2
Aktobe 26E1
Aktsyabrski 23F5
Akune 31C6
Akure 32D4
Akureyri 10□2
Akwanga 32D4
Akyazı 21N4
Alabama *r.* 47J5
Alabama *state* 47J5
Alaçam 23G8
Alagir 23J8
Alagoinhas 55D1
Al Aḩmadī 26D4
Alajärvi 10M5
Al 'Alayyah 34E2
Alaşehir 21M5
Alaska *state* 44D3
Alaska, Gulf of 44D4
Alaska Peninsula 44B4
Alaska Range *mts* 44D3
Alatyr' 23J5
Alausí 52C4
Alaverdi 23J8
Alavus 10M5
Alba 20C2
Albacete 19F4
Alba Iulia 21J1
Albania *country* 21H4
Albany 40D6
Albany 46C3
Albany 47K5
Albany 48E1
Albany *r.* 45J4
Al Bayḑā' 33F1
Al Bayḑā' 34E2
Albenga 20C2
Albert, Lake 34D3
Alberta *prov.* 44G4
Albert Lea 47I3
Albert Nile *r.* 33G4
Alberton 37I4
Albertville 18H4
Albi 18F5
Albina 53H2
Albion 48B1
Al Birk 34E2
Al Biyāḑh *reg.* 34E1
Alborán, Isla de *i.* 19E6
Albufeira 19B5
Albuquerque 46F4
Al Buraymī 26E4
Albury 42C6
Alcalá de Henares 19E3
Alcalá la Real 19E5
Alcamo 20E6
Alcántara 19C4
Alcaraz 19E4
Alcázar de San Juan 19E4
Alchevs'k 23H6
Alcobaça 55D2
Alcoy-Alcoi 19F4
Alcúdia 19H4
Aldabra Islands 35E4
Aldan 25N4
Aldan *r.* 25N3
Aldeburgh 15I6
Aldershot 15G7
Aldridge 15F6
Aleg 32B3
Alegre 55C3
Alegrete 54E3
Aleksandrov 22H4
Aleksandrov Gay 23K6
Aleksandrovskoye 23I7
Aleksandrovsk-Sakhalinskiy 30F2
Aleksandry, Zemlya *i.* 24F1
Alekseyevka 23H6
Alekseyevka 23H6
Alekseyevskaya 22K5
Aleksin 23H5
Aleksinac 21I3
Alençon 18E2
Alenquer 53H4
'Alenuihāhā Channel 46□
Aleppo 33G1
Alès 18G4
Aleşd 21J1
Alessandria 20C2
Ålesund 10E5
Aleutian Islands 44A4
Aleutian Range *mts* 44C4
Alexander Bay 36C5
Alexandra 42B6
Alexandria 16E5
Alexandria 21K3
Alexandria 33F1
Alexandria 47I5
Alexandria 48C3
Alexandroupoli 21K4
Aleysk 24J4
Al Fayyūm 33G2
Alfenas 55B3
Alford 14H5
Alfred 48C1
Algarve *reg.* 19B5
Algeciras 19D5
Algemesí 19F4
Algeria *country* 32C2
Al Ghayḑah 34F2
Alghero 20C4
Al Ghurdaqah 33G2
Algiers 19H5
Algoa Bay 37G7
Algona 47I3
Algorta 19E2
Al Ḩadīthah 33H1
Alhama de Murcia 19F5
Al Ḩanākīyah 34E1
Al Ḩasakah 33H1
Al Ḩayy 33H1
Al Ḩazm al Jawf 34E2
Al Ḩinnāh 34E1
Al Hoceima 19E6
Al Hufūf 34E1
Aliağa 21L5
Alicante 19F4
Alice 46H6
Alice Springs 40G4
Alihe 30A2
Alindao 34C3
Alingsås 11H8
Aliquippa 48A2
Al Isma'īlīyah 33G1
Aliveri 21K5
Al Jahrah 26D4
Al Jamalīyah 34F1
Al Jawf 26C4
Al Jawf 33F2
Al Jufra Oasis 33E2
Aljustrel 19B5
Al Kahfah 34E1
Al Khārijah 33G2
Al Khaşab 26E4
Al Khawr 34F1
Al Khums 33E1
Al Khunn 34E1
Alkmaar 12J4
Al Kūt 33H1
Allahabad 27H4
Allakh-Yun' 25O3
Allegheny *r.* 48B2
Allegheny Mountains 48A4
Allende 46G6
Allentown 48D2
Alliance 46G3
Alliance 48A2
Allier *r.* 18F3
Al Līth 34E1
Alloa 16F4
Alma 47M2
Almada 19B4
Al Maḩwīt 34E2
Al Mansa 19F4
Al Manşūrah 33G1
Al Marj 33F1
Almaty 27G2
Almazny 25M3
Almeirim 19B4
Almeirim 53H4
Almelo 13K4
Almenara 55C2
Almendralejo 19C4
Almería 19E5
Almería, Golfo de *b.* 19E5
Al'met'yevsk 24G4
Älmhult 11I8
Al Mindak 34E1
Al Minyā 33G2
Al Mubarrez 34E1
Alofi 39J3
Alor Setar 29C7
Alotau 41K2
Alpena 47K2
Alpine 46G5
Alps *mts* 18H4
Al Qā'īyah 34E1
Al Qāmishlī 33H1
Al Qaţn 34E2
Al Qunfidhah 34E2
Al Quşayr 33G2
Al Quwayīyah 34E1
Alsager 15E5
Alstonville 42F2
Alta 10M2
Alta Floresta 53G5
Altai Mountains 27H2
Altamira 53H4
Altamura 20G4
Altay 27H2
Altay 27I2
Altdorf 18I3
Altıntaş 21N5
Altiplano *plain* 52E7
Alto Garças 53H7
Altoona 48B2
Alto Parnaíba 53I5
Altrincham 14E5
Altun Shan *mts* 27H3
Altus 46H5
Alüksne 11O8
Alva 46H4
Alvesta 11I8
Älvsbyn 10L4
Al Wajh 34D1
Al Widyān *plat.* 33H1
Alyangula 41H2
Alyth 16F4
Alytus 11N9
Amadeus, Lake *salt flat* 40G4
Amadora 19B4
Åmål 11H7
Amambaí 54E2
Amanzimtoti 37J6
Amarante 53J5
Amareleja 19C4
Amargosa 55D1
Amarillo 46G4
Amasra 23G8
Amazar 30A1
Amazon *r.* 52F4
Amazon, Mouths of the 53I3
Ambalavao 35E6
Ambam 34B3
Ambato 52C4
Ambato Boeny 35E5
Ambato Finandrahana 35E6
Ambatolampy 35E5
Ambatondrazaka 35E5
Amberg 13M6
Ambilobe 35E5
Ambleside 14E4
Amboasary 35E6
Ambohimahasoa 35E6
Ambon 29E8
Ambositra 35E6
Ambovombe 35E6
Ambriz 35B4
Americana 55B3
American Fork 46E3
American Samoa *terr.* 39J3
Americus 47K5
Amersfoort 12J4
Amersham 15G7
Ames 47I3
Amesbury 48F1
Amfissa 21J5
Amga 25O3
Amherst 48E1
Amiens 18F2
Amistad Reservoir 46G6
Amlwch 14C5
'Ammān 33G1
Ammanford 15D7
Ämmänsaari 10P4
Amorgos *i.* 21K6
Amos 45K5
Ampanihy 35E6
Amparo 55B3
Ampasimanolotra 35E5
Amravati 27G4
Amritsar 27G3
Amstelveen 12J4
Amsterdam 12J4
Amsterdam 48D1
Amstetten 13O6
Am Timan 33F3
Amudar'ya *r.* 26E2
Amundsen Gulf 44F2
Amundsen Sea 56C4
Amuntai 29D8
Amur *r.* 30F1
Amursk 30E2
Amurskaya Oblast' *admin. div.* 30C1
Amurzet 30C3
Amvrosiyivka 23H7
Anabanua 29E8
Anaconda 46E2
Anadolu Dağları *mts* 26C2
Anadyr' 25S3
Anagé 55C1
'Ānah 33H1
Anaheim 49D4
Anajás 53I4
Analalava 35E5
Anamur 33G1
Anan 31D6
Anantapur 27G5
Anan'yiv 23F7
Anapa 23H7
Anápolis 55A2
Añatuya 54D3
Anbyon 31B5
Anchorage 44D3
Ancona 20E3
Anda 30B3
Andacollo 54B4
Andalucía *aut. comm.* 19D5
Andaman Islands 27I5
Andaman Sea 29B6
Andapa 35E5
Andenne 12J5
Andéramboukane 32D3
Anderlecht 12J5
Anderson 47J3
Anderson 47K5
Andes *mts* 54C4
Andijon 27G2
Andilamena 35E5
Andilanatoby 35E5
Andoany 35E5
Andong 31C5
Andorra *country* 19G2
Andorra la Vella 19G2
Andover 15F7
Andradina 55A3
Andreapol' 22G4
Andrelândia 55B3
Andrews 46G5
Andria 20G4
Andros *i.* 21K6
Andros *i.* 47L7
Andselv 10K2
Andújar 19D4
Andulo 35B5
Anegada, Bahía *b.* 54D6
Aného 32D4
Ang'angxi 30A3
Angara *r.* 25K4
Angarsk 25L4
Angatuba 55A3
Ängelholm 11H8
Angers 18D3
Anglesey *i.* 14C5
Angoche 35D5
Angol 54B5
Angola 48B1
Angola *country* 35B5
Angoulême 18E4
Angra dos Reis 55B3
Angren 27G2
Anguang 30A3
Anguilla *terr.* 51L5
Anjalankoski 11O6
Ankara 26C3
Ankazoabo 35E6
Anna 23I6
Annaba 20B6
An Nafūd *des.* 26D4
An Najaf 33H1
Annandale 48C3
Annapolis 48C3
Ann Arbor 47K3
Anna Regina 53G2
An Nāşirīyah 33H1
Annecy 18H4
An Nimāş 34E2
Anniston 47J5
Ansbach 13M6
Anshan 30A4
Anshun 27J4
Antakya 33G1
Antalaha 35F5
Antalya 21N6
Antalya Körfezi *g.* 21N6
Antananarivo 35E5
Antarctica 56
Antarctic Peninsula 56D4
Antequera 19D5
Anti Atlas *mts* 32C2
Antibes 18H5
Anticosti, Île d' *i.* 45L5
Antigua and Barbuda *country* 51L5
Antikythiro, Steno *sea chan.* 21J7
Antioch 49B1
Antipodes Islands 39H6
Antofagasta 54B2
Antrim 17F3
Antrim Hills 17F2
Antsalova 35E5
Antsirabe 35E5
Antsirañana 35E5
Antsohihy 35E5
Antwerp 12J5
Anuchino 30D4
Anuradhapura 27H6
Anxious Bay 40G6
Anyang 27K3
Anyang 31B5
Anzhero-Sudzhensk 24J4
Anzio 20E4
Aomori 30F4
Aoraki *mt.* 43C6
Aosta 20B2
Aoukâr *reg.* 32C2
Aparecida do Tabuado 55A3
Apatity 10R3
Apatzingán 50D5
Apeldoorn 13J4
Apennines *mts* 20C2
Apia 39I3
Apiaí 55A4
Aporé 55A2
Appalachian Mountains 47K4
Appennino Abruzzese *mts* 20E3
Appennino Tosco-Emiliano *mts* 20D3
Appennino Umbro-Marchigiano *mts* 20E3
Appleton 47J3
Apple Valley 49D3
Aprilia 20E4
Apsheronsk 23H7
Apt 18G5
Apucarana 55A3
Aqaba, Gulf of 26C4
Aquaviva delle Fonti 20G4
Aquidauana 54E2
Arabian Gulf *see* The Gulf
Arabian Peninsula 26D4
Arabian Sea 26F5
Aracaju 53K6
Aracati 53K4
Aracatu 55C1
Araçatuba 55A3
Aracruz 55C2
Araçuaí 55C2
Arad 21I1
Arafura Sea 38D2
Aragarças 53H7
Araguaçu 55A1
Araguaina 53I5
Araguari 55A2
Araguatins 53I5
Araiosos 53J4
Arāk 33H1
Arakan Yoma *mts* 27I4
Aral Sea *salt l.* 26F2
Aral'sk 26F2
Aranda de Duero 19E3
Arandelovac 21I2
Aranjuez 19E3
Arao 31C6
Arapiraca 53K5
Arapongas 55A3
Araquari 55A4
'Ar'ar 26D3
Araranguá 55A5
Araraquara 55A3
Araripina 53J5
Arataca 55D1
Arauca 52D2
Arawa 38F2
Araxá 55B2
Arayıt Dağı *mt.* 21N5
Arbil 33H1
Arboga 11I7
Arbroath 16G4
Arcachon 18D4
Arcade 48B1
Arcadia 47K6
Arcelia 50D5
Archangel 22I2
Arcos 55B3
Arcos de la Frontera 19D5
Arctic Ocean *ocean* 56
Ardabil 26D3
Ardahan 23I8
Ardatov 23I5
Ardatov 23J5
Ardee 17F4
Ardennes *plat.* 12J6
Arden Town 49B1
Ardestān 26E3
Ardmore 47H5
Ardrossan 16E5
Areia Branca 53K4
Arendal 11F7
Arequipa 52D7
Arezzo 20D3
Arganda 19E3
Argentan 18D2
Argentina *country* 54C5
Argentino, Lago *l.* 54B8
Argos 21J6
Argostoli 21I5
Argun' 23J8
Argun' *r.* 28E2
Argungu 32D3
Argyle, Lake 40F3
Århus 11G8
Ariano Irpino 20F4
Aribinda 32C3
Arica 52D7
Arima 51L6
Arinos 55B1
Aripuanã 53G6
Ariquemes 52F5
Arisaig, Sound of *sea chan.* 16D4
Arizona *state* 46E5
'Arjah 34E1
Arkadak 23I6
Arkadelphia 47I5
Arkalyk 26F1
Arkansas *r.* 47I5
Arkansas *state* 47I4
Arkansas City 47H4
Arkhara 30C2
Arklow 17F5
Arkul' 22K4
Arles 18G5
Arlington 48C3
Arlington 48E2
Arlon 13J6
Armagh 17F3
Armant 33G2
Armavir 23I7
Armenia 52C3
Armenia *country* 26D2
Armeria 50D5
Armidale 42E3
Arnhem 13J5
Arnhem Land *reg.* 40G2
Arnold 15F5
Arnsberg 13L5
Arquipélago da Madeira *aut. reg.* 32B1
Arraias 55B1
Ar Ramādī 33H1
Arran *i.* 16D5
Ar Raqqah 33G1
Arras 18F1
Ar Rayyān 34F1
Arrecife 32B2
Arriagá 50F5
Ar Rifā'ī 33H1
Arroyo Grande 49B3
Arsen'yev 30D3
Arsk 22K4
Arta 21I5
Artem 30D4
Artemivs'k 23H6
Artesia 46G5
Artigas 54E4
Art'ik 23I8
Artsyz 21M2
Artvin 23I8
Arua 34D3
Aruba *terr.* 51K6
Arundel 15G8
Arusha 34D4
Arvayheer 27J2
Arviat 45I3
Arvidsjaur 10K4
Arvika 11H7
Arzamas 23I5
Arzew 19F6
Arzgir 23J7
Asaba 32D4
Asahikawa 30F4
Āsalē *l.* 34E2
Asansol 27H4
Āsayita 34E2
Asbury Park 48D2
Ascensión 52F7
Ascension *i.* 6
Aschaffenburg 13L6
Ascoli Piceno 20E3
Åseda 11I8
Asenovgrad 21K3
Asgabat 26E3
Asheville 47K4
Ashford 15H7
Ashibetsu 30F4
Ashikaga 31E5
Ashington 14F3
Ashland 46C3
Ashland 47I2
Ashmore and Cartier Islands *terr.* 40E2
Ashmyany 11N9
Ash Shiḩr 34E2
Ashtabula 48A2
Ashton-under-Lyne 14E5
Asilah 19C6
Asinara, Golfo dell' *b.* 20C4
Asino 24J4
Asipovichy 23F5
'Asīr *reg.* 34E1
Asker 11G7
Askim 11G7
Asmara 33G3
Åsosa 34D2
Aspatria 14D4
Aspen 46F4
Assab 33H3
As Samāwah 33H1
Assen 13K4
Assiniboine *r.* 44I5
Assis 55A3
Assisi 20E3
As Sulaymānīyah 33H1
Assynt, Loch *l.* 16D2
Astakos 21I5
Astana 27G1
Āstārā 26D3
Asti 20C2
Astorga 19C2
Astoria 46C2
Åstorp 11H8
Astrakhan' 23K7
Astravyets 11N9
Asturias *aut. comm.* 19C2
Asunción 54E3
Aswān 33G2
Asyūţ 33G2
Atacama, Salar de *salt flat* 54C2
Atacama Desert 54C3
Atakpamé 32D4
Ataléia 55C2
Atamyrat 26F3
'Ataq 34E2
Atâr 32B2
Atascadero 49B3
Atasu 27G2
Atbara 33G3
Atbara *r.* 33G3
Atbasar 26F1
Atchison 47H4
Athabasca, Lake 44H4
Athens 21J6
Athens 47K4
Athens 47K5
Athens 48C2
Atherstone 15F6
Athlone 17E4
Athol 48E1
Athy 17F5
Ati 33E3
Atico 52D7
Atka 25Q3
Atkarsk 23J6
Atlanta 47K5
Atlantic City 48D3
Atlantis 36D7
Atlas Mountains 32C1
Atlas Saharien *mts* 32D1
Atlas Tellien *mts* 19H6
Aţ Ţā'if 34E1
Attu Island 25S4
Aţ Ţūr 33G2
Åtvidaberg 11I7
Atwater 49B2
Atyashevo 23J5
Atyrau 26E2
Atyrauskaya Oblast' *admin. div.* 23K7
Aubagne 18G5
Auburn 48C1
Auburn 49B1
Auch 18E5
Auchterarder 16F4
Auckland 43E3
Auckland Islands 39G7
Audo *mts* 34E3
Augsburg 13M6
Augusta 20F6
Augusta 40D6
Augusta 47K5
Augusta 47N3
Auki 41M1
Aurangabad 27G5
Aurich 13K4
Aurillac 18F4
Aurora 46G4
Aurora 47J3
Austin 46H5
Austin 47I3
Austintown 48A2
Australia *country* 40F5
Australian Capital Territory *admin. div.* 42D5
Austria *country* 13N7
Autazes 53G4
Auvergne, Monts d' *mts* 18F4
Auxerre 18F3
Avaré 55A3
Aveiro 19B3
Avellino 20F4
Aversa 20F4
Avesta 11J6
Avezzano 20E3
Aviemore 16F3
Avignon 18G5
Ávila 19D3
Avilés 19D2
Avoca 42A6
Avola 20F6
Avon 48C1
Avon *r.* 15F8
Avon *r.* 16F3
Awbārī 32E2
Awe, Loch *l.* 16D4
Aweil 33F4
Awka 32D4
Axminster 15E8
Ayacucho 52D6
Ayacucho 54E5
Ayagoz 27H2
Ayancık 23G8
Ayang 31B5
Aydın 21L6
Aylesbury 15G7
'Ayoûn el 'Atroûs 32C3
Ayr 16E5
Aytos 21L3
Ayutthaya 29C6
Ayvacık 21L5
Ayvalık 21L5
Azaouâd *reg.* 32C3
Azare 32E3
Azerbaijan *country* 26D2
Azogues 52C4
Azores *terr.* 6
Azov 23H7
Azov, Sea of 23H7
Azzaba 20B6
Az Zaqāzīq 33G1
Az Zarqā' 33G1
Azzeffāl *hills* 32B2

B

Baardheere 34E3
Babadag 21M2
Babaeski 21L4
Babahoyo 52C4
Bāb al Mandab *strait* 34E2
Babanusa 33F3
Babati 35D4
Babayevo 22G4
Babayurt 23J8
Babruysk 23F5
Bacabal 53J4
Bacău 21L1
Bačka Palanka 21H2
Bac Liêu 29C7
Bacolod 29E6
Badajoz 19C4
Baden 13P6
Baden 18I3
Baden-Baden 13L6
Bad Hersfeld 13L5
Bad Ischl 13N7
Bad Kissingen 13M5
Badou 32D4
Badr Ḩunayn 34D1
Bad Salzungen 13M5
Bad Schwartau 13M4
Badulla 27H6
Bafatá 32B3
Baffin Bay *sea* 45L2
Baffin Island 45L3
Bafia 32E4
Bafilo 32D4
Bafoussam 32E4
Bāfq 26E3
Bafra 23G8
Bāft 26E4
Bafwasende 34C3
Bagamoyo 35D4
Bagé 54F4
Baghdād 33H1
Baghlān 27F3
Bagrationovsk 11L9
Bahia *state* 55C1
Bahía Blanca 54D5
Bahir Dar 34D2
Bahrain *country* 34F1
Bahrīyah, Wāḩāt al *oasis* 33F2
Baia Mare 21J1
Baicheng 30A3
Baie-Comeau 45L5
Baikal, Lake 25L4
Băileşti 21J2
Bainbridge 47K5
Baiquan 30B3
Bairnsdale 42C6
Baishan 30B4
Baisogala 11M9
Bajaur Desert 33G3
Baja 20H1
Baja California *pen.* 46D5
Bajoga 32E3
Bakel 32B3
Baker 46D3
Baker Island *terr.* 39I1
Baker Lake 45I3
Baker Lake 45I3
Bakersfield 49C3
Bakhmach 23G6
Bakırköy 21M4
Baksan 23I8
Baku 26D2
Balabac Strait *strait* 29D7
Balakān 23J8
Balakhna 22I4
Balakliya 23H6
Balakovo 23J5
Balanga 29E6
Balashov 23I6
Balaton, Lake 20G1
Balatonboglár 20G1
Balatonfüred 20G1
Balbina, Represa de *resr* 53G4
Balchik 21M3
Baldwin 48B2
Baléa 32B3
Balearic Islands *is* 19G4
Baleshwar 27H4
Baléyara 32D3
Bali *i.* 29D8
Bali, Laut *sea* 29D8
Balige 27I6
Balıkesir 21L5
Balikpapan 29D8
Balimo 38E2
Balingen 13L6
Balkanabat 26E3
Balkan Mountains 21J3
Balkhash 27G2
Balkhash, Lake 27G2
Ballarat 42A6
Ballé 32C3
Ballina 17C3
Ballina 42F2
Ballinasloe 17D4
Ballyclare 17G3
Ballymena 17F3
Ballymoney 17F2
Ballynahinch 17G3
Ballyshannon 17D3
Balranald 42A5
Balş 21K2
Balsas 53I5
Balta 23F7
Bălţi 23E7
Baltic Sea *g.* 11J9
Baltimore 48C3
Baltiysk 11K9
Balvi 11O8
Balykchy 27G2
Bam 26E4
Bamako 32C3
Bamba 32C3
Bambari 34C3
Bamberg 13M6
Bambuí 55B3
Bamenda 32E4
Bañados del Izozog *swamp* 52F7
Banamba 32C3
Banaz 21M5
Banbridge 17F3
Banbury 15F6
Banda, Laut *sea* 29F8
Banda Aceh 27I6
Bandar-e 'Abbās 26E4
Bandar-e Lengeh 26E4
Bandar Lampung 29C8
Bandar Seri Begawan 29D7
Bandiagara 32C3
Bandırma 21L4
Bandon 17D6
Bandundu 34B4
Bandung 29C8
Banes 51I4
Banff 16G3
Banff 44G4
Banfora 32C3
Bangalore 27G5
Bangassou 34C3
Bangka *i.* 29C8
Bangko 29C8
Bangkok 29C6
Bangladesh *country* 27H4
Bangolo 32C4
Bangor 14C5
Bangor 17G3
Bangor 47N3
Bangui 34B3
Banī Suwayf 33G2
Banī Walīd 33E1
Banja Luka 20G2
Banjarmasin 29D8
Banjul 32B3
Bankilaré 32D3
Banks Peninsula 43D6
Bann *r.* 17F2
Banning 49D4
Banská Bystrica 13Q6
Bantry 17C6
Bantry Bay 17C6
Banyo 32E4
Baochang 27K2
Baoding 27K3
Baoji 27J3
Baoqing 30D3
Baoshan 27I4
Baotou 27K2
Ba'qūbah 33H1
Bar 21H3
Baracoa 51J4
Barahona 51J5
Barakaldo 19E2
Baranavichy 11O10
Baranis 33G2
Baraouéli 32C3
Barbacena 55C3
Barbados *country* 51M6
Barbate de Franco 19D5
Barcaldine 41J4
Barcelona 19H3
Barcelona 52F1
Barcelos 52F4
Barclayville 32C4
Barcs 20G2
Bārdā 23J8
Bardejov 23D6
Bareilly 27G4
Barents Sea 24F2
Barentu 33G3
Barham 42B5
Bari 20G4
Barinas 52D2
Bariri 55A3
Barisan, Pegunungan *mts* 29C8
Barkly East 37H6
Barkly Tableland *reg.* 41H3
Barkly West 36G5
Barkol 27I2
Bârlad 21L1
Bar-le-Duc 18G2
Barlee, Lake *salt flat* 40D5
Barletta 20G4
Barmer 27G4
Barmouth 15C6
Barnaul 24J4
Barnsley 14F5
Barnstaple 15C7
Barnstaple Bay 15C7
Baro 32D4
Barquisimeto 52E1
Barra 55C1
Barra *i.* 16B4
Barra, Sound of *sea chan.* 16B3
Barraba 42E3
Barra Bonita 55A3
Barra do Bugres 53G7
Barra do Corda 53I5
Barra do Garças 53H7
Barra do Piraí 55C3
Barra Mansa 55B3
Barranqueras 54E3
Barranquilla 52D1
Barreiras 53J6
Barreirinha 53G4
Barreirinhas 53J4
Barreiro 19B4
Barreiros 53K5
Barretos 55A3
Barrhead 16E5
Barrier Range *hills* 41I6
Barro Alto 55A1
Barrow-in-Furness 14D4
Barry 15D7
Barstow 49D3
Bartica 53G2
Bartın 23G8
Bartoszyce 13R3
Baruun-Urt 27K2
Barwon *r.* 42C3
Barysaw 11P9
Barysh 23J5
Basarabi 21M2
Basel 18H3
Bashmakovo 23I5
Bashtanka 23G7
Basildon 15H7
Basingstoke 15F7
Basra 33H1
Bassano del Grappa 20D2
Bassar 32D4
Bassein 27I5
Basse-Normandie *admin. reg.* 15F9
Basse Santa Su 32B3
Basse-Terre 51L5
Basseterre 51L5
Bass Strait *strait* 42C7
Bastia 18I5
Bastogne 13J5
Bastrop 47I5
Bata 32D4
Batabanó, Golfo de *b.* 51H4
Batagay 25O3
Batangafo 34B3
Batangas 29E6
Batavia 48B1
Bataysk 23H7
Bătdâmbâng 29C6
Batemans Bay 42E5
Batesville 47I4
Bath 15E7
Bathgate 16F5
Bathurst 42D4
Bathurst 47N2
Bathurst Inlet 44H3
Bathurst Island 40G2
Bathurst Island 45I2
Batié 32C4
Batı Menteşe Dağları *mts* 21L6
Batı Toroslar *mts* 21N6
Batley 14F5
Batlow 42D5
Batna 32D1
Baton Rouge 47I5
Batouri 33E4
Batticaloa 27H6
Battipaglia 20F4
Battle Creek 47J3
Bat'umi 23I8
Baturite 53K4
Batyrevo 23J5
Baubau 29E8
Bauchi 32D3
Bauru 55A3
Bauska 11N8
Bautzen 13O5
Bayamo 51I4
Bayan 30B3
Bayanhongor 27J2
Bayan Hot 27J3
Bay City 47H6
Bay City 47K3
Baydhabo 34E3
Bayerischer Wald *mts* 13N6
Bayeux 15G9
Bayındır 21L5
Baykonyr 26F2
Baymak 24G4
Bayombong 29E6
Bayonne 18D5
Bayonne 48D2
Bayramiç 21L5
Bayreuth 13M6
Bay Shore 48E2
Baza 19E5
Bazarnyy Karabulak 23J5
Beachy Head 15H8
Beacon 48E2
Beacon Bay 37H7
Beaconsfield 15G7
Beagle Gulf 40F2
Bealanana 35E5
Beaminster 15E8
Beatrice 47H3
Beaufort 42A6
Beaufort Sea 44D2
Beaufort West 36F7
Beaumont 47I5
Beaune 18G3
Beauvais 18F2
Beaver 48A2
Beaver Falls 48A2
Beawar 27G4
Bebedouro 55A3
Bebington 14D5
Beccles 15I6
Bečej 21I2
Becerreá 19C2
Béchar 32C1
Beckley 48A4
Bedale 14F4
Bedford 15G6
Bedford 37J5
Bedford 47J4
Bedford 48B2
Bedford 48B4
Bedlington 14F3
Bedworth 15F6
Beechworth 42C6
Beenleigh 42F1
Beersheba 33G1
Beeville 46H6
Bega 42D6
Behshahr 26E3
Bei'an 30B2
Beihai 27J4
Beijing 27K3
Beira 35D5
Beirut 33G1
Beja 19C4
Béja 20C6
Bejaïa 19I5
Békés 21I1
Békéscsaba 21I1
Bekovo 23I5
Bela 26F4
Bela-Bela 37I3
Bélabo 32E4
Bel Air 48C3
Belalcázar 19D4
Belarus *country* 23E5
Bela Vista 54E2
Bela Vista de Goiás 55A2
Belaya Glina 23I7
Belaya Kalitva 23I6
Belaya Kholunitsa 22K4
Bełchatów 13Q5
Beledweyne 34E3
Belém 53I4
Belev 23H5
Belfast 17G3
Belfast 47N3
Belfast Lough *inlet* 17G3
Belfort 18H3
Belgaum 27G5
Belgium *country* 12J5
Belgorod 23H6
Belgrade 21I2
Belinskiy 23I5
Belinyu 29C8
Belize 35B4
Belize 50G5
Belize *country* 50G5
Bellary 27G5
Bella Unión 54E4
Belledonne *mts* 18G4
Bellefonte 48C2
Belle Glade 47K6
Belle Isle, Strait of 45M4
Bellevue 46C2
Bellingham 46C2
Bellinzona 18I3
Belluno 20E1
Bellville 36D7
Bell Ville 54D4
Belmont 42E4
Belmonte 55D1
Belmopan 50G5
Belo Campo 55C1
Belogorsk 30C2
Belo Horizonte 55C2
Beloit 47J3
Belomorsk 22G2
Beloretsk 24G4
Belo Tsiribihina 35E5
Beloye, Ozero *l.* 22H3
Belozersk 22H3
Belyy 22G5
Bemidji 47I2
Ben Arous 20D6
Benavente 19D2
Benbecula *i.* 16B3
Bend 46C3
Bendigo 42B6
Benešov 13O6
Benevento 20F4
Bengal, Bay of *sea* 27H5
Bengbu 27K3
Benghazi 33F1
Bengkulu 29C8
Benguela 35B5
Beni 34C3
Benidorm 19F4
Beni Mellal 32C1
Benin *country* 32D4
Benin, Bight of *g.* 32D4
Benin City 32D4
Beni-Saf 19F6
Benito Juárez 54E5
Benjamim Constant 52E4
Ben Nevis *mt.* 16D4
Bennington 48E1
Benoni 37I4
Bentiu 33F4
Bento Gonçalves 55A5
Benton Harbor 47J3
Bentonville 47I4
Benue *r.* 32D4
Benxi 30A4
Béoumi 32C4
Beppu 31C6
Berat 21H4
Berber 33G3
Berbera 34E2
Berbérati 34B3
Berdyans'k 23H7
Berdychiv 23F6
Berehove 23D6
Berekum 32C4
Berezivka 23F7
Berezne 23E6
Bereznik 22I3
Berezniki 24G4
Berezovo 24H3
Bergama 21L5
Bergamo 20C2
Bergen 11D6
Bergerac 18E4
Bergheim (Erft) 13K5
Bergsviken 10L4
Beringovskiy 25S3
Bering Sea 25S4
Bering Strait *strait* 44B3
Berkane 19E6
Berkeley 49A2
Berkovitsa 21J3
Berlin 13N4
Bermagui 42E6
Bermejo 52F8
Bermuda *terr.* 51L2
Bern 18H3
Bernardino de Campos 55A3
Berner Alpen *mts* 18H3
Beroun 13O6
Berrouaghia 19H5
Berry 42E5
Bertolinía 53J5
Bertoua 32E4
Beruri 52F4
Berwick-upon-Tweed 14E3
Beryslav 21O1
Besalampy 35E5
Besançon 18H3
Beslan 23J8
Bessbrook 17F3
Bessemer 47J5
Bessonovka 23J5
Bethel Park 48A2
Bethesda 14C5
Bethesda 48C3
Bethlehem 37I5
Bethlehem 48D2
Betim 55B2
Betpak-Dala *plain* 26G2
Betroka 35E6
Bettiah 27H4
Bettystown 17F4
Beverley 14G5
Beverly 48F1
Beverly Hills 49C3
Bexhill 15H8
Beykoz 21M4
Beyla 32C4
Beyneu 26E2
Beypazarı 21N4
Beyşehir 33G1
Bezhanitsy 22F4
Bezhetsk 22H4
Béziers 18F5
Bhamo 27I4
Bhavnagar 27G4
Bhawanipatna 27H5
Bhilwara 27G4
Bhopal 27G4
Bhubaneshwar 27H4
Bhuj 27F4

Hamamatsu 31E6
Hamar 11G6
Hambantota 27H6
Hamburg 13L4
Hamburg 48B1
Hamden 48E2
Hämeenlinna 11N6
Hameln 13L4
Hamersley Range *mts* 40D4
Hamhŭng 31B5
Hami 27I2
Hamilton 16E5
Hamilton 43E3
Hamilton 47K4
Hamilton 48B1
Hamilton 51L2
Hamina 11O6
Hamju 31B5
Hamm 13K5
Hammada du Drâa *plat.* 32C2
Hammamet 20D6
Hammamet, Golfe de *g.* 20D6
Hammerfest 10M1
Hammonton 48D3
Hampshire Downs *hills* 15F7
Hampton 48C4
Ḩanak 34D1
Hanamaki 31F5
Handan 27K3
Handeni 35D4
Hanford 49C2
Hangayn Nuruu *mts* 27I2
Hangzhou 28E4
Hangzhou Wan *b.* 28E4
Hanko 11M7
Hanna 44G4
Hannibal 47I4
Hannover 13L4
Hanöbukten *b.* 11I9
Ha Nôi 28C5
Hanover 48C3
Hantsavichy 11O10
Hanzhong 27J3
Haparanda 10N4
Happy Valley-Goose Bay 45L4
Ḩaraḑh 34E1
Haradok 23F5
Haramachi 31F5
Harare 35D5
Harbin 30B3
Hardangerfjorden *sea chan.* 11D7
Hardap *admin. reg.* 36C3
Hārer 34E3
Hargeysa 34E3
Harima-nada *b.* 31D6
Harjavalta 11M6
Harleston 15I6
Harlow 15H7
Harney Basin 46C3
Härnösand 10J5
Harper 32C4
Harris, Sound of *sea chan.* 16B3
Harrisburg 48C2
Harrison 47I4
Harrisonburg 48B3
Harrisonville 47I4
Harrogate 14F5
Hârşova 21L2
Harstad 10J2
Hartberg 13O7
Hartford 48E2
Hartlepool 14F4
Harvey 46G2
Harwich 15I7
Haslemere 15G7
Hassan 27G5
Hasselt 12J5
Hässleholm 11H8
Hastings 15H8
Hastings 43F4
Hastings 46H3
Hastings 47I3
Hatfield 14G5
Hatteras, Cape 47L4
Hattiesburg 47J5
Hat Yai 29C7
Haud *reg.* 34E3
Haugesund 11D7
Haukivesi *l.* 10P5
Hauraki Gulf 43E3
Haut Atlas *mts* 32C1
Haute-Normandie *admin. reg.* 15I9
Hauts Plateaux 32C1
Havana 51H4
Havant 15G8
Haverfordwest 15C7
Haverhill 48F1
Havlíčkův Brod 13O6
Havran 21L5
Havre 46F2
Havre Rock *i.* 39I5
Havza 23G8
Hawai'i *i.* 46□
Hawick 16G5
Hawke Bay 43F4
Haxby 14F4
Hay 42B5
Hay *watercourse* 41H4
Haymā' 26E5
Hayrabolu 21L4
Hay River 44G3
Hays 46H4
Haysyn 23F6
Hayward 49A2
Haywards Heath 15G8
Hazleton 48D2
Heanor 15F5
Heard and McDonald Islands *terr.* 7
Hearst 45J5
Heathcote 42B6
Hechi 27J4
Hedemora 11I6
Hefei 27K3
Hegang 30C3
Heide 13L3
Heidelberg 13L6
Heidelberg 37I4
Heihe 30B2
Heilbronn 13L6
Heilongjiang *prov.* 30C3
Heilong Jiang *r.* 30D2
Heinola 11O6
Hekla *vol.* 10□ 2
Helena 46E2
Helensburgh 16E4
Helgoländer Bucht *g.* 13L3
Hellín 19F4
Helmand *r.* 26F3
Helmond 13J5
Helmstedt 13M4
Helong 30C4
Helsingborg 11H8
Helsingør 11H8
Helsinki 11N6
Hemel Hempstead 15G7
Hemet 49D4
Hendek 21N4
Henderson 47I5
Henderson 47L4
Henderson 49E2
Hengelo 13K4
Hengshan 30C3
Hengyang 27K4
Heniches'k 23G7
Henley-on-Thames 15G7
Herāt 26F3
Hereford 15E6
Hereford 46G5
Herford 13L4
Herisau 18I3
Herkimer 48D1
Hermes, Cape 37I6
Hermosillo 46E6
Hernandarias 54F3
Herne Bay 15I7
Herning 11F8
Hérouville-St-Clair 15G9
Herrera del Duque 19D4
Hershey 48C2
Hertford 15G7
Hesperia 49D3
Hettstedt 13M5
Hexham 14E4
Heysham 14E4
Heywood 14E5
Heze 27K3
Hibbing 47I2
Hidalgo del Parral 46F6
Hidrolândia 55A2
Highlands 48E2
Highland Springs 48C4
High Level 44G4
High Point 47L4
High Prairie 44G4
High Wycombe 15G7
Higüey 51K5
Hiiumaa *i.* 11M7
Hijaz *reg.* 34D1
Hikone 31E6
Hildesheim 13L4
Hillah 33H1
Hillerød 11H9
Hillston 42B4
Hilo 46□
Hilton Head Island 47K5
Hilversum 12J4
Himalaya *mts* 27G3
Himarë 21H4
Himeji 31D6
Hinckley 15F6
Hindley 14E5
Hindu Kush *mts* 26F3
Hinesville 47K5
Hinthada 27I5
Hirosaki 30F4
Hiroshima 31D6
Hirson 18G2
Hirtshals 11F8
Hisar 27G4
Hispaniola *i.* 51J4
Hitachi 31F5
Hitachinaka 31F5
Hjälmaren *l.* 11I7
Hjo 11I7
Hjørring 11G8
Hlobyne 23G6
Hlukhiv 23G6
Hlybokaye 11O9
Ho 32D4
Hobart 41J8
Hobbs 46G5
Hobro 11F8
Ho Chi Minh City 29C6
Hoddesdon 15G7
Hodeidah 34E2
Hódmezővásárhely 21I1
Hoeryŏng 30C4
Hof 13M5
Hofors 11J6
Hofsjökull *ice cap* 10□ 2
Hōfu 31C6
Höganäs 11H8
Hoggar *plat.* 32D2
Hohhot 27K2
Hoh Xil Shan *mts* 27H3
Hoima 34D3
Hokkaidō *i.* 30F4
Hokksund 11F7
Holbæk 11G9
Holbrook 42C5
Holdrege 46H3
Holguín 51I4
Hollidaysburg 48B2
Hollister 49B2
Holly Springs 47J5
Hollywood 47K6
Hollywood 49C4
Holmestrand 11G7
Holmsund 10L5
Holstebro 11F8
Holt 15I6
Holyhead 14C5
Holyhead Bay 14C5
Holy Island 14C5
Holy Island 14F3
Hombori 32C3
Home Bay 45L3
Homer 48C1
Homs 33G1
Homyel' 23F5
Honar 21M6
Hondo 46H6
Honduras *country* 51G6
Hønefoss 11G6
Hongjiang 27J4
Hong Kong 27K4
Hongwŏn 31B4
Hongze Hu *l.* 28D4
Honiara 41L1
Honiton 15D8
Honjō 31F5
Honolulu 46□
Honshū *i.* 31D6
Hoogeveen 13K4
Hoopstad 37G4
Höör 11H9
Hoorn 12J4
Hoover Dam 49E2
Hopa 23I8
Hope 47I5
Hopewell 48C4
Hopkinsville 47J4
Hörby 11H9
Horki 23F5
Horlivka 23H6
Hormuz, Strait of *strait* 26E4
Horn 13O6
Horn, Cape 54C9
Horncastle 14G5
Hörnefors 10K5
Hornsby 42E4
Horodenka 23E6
Horodnya 23F6
Horodok 23D6
Horodok 23E6
Horsens 11F9
Horsham 41I7
Horten 11G7
Hoshiarpur 27G3
Hotan 27F3
Hot Springs 47I5
Houghton 47J2
Houghton le Spring 14F4
Houma 47I6
Houston 47H6
Hovd 27I2
Hove 15G8
Hovmantorp 11I8
Hövsgöl Nuur *l.* 27J1
Howden 14G5
Howe, Cape 42D6
Howick 37J5
Howland Island *terr.* 39I1
Howlong 42C5
Höxter 13L5
Hoy *i.* 16F2
Hoyerswerda 13O5
Hradec Králové 13O5
Hrazdan 23J8
Hrebinka 23G6
Hrodna 11M10
Hsinchu 28E5
Huacho 52C6
Huadian 30B4
Huaibei 27K3
Huaihua 27J4
Huainan 27K3
Huajuápan de León 50E5
Huambo 35B5
Huanan 30C3
Huancavelica 52C6
Huancayo 52C6
Huanren 30B4
Huánuco 52C5
Huaráz 52C5
Huarmey 52C6
Huasco 54B3
Huatabampo 46F6
Hubli 27G5
Hucknall 15F5
Huddersfield 14F5
Huder 30A2
Hudiksvall 11J6
Hudson 48E1
Hudson 48F1
Hudson *r.* 48E2
Hudson Bay *sea* 45J4
Hudson Falls 48E1
Hudson Strait *strait* 45K3
Huê 29C6
Huehuetenango 50F5
Huelva 19C5
Huesca 19F2
Hughenden 41I4
Hughson 49B2
Hugo 47H5
Huhudi 36G4
Huib-Hoch Plateau 36C4
Huíla Plateau 35B5
Huimanguillo 50F5
Huittinen 11M6
Hulan 30B3
Hulan Ergi 30A3
Hulayfah 34E1
Hulin 30D3
Hull 45K5
Hultsfred 11I8
Hulun Buir 27K2
Ḩulwān 33G2
Humaitá 52F5
Humber, Mouth of the 14H5
Hume Reservoir 42C5
Hŭn 33E2
Húnaflói *b.* 10□ 2
Hunedoara 21J2
Hungary *country* 20H1
Hŭngnam 31B5
Hunstanton 15H6
Huntingdon 15G6
Huntingdon 48C2
Huntington 47J3
Huntington 47K4
Huntington Beach 49C4
Huntly 16G3
Huntsville 45K5
Huntsville 47H5
Huntsville 47J5
Huolin Gol 30A3
Huron 46H3
Huron, Lake 48A1
Húsavík 10□ 2
Huşi 21M1
Husnes 11D7
Husum 10K5
Husum 13L3
Hutchinson 46H4
Huzhou 28E4
Hvar *i.* 20G3
Hwange 35C5
Hyderabad 26F4
Hyderabad 27G5
Hyères 18H5
Hyesan 30C4
Hythe 15I7
Hyūga 31C6
Hyvinkää 11N6

I

Iaçu 55C1
Ianca 21L2
Iaşi 21L1
Ibadan 32D4
Ibagué 52C3
Ibaiti 55A3
Ibarra 52C3
Ibb 34E2
Iberian Peninsula 19
Ibiá 55B2
Ibiapaba, Serra da *hills* 53J4
Ibiassucê 55C1
Ibicaraí 55D1
Ibirama 55A4
Ibitinga 55A3
Ibiza 19G4
Ibiza *i.* 19G4
Ibotirama 53J6
Ibrā' 26E4
Ibrī 26E4
Ica 52C6
Içana 52E3
Icatu 53J4
Iceland *country* 10□ 2
Ichinomiya 31E6
Ichinoseki 31F5
Ichnya 23G6
Icó 53K5
Iconha 55C3
Idah 32D4
Idaho *state* 46E3
Idaho Falls 46E3
Idar-Oberstein 13K6
Idfū 33G2
Idiofa 35B4
Idlib 33G1
Iepê 55A3
Ifakara 35D4
Ifanadiana 35E6
Ife 32D4
Ifenat 33E3
Iferouâne 32D3
Ifôghas, Adrar des *hills* 32D3
Iganga 33G4
Igarapava 55B3
Igarka 24J3
Iggesund 11J6
Iglesias 20C5
Ignalina 11O9
Igoumenitsa 21I5
Iguaí 55C1
Iguala 50E5
Igualada 19G3
Iguape 55B4
Iguatemi 54F2
Iguatu 53K5
Ihosy 35E6
Iisalmi 10O5
Iizuka 31C6
Ijebu-Ode 32D4
Ijevan 23J8
IJssel *r.* 13J4
Ikageng 37H4
Ikare 32D4
Ikaria *i.* 21L6
Ikast 11F8
Ikhtiman 21J3
Ikom 32D4
Iksan 31B6
Ikungu 35D4
Ilagan 29E6
Īlām 33H1
Iława 13Q4
Ilebo 35C4
Ileza 22I3
Ilfeld 13M5
Ilford 15H7
Ilfracombe 15C7
Ilgaz 23G8
Ilha Grande, Represa *resr* 54F2
Ílhavo 19B3
Ilhéus 55D1
Ilkeston 15F6
Ilkley 14F5
Illapel 54B4
Illéla 32D3
Iller *r.* 13L6
Illichivs'k 21N1
Illinois *r.* 47I4
Illinois *state* 47J4
Illizi 32D2
Il'men', Ozero *l.* 22F4
Ilminster 15E8
Ilo 52D7
Iloilo 29E6
Ilorin 32D4
Ilovlya 23I6
Ilulissat 45M3
Imabari 31D6
Imaichi 31E5
Imari 31C6
Imaruí 55A5
Imatra 11P6
Imbituva 55A4
Imola 20D2
Imperatriz 53I5
Imperia 20C3
Imperial 49E4
Imperial Beach 49D4
Impfondo 34B3
Imphal 27I4
İmroz 21K4
Ina 31E6
Inarijärvi *l.* 10O2
Inca 19H4
Inch'ŏn 31B5
Indaal, Loch *b.* 16C5
Indalsälven *r.* 10J5
Inda Silasē 34D2
Independence 47I4
Inder 30A3
Inderborskiy 26E2
India *country* 27G4
Indiana 48B2
Indiana *state* 47J3
Indianapolis 47J4
Indianola 47I3
Indianola 47I5
Indigirka *r.* 25P2
Indija 21I2
Indio 49D4
Indonesia *country* 29D8
Indore 27G4
Indus *r.* 27F4
Indus, Mouths of the 26F4
İnebolu 23G8
İnegöl 21M4
Inglewood 42E2
Inglewood 49C4
Ingoldmells 14H5
Ingolstadt 13M6
Inhambane 37L2
Inhambane *prov.* 37L2
Inhumas 55A2
Inner Sound *sea chan.* 16D3
Innisfail 41J3
Innsbruck 13M7
Inongo 34B4
Inowrocław 13Q4
In Salah 32D2
Inscription, Cape 40C5
Inta 24H3
International Falls 47I2
Inuvik 44E3
Invercargill 43B8
Invergordon 16E3
Inverkeithing 16F4
Inverness 16E3
Investigator Group *is* 40G6
Investigator Strait 41H7
Inyonga 35D4
Inza 23J5
Inzhavino 23I5
Ioannina 21I5
Iola 47H4
Iona *i.* 16C4
Ionian Islands 21H5
Ionian Sea 20H5
Ios *i.* 21K6
Iowa *state* 47I3
Iowa City 47I3
Ipameri 55A2
Ipanema 55C2
Ipatinga 55C2
Ipatovo 23I7
Ipelegeng 37G4
Ipiales 52C3
Ipiaú 55D1
Ipirá 55D1
Ipiranga 55A4
Ipoh 29C7
Iporá 55A2
Ippy 34C3
Ipsala 21L4
Ipswich 15I6
Ipswich 42F1
Ipu 53J4
Iqaluit 45L3
Iquique 54B2
Iquitos 52D4
Irai 54F3
Iraklion 21K7
Iramaia 55C1
Iran *country* 26E3
Īrānshahr 26F4
Irapuato 50D4
Iraq *country* 33H1
Irara 55D1
Irati 55A4
Irbid 33G1
Irbit 24H4
Irecê 53J6
Ireland *i.* 17
Ireland, Republic of *country* 17E4
Irgiz 26F2
Iringa 35D4
Iriri *r.* 53H4
Irish Sea 17G4
Irituia 53I4
Irkutsk 25L4
Irondequoit 48C1
Iron Mountain 47J2
Irosin 29E6
Irpin' 23F6
Irrawaddy *r.* 27I5
Irtysh *r.* 27G1
Irún 19F2
Irvine 16E5
Irvine 49D4
Isa 32D3
Isabela 29E7
Ísafjarðardjúp *est.* 10□ 2
Ísafjörður 10□ 2
Ise 31E6
Isère *r.* 18G4
Isernia 20F4
Ise-wan *b.* 31E6
Iseyin 32D4
Ishinomaki 31F5
Ishioka 31F5
Isil'kul' 24I4
Isipingo 37J5
Isiro 34C3
İskenderun 33G1
Iskitim 24J4
Islamabad 27G3
Islands, Bay of 43E2
Islay *i.* 16C5
Isoka 35D5
Isparta 21N6
Isperikh 21L3
Israel *country* 33G1
Issia 32C4
Issoire 18F4
İstanbul 21M4
Istiaia 21J5
Istres 18G5
Istria *pen.* 20E2
Itaberá 55A3
Itaberaba 55C1
Itaberaí 55A2
Itabira 55C2
Itabirito 55C3
Itabuna 55D1
Itacajá 53I5
Itacarambi 55B1
Itacoatiara 53G4
Itaetê 55C1
Itaguaçu 55C2
Itaí 55A3
Itaiópolis 55A4
Itaituba 53G4
Itajaí 55A4
Itajubá 55B3
Itajuípe 55D1
Italy *country* 20E3
Itamarandiba 55C2
Itambé 55C1
Itanhaém 55B4
Itanhém 55C2
Itaobim 55C2
Itapaci 55A1
Itapajipe 55A2
Itapebi 55D1
Itapecerica 55B3
Itapemirim 55C3
Itaperuna 55C3
Itapetinga 55C1
Itapetininga 55A3
Itapeva 55A3
Itapicuru 53J6
Itapicuru Mirim 53J4
Itapipoca 53K4
Itapira 55B3
Itaporanga 55A3
Itapuã 55A5
Itaqui 54E3
Itararé 55A4
Itatiba 55B3
Itaúna 55B3
Itea 21J5
Ithaca 48C1
Itinga 55C2
Itiquira 53H7
Itiruçu 55C1
Itō 31E6
Itu 55B3
Ituaçu 55C1
Ituberá 55D1
Ituiutaba 55A2
Itumbiara 55A2
Itupiranga 53I5
Ituporanga 55A4
Iturama 55A2
Itzehoe 13L4
Iul'tin 25T3
Ivalo 10O2
Ivanava 11N10
Ivankiv 23F6
Ivano-Frankivs'k 23E6
Ivanovka 30B2
Ivanovo 22I4
Ivanteyevka 23K5
Ivatsevichy 11N10
Ivaylovgrad 21L4
Ivdel' 24H3
Ivrea 20B2
İvrindi 21L5
Ivujivik 45K3
Ivyanyets 11O10
Iwaki 31F5
Iwakuni 31D6
Iwamizawa 30F4
Iwo 32D4
Iwye 11N10
Ixmiquilpán 50E4
Ixtlán 50D4
Ixworth 15H6
Izberbash 23J8
Izhevsk 24G4
Izmayil 21M2
İzmir 21L5
İzmir Körfezi *g.* 21L5
İzmit 21M4
Iztochni Rodopi *mts* 21K4
Izumo 31D6
Izyaslav 23E6
Iz"yayu 22M2
Izyum 23H6

J

Jabalpur 27G4
Jablanica 20G3
Jaboatão 53L5
Jaboticabal 55A3
Jacaraci 55C1
Jacareí 55B3
Jacarézinho 55A3
Jacinto 55C2
Jackson 47I5
Jackson 47J4
Jackson 47K3
Jacksonville 47I4
Jacksonville 47K5
Jacksonville 47L5
Jacmel 51J5
Jacobabad 26F4
Jacobina 53J6
Jacunda 53I4
Jaén 19E5
Jaffa, Cape 41H7
Jaffna 27G6
Jagdalpur 27H5
Jaguariaíva 55A4
Jaguaripe 55D1
Jahrom 26E4
Jaicós 53J5
Jaipur 27G4
Jaisalmer 27G4
Jakarta 29C8
Jakobstad 10M5
Jalālābād 27G3
Jalandhar 27G3
Jalapa 50E5
Jales 55A3
Jalgaon 27G4
Jalingo 32E4
Jalna 27G5
Jalpa 50D4
Jalpaiguri 27H4
Jamaica *country* 51I5
Jamaica Channel 51I5
Jambi 29C8
James *r.* 46H3
James Bay 45J4
Jamestown 41H6
Jamestown 46H2
Jamestown 48B1
Jammu 27G3
Jämsä 11N6
Jämsänkoski 10N6
Jamshedpur 27H4
Janaúba 55C1
Janesville 47J3
Januária 55B1
Japan *country* 31D5
Japan, Sea of 31D5
Japurá *r.* 52F4
Jaraguá 55A1
Jaraguá do Sul 55A4
Jardinópolis 55B3
Jarocin 13P5
Jarosław 23D6
Jarrettsville 48C3
Jarú 52F6
Järvenpää 11N6
Jāsk 26E4
Jasło 23D6
Jasper 44G4
Jasper 47I5
Jastrzębie-Zdrój 13Q6
Jászberény 21H1
Jataí 55A2
Jaú 55A3
Jauja 52C6
Java *i.* 29C8
Jawa, Laut *sea* 29D8
Jawhar 34E3
Jawor 13P5
Jaya, Puncak *mt.* 29F8
Jayapura 29G8
Jebel Marra *plat.* 33F3
Jedburgh 16G5
Jeddah 34D1
Jefferson City 47I4
Jeffreys Bay 36G8
Jēkabpils 11N8
Jelenia Góra 13O5
Jelgava 11M8
Jember 29D8
Jena 13M5
Jendouba 20C6
Jennings 47I5
Jequié 55C1
Jequitinhonha 55C2
Jérémie 51J5
Jerez 50D4
Jerez de la Frontera 19C5
Jerome 46E3
Jersey *terr.* 15E9
Jersey City 48D2
Jerumenha 53J5
Jerusalem 33G1
Jervis Bay 42E5
Jervis Bay Territory *admin. div.* 42E5
Jesenice 20F1
Jesi 20E3
Jessheim 11G6
Jesup 47K5
Jhansi 27G4
Jiamusi 30C3
Ji'an 27K4
Ji'an 30B4
Jianyang 28D5
Jiaohe 30B4
Jiaxing 28E4
Jiayuguan 27I3
Jieznas 11N9
Jihlava 13O6
Jijel 32D1
Jijiga 34E3
Jilib 34E3
Jilin 30B4
Jilin *prov.* 30B4
Jīma 34D3
Jiménez 46G6
Jiménez 46H7
Jim Thorpe 48D2
Jinan 27K3
Jindřichův Hradec 13O6
Jingdezhen 28D5
Jingellic 42C5
Jingyu 30B4
Jingyuan 27J3
Jingzhou 27K3
Jinhua 28D5
Jining 27K2
Jining 27K3
Jinja 34D3
Jinotepe 51G6
Jinxi 28D5
Jinzhong 27K3
Jinzhou 27L2
Ji-Paraná 52F6
Jipijapa 52B4
Jiquiriçá 55D1
Jishou 27J4
Jiwen 30A2
Jixi 30C3
Jixian 30C3
Jīzān 34E2
Jizzax 26F2
Joaçaba 55A4
Joaíma 55C2
João Pessoa 53L5
João Pinheiro 55B2
Jodhpur 27G4
Joensuu 10P5
Jōetsu 31E5
Jõgeva 11O7
Johannesburg 37H4
John Day 46D3
John o'Groats 16F2
Johnsonburg 48B2
Johnstone 16E5
Johnstown 48B2
Johnstown 48D1
Johor Bahru 29C7
Jõhvi 11O7
Joinville 18G2
Joinville 55A4
Joliet 47J3
Jonava 11N9
Jonesboro 47I4
Jones Sound *sea chan.* 45J2
Jönköping 11I8
Jonquière 45K5
Joplin 47I4
Jordan *country* 33G1
Jorhat 27I4
Jos 32D4
José de San Martín 54B6
Joseph Bonaparte Gulf 40F2
Jos Plateau 32D4
Jouberton 37H4
Joutseno 11P6
Juan Aldama 46G7
Juan de Fuca Strait *strait* 44F5
Juàzeiro 53J5
Juàzeiro do Norte 53K5
Juba 33G4
Jubba *r.* 34E4
Júcar *r.* 19F4
Juchitán 50E5
Judenburg 13O7
Juigalpa 51G6
Juína 53G6
Juiz de Fora 55C3
Juliaca 52D7
Jumilla 19F4
Junagadh 27G4
Junction City 47H4
Jundiaí 55B3
Juneau 44E4
Junee 42C5
Jungfrau *mt.* 18H3
Junggar Pendi *basin* 27G2
Junín 54D4
Juodupė 11N8
Jura *i.* 16D4
Jura *mts* 18G4
Jura, Sound of *sea chan.* 16D5
Jurbarkas 11M9
Jūrmala 11M8
Juruti 53G4
Jussara 55A1
Jutaí 52E5
Jutiapa 50G6
Juticalpa 51G6
Jutland *pen.* 11F8
Jwaneng 36G3
Jyväskylä 10N5

K

K2 *mt.* 27G3
Kaarina 11M6
Kabale 34C4
Kabalo 35C4
Kabinda 35C4
Kabongo 35C4
Kābul 27F3
Kabwe 35C5
Kachchh, Rann of *marsh* 27G4
Kachia 32D4
Kachret'i 23J8
Kachug 25L4
Kadıköy 21M4
Kadoma 35C5
Kadugli 33F3
Kaduna 32D3
Kaduy 22H4
Kadzherom 22L2
Kaédi 32B3
Kaélé 33E3
Kaesŏng 31B5
Kafanchan 32D4
Kafue 35C5
Kafue *r.* 35C5
Kaga 31E5
Kaga Bandoro 34B3
Kagoshima 31C7
Kagoshima *pref.* 31C7
Kaharlyk 23F6
Kahramanmaraş 26C3
Kaifeng 27K3
Kainan 31D6
Kairouan 20D7
Kaiyuan 27J4
Kaiyuan 30B4
Kajaani 10O4
Kakamega 34D3
Kakata 32B4
Kakhovka 21O1
Kakinada 27H5
Kakogawa 31D6
Kala 35D4
Kalaâ Kebira 20D7
Kalach 23I6
Kalach-na-Donu 23I6
Kalahari Desert 35C6
Kalajoki 10M4
Kalamaria 21J4
Kalamata 21J6
Kalamazoo 47J3
Kalanchak 21O1
Kale 21M6
Kalemie 35C4
Kalevala 10Q4
Kalgoorlie 40E6
Kali 20F2
Kalima 34C4
Kaliningrad 11L9
Kalininsk 23J6
Kalininskaya 23H7
Kalinkavichy 23F5
Kalispell 46E2
Kalisz 13Q5
Kalix 10M4
Kalmar 11J8
Kaluga 23H5
Kalundborg 11G9
Kalush 23E6
Kalyazin 22H4
Kama 34C4
Kama *r.* 22L4
Kamaishi 31F5
Kambove 35C5
Kamchatka Peninsula 25Q4
Kamenka 23J5
Kamenka 23K6
Kamen'-na-Obi 24J4
Kamenolomni 23I7
Kamensk-Shakhtinskiy 23I6
Kamensk-Ural'skiy 24H4
Kamina 35C4
Kamloops 44F4
Kampala 34D3
Kampene 34C4
Kâmpóng Cham 29C6
Kâmpóng Spœ 29C6
Kâmpóng Thum 29C6
Kâmpôt 29C6
Kamuli 34D3
Kam"yanets'-Podil's'kyy 23E6
Kam"yanka-Buz'ka 23E6
Kāmyārān 33H1
Kamyshin 23J6
Kamyzyak 23K7
Kananga 35C4
Kanash 22J5
Kanazawa 31E5
Kanchipuram 27G5
Kandahār 26F3
Kandalaksha 10R3
Kandé 32D4
Kandi 32D3
Kandıra 21N4
Kandos 42D4
Kandy 27H6
Kandyagash 26E2
Kāne'ohe 46□
Kanevskaya 23H7
Kangān 26E4
Kangar 29C7
Kangaroo Island 41H7
Kanggye 30B4
Kangnŭng 31C5
Kangping 30A4
Kaniñg 32B3
Kanin, Poluostrov *pen.* 22J2
Kankaanpää 11M6
Kankakee 47J3
Kankan 32C3
Kano 32D3
Kanoya 31C7
Kanpur 27H4
Kansas *state* 46H4
Kansas City 47I4
Kansk 25K4
Kantchari 32D3
Kantemirovka 23H6
Kanyamazane 37J3
Kanye 37G3
Kaohsiung 28E5
Kaolack 32B3
Kapiri Mposhi 35C5
Kapoeta 33G4
Kaposvár 20G1
Kapuskasing 45J5
Kapuvár 20G1
Kapyl' 11O10
Kara 32D4
Karabalyk 26F1
Karabük 23G8
Karacabey 21M4
Karacasu 21M6
Karachayevsk 23I8
Karachev 23G5
Karachi 26F4
Karaganda 27G2
Karaguyly 27G2
Karahallı 21M5
Karaj 26E3
Kara-Köl 27G2
Karakol 27G2
Karakoram Range *mts* 27G3
Karakum Desert 26E2
Karakum Desert 26F3
Karaman 33G1
Karamanlı 21M6
Karamay 27H2
Karamea Bight *b.* 43C5
Karamürsel 21M4
Karas *admin. reg.* 36C4
Karasburg 36D5
Kara Sea 24I2
Karasu 21N4
Karasuk 24I4
Karatau 27G2
Karatsu 31C6
Karbalā' 33H1
Karcag 21I1
Karditsa 21I5
Kärdla 11M7
Kareima 33G3
Kareliya, Respublika *aut. rep.* 10R5
Karema 35D4
Kargalinskaya 23J8
Kargopol' 22H3
Kari 32E3
Kariba 35C5
Kariba, Lake *resr* 35C5
Kariba Dam 35C5
Karimata, Selat *strait* 29C8
Karksi-Nuia 11N7
Karlivka 23G6
Karlovac 20F2
Karlovo 21K3
Karlovy Vary 13N5
Karlshamn 11I8
Karlskoga 11I7
Karlskrona 11I8
Karlsruhe 13L6
Karlstad 11H7
Karnal 27G4
Karnobat 21L3
Karoi 35C5
Karonga 35D4
Karpenisi 21I5
Karpogory 22J2
Karratha 40D4
Kars 23I8
Kärsava 11O8
Karsun 23J5
Kartal 21M4
Kartaly 24H4
Karviná 13Q6
Karwar 27G5
Karymskoye 25M4
Karystos 21K5
Kasaï, Plateau du 35C4
Kasama 35D5
Kasane 35C5
Kasese 34D3
Kāshān 26E3
Kashary 23I6
Kashi 27G3
Kashihara 31D6
Kashin 22H4
Kashira 23H5
Kashiwazaki 31E5
Kashmar 26E3
Kasimov 23I5
Kasongo 35C4
Kasongo-Lunda 35B4
Kaspiysk 23J8
Kassala 33G3
Kassel 13L5
Kasserine 20C7
Kastamonu 23G8
Kastelli 21J7
Kastoria 21I4
Kastsyukovichy 23G5
Kasulu 35D4
Kasungu 35D5
Katakwi 34D3
Katerini 21J4
Katete 35D5
Kathmandu 27H4
Kati 32C3
Katihar 27H4
Katima Mulilo 35C5
Katiola 32C4
Katlehong 37I4
Kato Achaïa 21I5
Katoomba 42E4
Katowice 13Q5
Kātrīnā, Jabal *mt.* 33G2
Katrine, Loch *l.* 16E4
Katrineholm 11J7
Katsina 32D3
Katsina-Ala 32D4
Katsuura 31F6
Kattegat *strait* 11G8
Kaua'i Channel 46□
Kauhajoki 10M5
Kauhava 10M5
Kaunas 11M9
Kaura-Namoda 32D3
Kavadarci 21J4
Kavak 23H8
Kavala 21K4
Kavalerovo 30D3
Kavarna 21M3
Kavīr, Dasht-e *des.* 26E3
Kawagoe 31E6
Kawaguchi 31E6
Kawasaki 31E6
Kawm Umbū 33G2
Kaya 32C3
Kayes 32B3
Kayseri 26C3
Kazakhskiy Melkosopochnik *plain* 27G1
Kazakhstan *country* 26F2
Kazan' 22K5
Kazanlŭk 21K3
Kaz Dağı *mts* 21L5
Kazincbarcika 23D6
Keady 17F3
Kearney 46H3
Kebili 32D1
Keçiborlu 21N6
Kecskemét 21H1
Kėdainiai 11M9
Kedong 30B3
Kędzierzyn-Koźle 13Q5
Keene 48E1
Keetmanshoop 36D4
Keffi 32D4
Keflavík 10□ 2
Kegen 27G2
Kehra 11N7
Keighley 14F5
Keith 16G3
Keith 41I7
Kelibia 20D6
Kelkit *r.* 26C2
Kelmė 11M9
Kelo 33E4
Kelowna 44G5
Keluang 29C7
Kem' 22G2
Kemalpaşa 21L5
Kemer 21N6
Kemerovo 24J4
Kemi 10N4
Kemijärvi 10O3
Kemnay 16G3
Kempele 10N4
Kempten (Allgäu) 13M7
Kempton Park 37I4
Kendal 14E4
Kendari 29E8
Kendawangan 29D8
Kenema 32B4
Kenge 35B4
Kenhardt 36E5
Kénitra 32C1
Kenmore 48B1
Kennewick 46D2
Kenosha 47J3
Kent 48A2
Kentucky *state* 47K4
Kenya *country* 34D3
Kenya, Mount 34D4
Keokuk 47I3
Keppel Bay 41K4
Kepsut 21M5
Kerang 42A5
Kerava 11N6
Kerba 19G5
Kerch 23H7
Kerema 38E2
Keren 33G3
Kerewan 32B3
Kericho 34D4
Kerkyra 21H5
Kermadec Islands 39I5
Kermān 26E3
Kermānshāh 33H1
Kermit 46G5
Kerrville 46H5
Kerteminde 11G9
Keşan 21L4
Keşap 23H8
Kesennuma 31F5
Keshan 30B2
Kesten'ga 10Q4
Keswick 14D4
Keszthely 20G1
Ketapang 29D8
Kettering 15G6
Keuruu 10N5
Keyihe 30A2
Key Largo 47K6
Keynsham 15E7
Keyser 48B3
Key West 47K7
Kgalagadi *admin. dist.* 36E3
Kgalagadi Transfrontier Park *nat. park* 35C6
Kgatleng *admin. dist.* 37H3
Kgotsong 37H4
Khabarovsk 30D2
Khabarovskiy Kray *admin. div.* 30D2
Khairpur 27F4
Khamar-Daban, Khrebet *mts* 25L4
Khamgaon 27G4
Khamis Mushayt 34E2
Khandyga 25O3
Khanka, Lake 30D3
Khanpur 27G4
Khanty-Mansiysk 24H3
Kharabali 23J7
Kharagpur 27H4
Khārijah, Wāḩāt al *oasis* 33G2
Kharkiv 23H6
Kharmanli 21K4
Kharovsk 22I4
Khartoum 33G3
Khasavyurt 23J8
Khāsh 26F4
Khashuri 23I8
Khaskovo 21K4
Khaybar 34D1
Khayelitsha 36D8
Khemis Miliana 19H5
Khenchela 20B7
Khenifra 32C1
Kherson 21O1
Khilok 25M4
Khlevnoye 23H5
Khmel'nyts'kyy 23E6
Khmil'nyk 23E6
Khomas *admin. reg.* 36C2
Khon Kaen 29C6
Khor 30D3
Khorol 23G6
Khorol 30D3
Khorramābād 33H1
Khorramshahr 33H1
Khorugh 27G3
Khouribga 32C1
Khromtau 26E1
Khrystynivka 23F6
Khŭjand 27F2
Khulays 34D1
Khulna 27H4
Khuma 37H4
Khurays 34E1
Khust 23D6
Khutsong 37H4
Khvalynsk 23K5
Khvoynaya 22G4
Khyber Pass 27G3
Kiama 42E5
Kibaha 35D4
Kiboga 34D3
Kibre Mengist 33G4
Kibungo 34D4
Kičevo 21I4
Kichmengskiy Gorodok 22J4
Kidal 32D3
Kidderminster 15E6
Kidsgrove 15E5
Kiel 13M3
Kielce 13R5
Kielder Water *resr* 14E3
Kieler Bucht *b.* 13M3
Kiev 23F6
Kiffa 32B3
Kifisia 21J5
Kigali 34D4
Kigoma 35C4
Kikinda 21I2
Kiknur 22J4
Kikwit 35B4
Kilchu 30C4
Kilcoole 17F4
Kilcoy 42F1
Kildare 17F4
Kil'dinstroy 10R2
Kilimanjaro *vol.* 34D4
Kilingi-Nõmme 11N7
Kiliya 21M2
Kilkeel 17G3
Kilkenny 17E5
Kilkis 21J4
Killarney 17C5
Killeen 46H5
Kilmarnock 16E5
Kil'mez' 22K4
Kilmore 42B6
Kilosa 35D4
Kilwinning 16E5
Kimbe 38F2
Kimberley 36G5
Kimberley Plateau 40F3
Kimch'aek 31C4
Kimch'ŏn 31C5
Kimhae 31C6
Kimovsk 23H5
Kimpese 35B4
Kimry 22H4
Kinabalu, Gunung *mt.* 29D7
Kincardine 16F4
Kindersley 46F1
Kindia 32B3
Kindu 34C4
Kinel' 23K5
Kineshma 22I4
Kingisepp 11P7
King Island 41I7
King Leopold Ranges *hills* 40E3
Kingman 49E3
King's Lynn 15H6
King Sound *b.* 40E3
Kingsport 47K4
Kingston 39G4
Kingston 45K5
Kingston 48D2
Kingston 48D2
Kingston 51I5
Kingston upon Hull 14G5
Kingstown 51L6
Kingsville 46H6
Kington 15D6
King William Island 45I3
King William's Town 37H7
Kinloss 16F3
Kinna 11H8
Kinross 16F4
Kinshasa 35B4
Kinston 47L4
Kintore 16G3
Kintyre *pen.* 16D5
Kipushi 35C5
Kirakira 39G3
Kirensk 25L4
Kireyevsk 23H5
Kiribati *country* 39J2
Kırıkkale 26C3
Kirillov 22H4
Kirishi 22G4
Kırkağaç 21L5
Kirkby 14E5
Kirkby in Ashfield 15F5
Kirkcaldy 16F4
Kirkcudbright 16E6
Kirkenes 10Q2
Kirkintilloch 16E5
Kirkkonummi 11N6
Kirkland Lake 45J5
Kırklareli 21L4
Kirksville 47I3
Kirkūk 33H1
Kirkwall 16G2
Kirov 22K4
Kirov 23G5
Kirovo-Chepetsk 22K4
Kirovohrad 23G6
Kirovsk 10R3
Kirovsk 22F4
Kirovs'ke 23G7
Kirovskiy 30D3
Kirs 22L4
Kirsanov 23I5
Kiruna 10L3
Kiryū 31E5
Kisangani 34C3
Kiselevsk 24J4
Kishi 32D4
Kishkenekol' 27G1
Kisii 34D4
Kiskunfélegyháza 21H1
Kiskunhalas 21H1
Kislovodsk 23I8
Kismaayo 34E4
Kisoro 33F5
Kissidougou 32B4
Kissimmee 47K6
Kisumu 34D4
Kita 32C3
Kitaibaraki 31F5
Kitakami 31F5
Kita-Kyūshū 31C6
Kitale 34D3
Kitami 30F4
Kitchener 48A1
Kitee 10Q5
Kitgum 34D3
Kittanning 48B2
Kitwe 35C5
Kiuruvesi 10O5
Kivu, Lake 34C4
Kizel 24G4
Kizilyurt 23J8
Kizlyar 23J8
Kizner 22K4
Kladno 13O5
Klagenfurt 13O7
Klaipėda 11L9
Klaksvík 10□ 1
Klamath *r.* 44F5
Klamath Falls 46C3
Klatovy 13N6
Klerksdorp 37H4
Kletnya 23G5
Kletskaya 23I6
Klimovo 23G5
Klin 22H4
Klintsy 23G5
Ključ 20G2
Kłodzko 13P5
Klosterneuburg 13P6
Kluczbork 13Q5
Klyetsk 11O10
Klyuchevskaya, Sopka *vol.* 25R4
Knaresborough 14F4
Knighton 15D6
Knittelfeld 13O7
Knjaževac 21J3
Knockmealdown Mts *hills* 17D5
Knoxville 47K4
Knysna 36F8
Kōbe 31D6
Koblenz 13K5
Kobryn 11N10
K'obulet'i 23I8
Kočani 21J4
Kočevje 20F2
Kōchi 31D6
Kochubeyevskoye 23I7
Kodiak 44C4
Kodiak Island 44C4
Kodino 22H3
Kodyma 23F6
Kōfu 31E6
Køge 11H9
Kohila 11N7
Kohima 27I4
Kohtla-Järve 11O7
Kokkola 10M5
Kokomo 47J3
Kokosi 37H4
Kokpekti 27H2
Kokshetau 27F1
Kokstad 37I6
Kola 10R2
Kola Peninsula 22H2
Kol'chugino 22H4
Kolda 32B3
Kolding 11F9
Koléa 19H5
Kolhapur 27G5
Kolkata 27H4
Kołobrzeg 13O3
Kolokani 32C3
Kolomna 23H5
Kolomyya 23E6
Kolondiéba 32C3
Kolonedale 38C2
Kolpashevo 24J4
Koluli 33H3
Kolwezi 35C5
Kolyma *r.* 25R3
Kolymskiy, Khrebet *mts* 25R3
Kolyshley 23J5
Komaki 31E6
Komárno 13Q7
Komatsu 31E5
Kominternivs'ke 21N1
Komiža 20G3
Komló 20H1
Komotini 21K4
Komsomol's'k 23G6
Komsomol'sk-na-Amure 30E2
Kondoa 35D4
Kondopoga 22G3
Kondrovo 23G5
Kong Christian IX Land *reg.* 45P2
Kong Frederik IX Land *reg.* 45M3
Kongolo 35C4
Kongoussi 32C3
Kongsberg 11F7
Kongsvinger 11H6
Konin 13Q4
Konosha 22I3
Konotop 23G6
Konstantinovka 30B2
Konstanz 13L7
Konya 33G1
Koper 20E2
Köping 11J7
Koprivnica 20G1
Korablino 23I5
Korçë 21I4
Korčula 20G3
Korčula *i.* 20G3
Korea Bay *g.* 31B5
Korea Strait *strait* 31C6
Korenovsk 23H7
Korets' 23E6
Körfez 21M4
Korhogo 32C4
Kōriyama 31F5
Korkuteli 21N6
Korla 27H2
Körmend 20G1
Koro 32C3
Koro *i.* 39H3
Köroğlu Dağları *mts* 21O4
Korogwe 35D4
Koror 29F7
Korosten' 23F6
Korostyshiv 23F6
Korsakov 30F3
Korsør 11G9
Korsun'-Shevchenkivs'kyy 23F6
Kortrijk 12I5
Koryazhma 22J3
Koryŏng 31C6
Kos *i.* 21L6
Kosan 31B5
Kościan 13P4
Kosciuszko, Mount 42D6
Koshki 23K5
Košice 23D6
Kosŏng 31C5
Kosovo *prov.* 21I3
Kosovska Mitrovica 21I3
Kostanay 26F1
Kostenets 21J3
Kostinbrod 21J3
Kostomuksha 10Q4
Kostopil' 23E6
Kostroma 22I4
Kostyantynivka 23H6
Koszalin 13P3
Kőszeg 20G1
Kota 27G4
Kotabaru 29D8
Kota Bharu 29C7
Kota Kinabalu 29D7
Kotel'nich 22K4
Kotel'nikovo 23I7
Kotel'nyy, Ostrov *i.* 25O2
Kotido 33G4
Kotka 11O6
Kotlas 22J3
Kotorkoshi 32D3
Kotovo 23J6
Kotovsk 23I5
Koudougou 32C3
Koulikoro 32C3
Koumac 39G4
Koundâra 32B3
Koupéla 32C3
Kourou 53H2
Kouroussa 32C3
Kousséri 33E3
Koutiala 32C3
Kouvola 11O6
Kovdor 10Q3
Kovel' 23E6
Kovernino 22I4
Kovrov 22I4
Kovylkino 23I5
Kowanyama 41I3
Köyceğiz 21M6
Kozani 21I4
Kozara *mts* 20G2
Kozelets' 23F6
Kozel'sk 23G5
Kozlu 21N4
Koz'modem'yansk 22J4
Kožuf *mts* 21J4
Kozyatyn 23F6
Kpalimé 32D4
Krabi 29B7
Krâchéh 29C6
Kragerø 11F7
Kragujevac 21I2
Kraków 13Q5
Kramators'k 23H6
Kramfors 10J5
Kranidi 21J6
Kranj 20F1
Krāslava 11O9
Krasnaya Gorbatka 22I5
Krasnoarmeysk 23J6
Krasnoarmiys'k 23H6
Krasnoborsk 22J3
Krasnodar 23H7
Krasnodon 23H6
Krasnogorodskoye 11P8
Krasnogvardeyskoye 23I7
Krasnohrad 23G6
Krasnohvardiys'ke 23G7
Krasnoperekops'k 23G7
Krasnoslobodsk 23I5
Krasnoyarsk 24K4
Krasnyye Baki 22J4
Krasnyy Kholm 22H4
Krasnyy Kut 23J6
Krasnyy Luch 23H6
Krasnyy Lyman 23H6
Krasnyy Yar 23K7
Krasyliv 23E6
Krefeld 13K5
Kremenchuk 23G6
Krems an der Donau 13O6
Kresttsy 22G4
Kretinga 11L9
Kribi 32D4
Kristiansand 11E7
Kristianstad 11I8

Kristiansund 10E5
Kristinehamn 11I7
Krk *i.* 20F2
Krolevets' 23G6
Kronshtadt 11P7
Kroonstad 37H4
Kropotkin 23I7
Krosno 29D8
Krotoszyn 13P5
Krui 29C8
Krumovgrad 21K4
Krupki 23F5
Kruševac 21I3
Krychaw 23F5
Krymsk 23H7
Krytiko Pelagos *sea* 21K6
Kryvyy Rih 23G7
Ksar Chellala 19H6
Ksar el Boukhari 19H6
Ksar el Kebir 19D6
Ksour Essaf 20D7
Kstovo 22J4
Kuala Lipis 29C7
Kuala Lumpur 29C7
Kuala Terengganu 29C7
Kuandian 30B4
Kuantan 29C7
Kubrat 21L3
Kuching 29D7
Kuçovë 21H4
Kudat 29D7
Kufstein 13N7
Kugesi 22J4
Kuhmo 10P4
Kuito 35B5
Kujang 31B5
Kuji 31F4
Kukës 21I3
Kukmor 22K4
Kula 21M5
Kular 25O2
Kuldīga 11L8
Kulebaki 23I5
Kulmbach 13M5
Külob 27F3
Kul'sary 26E2
Kulunda 24I4
Kumagaya 31E5
Kumamoto 31C6
Kumano 31E6
Kumanovo 21I3
Kumasi 32C4
Kumba 32D4
Kumdah 34E1
Kumeny 22K4
Kumertau 24G4
Kumi 31C5
Kumi 33G4
Kumla 11I7
Kumo 32E3
Kumylzhenskiy 23I6
Kungälv 11G8
Kungsbacka 11H8
Kunlun Shan *mts* 27G3
Kunming 27J4
Kunsan 31B6
Kuopio 10O5
Kupang 40E2
Kupiškis 11N9
Kup"yans'k 23H6
Kuqa 27H2
Kurashiki 31D6
Kurayoshi 31D6
Kurchatov 23G6
Kŭrdzhali 21K4
Kure 31D6
Kuressaare 11M7
Kurgan 24H4
Kurganinsk 23I7
Kurikka 10M5
Kuril Islands 30H3
Kurkino 23H5
Kurmuk 33G3
Kurnool 27G5
Kuroiso 31F5
Kurri Kurri 42E4
Kursavka 23I7
Kursk 23H6
Kurskaya 23J7
Kurşunlu 23G8
Kuruman 36F4
Kurume 31C6
Kurunegala 27H6
Kuşadasi 21L6
Kushchevskaya 23H7
Kushiro 30G4
Kushmurun 26F1
Kusŏng 31B5
Kütahya 21M5
K'ut'aisi 23I8
Kutjevo 20G2
Kutno 13Q4
Kutu 34B4
Kutztown 48D2
Kuusamo 10P4
Kuusankoski 11O6
Kuvshinovo 22G4
Kuwait 26D4
Kuwait *country* 26D4
Kuybyshev 24I4
Kuybysheve 23H7
Kuybyshevskoye Vodokhranilishche *resr* 23K5
Kuytun 27H2
Kuyucak 21M6
Kuznetsk 23J5
Kuznetsovs'k 23E6
Kuzovatovo 23J5
Kvarnerić *sea chan.* 20F2
Kwale 32D4
KwaMashu 37J5
Kwa Mtoro 35D4
Kwangju 31B6
Kwanobuhle 37G7
Kwatinidubu 37H7
KwaZulu-Natal *prov.* 37J5
Kwekwe 35C5
Kweneng *admin. dist.* 36G2
Kwidzyn 13Q4
Kyakhta 25L4
Kyaukpyu 27I5
Kymi 21K5
Kyneton 42B6
Kyogle 42F2
Kyŏngju 31C6
Kyōto 31D6
Kyparissia 21I6
Kyrgyzstan *country* 27G2
Kythira *i.* 21J6
Kyūshū *i.* 31C7
Kyustendil 21J3
Kyzyl 24K4
Kyzylkum Desert 26F2
Kyzyl-Mazhalyk 24K4
Kyzylorda 26F2

L

Laagri 11N7
Laâyoune 32B2
La Banda 54D3
Labasa 39H3
Labé 32B3
Labinsk 23I7
Labouheyre 18D4
Laboulaye 54D4
Labrador *reg.* 45L4
Labrador City 45L4
Labrador Sea 45M3
Lábrea 52F5
Labuhanbilik 27J6
Labuna 29E8
Labytnangi 24H3
La Carlota 54D4
Laccadive Islands 27G5
Lac du Bonnet 47I1
La Ceiba 51G5
Lachlan *r.* 42A5
La Chorrera 51I7
Lachute 45K5
La Ciotat 18G5
Lac La Biche 44G4
Laconia 48F1
La Crosse 47I3
Ladainha 55C2
La Déroute, Passage de *strait* 15E9
Ladik 23G8
Ladoga, Lake 11Q6
Ladysmith 37I5
Lae 38E2
Lafayette 47I5
Lafayette 47J3
Lafia 32D4
Lafiagi 32D4
La Flèche 18D3
La Galite, Canal de *sea chan.* 20C6
Lagan' 23J7
Lagan *r.* 17G3
Lagarto 53K6
Lågen *r.* 11G7
Laghouat 32D1
Lago Agrio 52C3
Lagoa Santa 55C2
Lagoa Vermelha 55A5
Lagos 19B5
Lagos 32D4
Lagosa 35C4
La Grande 46D2
La Grande 4, Réservoir *resr* 45K4
La Grange 47J5
La Gran Sabana *plat.* 52F2
Laguna 55A5
Laha 30B2
La Habra 49D4
Lahad Datu 29D7
La Hague, Cap de *c.* 15F9
Lahat 29C8
Laḥij 34E2
Laholm 11H8
Lahore 27G3
Lahti 11N6
Laï 33E4
Laidley 42F1
Laihia 10M5
L'Aïr, Massif de *mts* 32D3
Laishevo 22K5
Laitila 11L6
Laiyang 28E4
Laizhou Wan *b.* 27K3
Lajeado 55A5
Lajes 53K5
Lajes 55A4
La Junta 46G4
La Juventud, Isla de *i.* 51H4
Lake Cargelligo 42C4
Lake Charles 47I5
Lake City 47K5
Lake Havasu City 49E3
Lakehurst 48D2
Lakeland 47K6
Lake Providence 47I5
Lakes Entrance 42D6
Lakeside 48C4
Lakewood 48B1
Lakewood 48D2
Lakhdenpokh'ya 10Q6
Lakota 32C4
Laksefjorden *sea chan.* 10O1
La Ligua 54B4
Lalín 19B2
La Línea de la Concepción 19D5
Lalitpur 27G4
La Louvière 12J5
Lamar 46G4
La Martre, Lac *l.* 44G3
Lambaréné 34B4
Lambayeque 52C5
Lambert's Bay 36D7
Lambeth 48A1
Lamego 19C3
La Merced 52C6
La Merced 54C3
Lamesa 46G5
La Mesa 49D4
Lamia 21J5
Lammermuir Hills 16G5
Lamont 49C3
Lampang 29B6
Lampazos 46G6
Lamu 34E4
Lancaster 14E4
Lancaster 47K5
Lancaster 48C2
Lancaster 49C3
Lancaster Sound *strait* 45J2
Landeck 13M7
Lander 46F3
Landsberg am Lech 13M6
Land's End *pt* 15B8
Landshut 13N6
Landskrona 11H9
Langenthal 18H3
Langjökull *ice cap* 10□[2]
Langport 15E7
Langres 18G3
Langsa 27I6
Långsele 10J5
Lannion 18C2
Lansing 47K3
Lanxi 30B3
Lanzarote *i.* 32B2
Lanzhou 27J3
Laoag 29E6
Lao Cai 27J4
Laon 18F2
La Oroya 52C6
Laos *country* 29C6
Laotougou 30C4
Lapa 55A4
La Palma 51I7
La Palma *i.* 32B2
La Paz 46E7
La Paz 50G6
La Paz 52E7
La Paz 54E4
La Pérouse Strait *strait* 30F3
La Plata 54E4
La Plata, Río de *sea chan.* 54E4
Lappeenranta 11P6
Lappland *reg.* 10M3
Lâpseki 21L4
Laptev Sea 25N2
Lapua 10M5
La Quiaca 54C2
L'Aquila 20E3
La Quinta 49D4
Larache 19C6
Laramie 46F3
Laranjal Paulista 55B3
Laranjeiras do Sul 54F3
Larba 19H5
Laredo 46H6
Largs 16E5
L'Ariana 20D6
La Rioja 54C3
La Rioja *aut. comm.* 19E2
Larisa 21J5
Larne 17G3
La Rochelle 18D3
La Roche-sur-Yon 18D3
La Romana 51K5
La Ronge 44H4
La Ronge, Lac *l.* 44H4
Larvik 11G7
Las Cruces 46F5
La Serena 54B3
Las Flores 54E5
Las Heras 54C4
Las Palmas de Gran Canaria 32B2
La Spezia 20C2
Las Tablas 51H7
Las Termas 54D3
Las Tunas 51I4
Las Varas 50C4
Las Varillas 54D4
Las Vegas 46F4
Las Vegas 49E2
Latacunga 52C4
Latakia 33G1
La Teste-de-Buch 18D4
Latina 20E4
La Tuque 47M2
Latvia *country* 11N8
Lauchhammer 13N5
Launceston 15C8
Launceston 41J8
Laurel 47J5
Laureldale 48D2
Laurel Hill *hills* 48B3
Laurinburg 47L5
Lausanne 18H3
Lautoka 39H3
Laval 18D2
La Vega 51J5
Lavras 55B3
Lawra 32C3
Lawrence 47H4
Lawrence 48F1
Lawrenceburg 47J4
Lazarev 30F1
Lazarevac 21I2
Lázaro Cárdenas 50D5
Lazdijai 11M9
Leamington Spa, Royal 15F6
Leatherhead 15G7
Lebanon 47I4
Lebanon 48C2
Lebanon 48E1
Lebanon *country* 33G1
Lebedyan' 23H5
Lębork 13P3
Lebowakgomo 37I3
Lebrija 19C5
Lebu 54B5
Lecce 20H4
Lecco 20C2
Lechaina 21I6
Le Creusot 18G3
Le Crotoy 15I8
Ledesma 19D3
Ledmozero 10R4
Leeds 14F5
Leek 15E5
Leesburg 48C3
Leesville 47I5
Leeuwarden 13J4
Leeuwin, Cape 40D6
Leeward Islands 51L5
Lefkada 21I5
Lefkada *i.* 21I5
Lefkimmi 21I5
Legnago 20D2
Legnica 13P5
Le Havre 15H9
Lehmo 10P5
Leibnitz 13O7
Leicester 15F6
Leiden 12J4
Leigh 14E5
Leigh Creek 41H6
Leighton Buzzard 15G7
Leipzig 13N5
Leiria 19B4
Leirvik 11D7
Leizhou Bandao *pen.* 27J4
Le Kef 20C6
Leksand 11I6
Lelystad 12J4
Le Mans 18E2
Le Mars 47H3
Leme 55B3
Lemmon 46G2
Lemore 49C2
Le Murge *hills* 20G4
Lemvig 11F8
Lena *r.* 25N2
Lenham 15H7
Lenine 23G7
Leningradskaya 23H7
Leningradskaya Oblast' *admin. div.* 11R7
Leningradskiy 25S3
Leninsk 23J6
Leninskiy 23H5
Leninsk-Kuznetskiy 24J4
Leninskoye 22J4
Leninskoye 30D3
Lens 18F1
Lensk 25M3
Lenti 20G1
Lentini 20F6
Léo 32C3
Leoben 13O7
Leominster 15E6
Leominster 48F1
León 19D2
León 50D4
León 51G6
Leongatha 42B7
Leonidi 21J6
Leonidovo 30F2
Leonora 40E5
Leopoldina 55C3
Lepontine, Alpi *mts* 18I3
Le Puy-en-Velay 18F4
Lerala 37H2
Léré 32C3
Lerma 19E2
Le Roy 48C1
Lerum 11H8
Lerwick 16□
Lesbos *i.* 21K5
Les Cayes 51J5
Leshan 27J4
Leshukonskoye 22J2
Leskovac 21I3
Lesosibirsk 24K4
Lesotho *country* 37I5
Lesozavodsk 30D3
L'Espérance Rock *i.* 39I5
Les Sables-d'Olonne 18D3
Lesser Antilles *is* 51K6
Lesser Caucasus *mts* 23I8
Lesser Slave Lake 44G4
Lesozno 13P5
Letchworth Garden City 15G7
Lethbridge 44G5
Leticia 52E4
Letnerechenskiy 22G2
Le Touquet-Paris-Plage 15I8
Letterkenny 17E3
Leuchars 16G4
Leuven 12J5
Levadeia 21J5
Levanger 10G5
Levashi 23J8
Levelland 46G5
Leven 14G5
Leven, Loch *l.* 16F4
Lévêque, Cape 40E3
Leverkusen 13K5
Levice 13Q6
Levittown 48D2
Levittown 48E2
Lev Tolstoy 23H5
Lewes 15H8
Lewis, Isle of *i.* 16C2
Lewisburg 48C2
Lewis Range *mts* 46E2
Lewiston 46D2
Lewistown 46F2
Lewistown 48C2
Lexington 46H3
Lexington 47K4
Lexington 48B4
Lezhë 21H4
L'gov 23G6
Lhasa 27I4
Lianyungang 28D4
Liaodong Wan *b.* 27L2
Liaoning *prov.* 30A4
Liaoyang 30A4
Liaoyuan 30B4
Liaozhong 30A4
Libenge 34B3
Liberal 46G4
Liberec 13O5
Liberia 51G6
Liberia *country* 32C4
Libourne 18D4
Libreville 34A3
Libya *country* 33E2
Libyan Desert 33F2
Libyan Plateau 33F1
Licata 20E6
Lichfield 15F6
Lichinga 35D5
Lichtenburg 37H4
Lida 11N10
Lidköping 11H7
Liebig, Mount 40G4
Liechtenstein *country* 18I3
Liège 13J5
Lieksa 10Q5
Lienz 13N7
Liepāja 11L8
Liezen 13O7
Liffey *r.* 17F4
Lifford 17E3
Lightning Ridge 42C2
Ligurian Sea 18I5
Lika *reg.* 20F2
Likasi 35C5
Likhoslavl' 22G4
Lilla Edet 11H7
Lille 18F1
Lillehammer 11G6
Lillestrøm 11G7
Lilongwe 35D5
Lima 47K3
Lima 48C1
Lima 52C6
Lima Duarte 55C3
Liman 23J7
Limassol 33G1
Limavady 17F2
Limbaži 11N8
Limeira 55B3
Limerick 17D5
Limmen Bight *b.* 41H2
Limnos *i.* 21K5
Limoeiro 53K5
Limoges 18E4
Limón 46G4
Limoux 18F5
Limpopo *prov.* 37I2
Limpopo *r.* 37K3
Linares 19E4
Linares 46H7
Linares 54B5
Lincoln 14G5
Lincoln 47H3
Lincoln 47J3
Lincoln 54D4
Lindau (Bodensee) 13L7
Linden 53G2
Lindi 35D4
Lindian 30B3
Line Islands 6
Linfen 27K3
Lingen (Ems) 13K4
Lingga, Kepulauan *is* 29C8
Linhares 55C2
Linhe 27J2
Linjiang 30B4
Linköping 11I7
Linkou 30C3
Linlithgow 16F5
Linnhe, Loch *inlet* 16D4
Lins 55A3
Linxi 27K2
Linxia 27J3
Linyi 27K3
Linz 13O6
Lion, Golfe du *g.* 18F5
Lipetsk 23H5
Lipova 21I1
Lira 34D3
Lisala 34C3
Lisbon 19B4
Lisburn 17F3
Lishu 30B4
Lisieux 18E2
Liski 23H6
Lismore 42F2
Lithgow 42E4
Lithuania *country* 11M9
Litoměřice 13O5
Little Andaman *i.* 27I5
Little Belt *sea chan.* 11F9
Little Cayman *i.* 51H5
Little Falls 47I2
Littlefield 46G5
Littlehampton 15G8
Little Minch *sea chan.* 16B3
Little Rock 47I5
Liuhe 30B4
Liuzhou 27J4
Livermore 49B2
Liverpool 14E5
Liverpool 42E4
Liverpool Plains 42E3
Liverpool Range *mts* 42D3
Livingston 16F5
Livingston 46E2
Livingston 47I5
Livingstone 35C5
Livno 20G3
Livny 23H5
Livorno 20D3
Livramento do Brumado 55C1
Lizard Point 15B9
Ljubljana 20F1
Ljungby 11H8
Ljusdal 11J6
Llandovery 15D7
Llandudno 14D5
Llanelli 15C7
Llangollen 15D6
Llano Estacado *plain* 46G5
Llanos *plain* 52E2
Llantrisant 15D7
Llay 15D5
Lleida 19G3
Llodio 19E2
Lobatse 37G3
Loberia 54E5
Lobito 35B5
Lobos 54E5
Loch Rannoch *l.* 16E4
Lochy, Loch *l.* 16E4
Lockerbie 16F5
Lock Haven 48C2
Lockport 48B1
Lodeynoye Pole 22G3
Lodi 20C2
Lodi 49B1
Lodja 34C4
Łódź 13Q5
Lofoten *is* 10H2
Log 23I6
Logan 46E3
Logan, Mount 44D3
Logansport 47J3
Logroño 19E2
Loima 11M6
Loire *r.* 18C3
Loja 19D5
Loja 52C4
Løkken 10F5
Loknya 22F4
Lokoja 32D4
Lokossa 32D4
Lokot' 23G5
Lolland *i.* 11G9
Lom 21J3
Lomas de Zamora 54E4
Lombok *i.* 40D1
Lombok, Selat *sea chan.* 29D8
Lomé 32D4
Lomond, Loch *l.* 16E4
Lomonosov 11P7
Lompoc 49B3
Łomża 13S4
London 15G7
London 47K4
London 48A1
Londonderry 17E3
Londonderry, Cape 40F2
Londrina 55A3
Longa, Proliv *sea chan.* 25S2
Long Ashton 15E7
Long Beach 49C4
Long Branch 48E2
Long Eaton 15F6
Longford 17E4
Long Island 48E2
Long Island Sound *sea chan.* 48E2
Longjiang 30A3
Longmeadow 48E1
Long Melford 15H6
Longmont 46F3
Long Point Bay 48A1
Longreach 41I4
Longtown 14E3
Longview 47I5
Long Xuyên 29C6
Longyan 28D5
Longyearbyen 24C2
Lönsboda 11I8
Lons-le-Saunier 18G3
Lop Buri 29C6
Lop Nur *salt flat* 27I2
Lorain 45J5
Lorca 19F5
Lord Howe Island 41L6
Lorena 55B3
Loreto 53J5
Lorient 18C3
Lorn, Firth of *est.* 16D4
Lorrain, Plateau 18H2
Los Alamos 46F4
Los Angeles 49C3
Los Ángeles 54B5
Los Banos 49B2
Los Chonos, Archipiélago de *is* 54A6
Los Juríes 54D3
Los Mochis 46F6
Los Mosquitos, Golfo de *b.* 51H7
Lossiemouth 16F3
Los Teques 52E1
Lostwithiel 15C8
Los Vilos 54B4
Lot *r.* 18E4
Lota 54B5
Louangnamtha 28C5
Louangphabang 29C6
Loubomo 35B4
Louga 32B3
Loughborough 15F6
Loughrea 17D4
Loughton 15H7
Louisiade Archipelago *is* 41K2
Louisiana *state* 47I5
Louisville 47J4
Loukhi 10R3
Loulé 19B5
Louny 13N5
Lourdes 18D5
Louth 14G5
Loutra Aidipsou 21J5
Lovech 21K3
Loviisa 11O6
Lovington 46G5
Lowell 48F1
Lower Hutt 43E5
Lower Lough Erne *l.* 17E3
Lowestoft 15I6
Łowicz 13Q4
Loxton 41I6
Loyauté, Îles *is* 39G4
Loyew 23F6
Loznica 21H2
Lozova 23H6
Luanda 35B4
Luanshya 35C5
Luau 35C5
Luba 32D4
Lubaczów 23D6
Lubango 35B5
Lubao 35C4
Lubartów 23D6
Lübbock 46G5
Lübeck 13M4
Lubin 13P5
Lublin 23D6
Lubny 23G6
Lubumbashi 35C5
Lucala 35B4
Lucapa 35C4
Lucca 20D3
Luce Bay 16E6
Lucélia 55A3
Lucena 19D5
Lucena 29E6
Lučenec 13Q6
Lucera 20F4
Lucerne 18I3
Luchegorsk 30D3
Luckenwalde 13N4
Lucknow 27H4
Lüdenscheid 13K5
Lüderitz 36B4
Ludhiana 27G3
Ludvika 11I6
Ludwigsburg 13L6
Ludwigshafen am Rhein 13L6
Ludza 11O8
Luebo 35C4
Luena 35B5
Lufkin 47I5
Luga 11P7
Lugano 18I3
Lugo 19C2
Lugo 20D2
Lugoj 21I2
Luhans'k 23H6
Lukhovitsy 23H5
Lukovit 21K3
Łuków 23D6
Lukoyanov 23J5
Luleå 10M4
Luleälven *r.* 10M4
Lüleburgaz 21L4
Lumberton 47L5
Lumbrales 19C3
Lumezzane 20D2
Lund 11H9
Lundy *i.* 15C7
Lune *r.* 14E4
Lüneburg 13M4
Lunéville 18H2
Luninyets 11O10
Lunsar 32B4
Luobei 30C3
Luohe 27K3
Luoyang 27K3
Lupane 35C5
Lupanshui 27J4
Lupeni 21J2
Lurgan 17F3
Lusaka 35C5
Lusambo 35C4
Lushnjë 21H4
Lut, Dasht-e *des.* 26E3
Lutherstadt Wittenberg 13N5
Luton 15G7
Luts'k 23E6
Lutzville 36D6
Luwero 34D3
Luwuk 29E8
Luxembourg 13K6
Luxembourg *country* 13K6
Luxor 33G2
Luza 22J3
Luzhou 27J4
Luziânia 55B2
Luzon *i.* 29E6
Luzon Strait *strait* 29E5
L'viv 23E6
Lyakhavichy 11O10
Lyckele 10K4
Lydd 15H8
Lyel'chytsy 23F6
Lyepyel' 11P9
Lyme Bay 15E8
Lyme Regis 15E8
Lymington 15F8
Lynchburg 48B4
Lynn 48F1
Lyon 18G4
Lyozna 23F5
Lysekil 11G7
Lyskovo 22J4
Lys'va 24G4
Lysychans'k 23H6
Lysyye Gory 23J6
Lytham St Anne's 14D5
Lyuban' 11P10
Lyubim 22I4
Lyudinovo 23G5

M

Ma'ān 33G1
Maastricht 13J5
Mabaruma 52G2
Mablethorpe 14H5
Mabopane 37I3
Macaé 55C3
Macajuba 55C1
Macapá 53H3
Macará 52C4
Macarani 55C1
Macas 52C4
Macau 27K4
Macau 53K5
Macclesfield 14E5
Macdonnell Ranges *mts* 40G4
Macduff 16G3
Macedonia *country* 21I4
Maceió 53K5
Macenta 32C4
Macerata 20E3
Machachi 52C4
Machakos 34D4
Machala 52C4
Machilipatnam 27H5
Machiques 52D1
Machu Picchu *tourist site* 52D6
Machynlleth 15D6
Măcin 21M2
Macintyre Brook *r.* 42E2
Maçka 23H8
Mackay 41J4
Mackenzie *r.* 44E3
Mackenzie Bay 44E3
Mackenzie Mountains 44E3
Macksville 42F3
Maclean 42F2
Macomb 47I3
Mâcon 18G3
Macon 47I4
Macon 47K5
Madadeni 37J4
Madagascar *country* 35E6
Madan 21K4
Madang 38E2
Madaoua 32D3
Madeira *r.* 52G4
Madeira *terr.* 32B1
Madera 46F6
Madgaon 27G5
Madingou 35B4
Madison 47H3
Madison 47J3
Madison 47J4
Madison Heights 48B4
Madisonville 47J4
Madona 11O8
Madra Dağı *mts* 21L5
Madrakah 33G2
Madre, Laguna *lag.* 47H6
Madre del Sur, Sierra *mts* 50D5
Madre Occidental, Sierra *mts* 46F6
Madre Oriental, Sierra *mts* 46G6
Madrid 19E3
Madurai 27G6
Maebashi 31E5
Maevatanana 35E5
Mafeteng 37H5
Maffra 42C6
Mafinga 35D4
Mafra 55A4
Magabeni 37J6
Magadan 25Q4
Magangue 52D2
Magaria 32D3
Magas 23J8
Magdagachi 30B1
Magdalena 46E5
Magdeburg 13M4
Magellan, Strait of 54B8
Maggiore, Lake 20C2
Magherafelt 17F3
Maghnia 19F6
Maghull 14E5
Magnitogorsk 24G4
Magnolia 47I5
Mago 30F1
Magta' Lahjar 32B3
Magwe 27I4
Mahābād 33H1
Mahajanga 35E5
Mahalapye 37H2
Mahalevona 35E5
Mahanoro 35E5
Maha Sarakham 27J5
Mahd adh Dhahab 34E1
Mahdia 19G6
Mahdia 20D7
Mahdia 53G2
Mahenge 35D4
Mahilyow 23F5
Mahón 19I4
Maicao 52D1
Maidenhead 15G7
Maidstone 15H7
Maiduguri 32E3
Maine *state* 47N2
Maine, Gulf of 45L5
Mainland *i.* 16F1
Mainland *i.* 16□
Maintirano 35E5
Mainz 13L5
Maitland 42E4
Maizuru 31D6
Majene 29D8
Majorca *i.* 19H4
Makabana 34B4
Makale 29D8
Makanchi 27H2
Makarov 30F2
Makar'yev 22I4
Makassar 29D8
Makassar, Selat *strait* 29D8
Makat 26E2
Makeni 32B4
Makgadikgadi *depr.* 35C6
Makhachkala 23J8
Makinsk 27G1
Makiyivka 23H6
Makó 21I1
Makokou 34B3
Maksatikha 22G4
Makunguwiro 35D5
Makurdi 32D4
Malabar Coast 27G5
Malabo 32D4
Malacca, Strait of *strait* 29B7
Maladzyechna 11O9
Málaga 19D5
Malaita *i.* 39G2
Malakal 33G4
Malang 29D8
Malanje 35B4
Mälaren *l.* 11J7
Malargüe 54C5
Malatya 26C3
Malawi *country* 35D5
Malaya Vishera 22G4
Malāyer 33H1
Malaysia *country* 29C7
Malbork 13Q3
Maldives *country* 27G6
Maldon 15H7
Maldon 42B6
Maldonado 54F4
Male 7
Malgobek 23J8
Malhada 55C1
Mali *country* 32C3
Malili 38C2
Malindi 34E4
Malin Head 17E2
Malkara 21L4
Mallawī 33G2
Mallét 55A4
Mallow 17D5
Malmédy 13K5
Malmesbury 15E7
Malmesbury 36D7
Malmö 11H9
Malmyzh 22K4
Maloshuyka 22H3
Maloyaroslavets 23H5
Malta 11O8
Malta *country* 20F7
Malta Channel 20F6
Maltby 14F5
Maluku, Laut *sea* 29E8
Malung 11H6
Maluti Mountains 37I5
Malvern 47I5
Malyn 23F6
Malyye Derbety 23J7
Mamadysh 22K5
Mamelodi 37I3
Mamfe 32D4
Mamoré *r.* 52E6
Mamou 32B3
Mamuju 38B2
Man 32C4
Man, Isle of *terr.* 14C4
Manacapuru 52F4
Manacor 19H4
Manado 29E7
Managua 51G6
Manakara 35E6
Manama 34F1
Mananara Avaratra 35E5
Mananjary 35E6
Manassas 48C3
Manaus 52F4
Manavgat 33G1
Manchester 14E5
Manchester 48C3
Manchester 48E2
Manchester 48F1
Mandal 11E7
Mandalay 27I4
Mandalgovĭ 27J2
Mandan 46G2
Mandeville 51I5
Mandritsara 35E5
Mandsaur 27G4
Mandurah 40D6
Manduria 20G4
Mandya 27G5
Manevychi 23E6
Manfredonia 20F4
Manga 32C3
Manga 55C1
Mangai 34B4
Mangalia 21M3
Mangalore 27G5
Mangaung 37H5
Mangotsfield 15E7
Mangualde 19C3
Manhattan 47H4
Manhica 37K3
Manhuaçu 55C3
Manicouagan, Réservoir *resr* 45L4
Maniitsoq 45M3
Manila 29E6
Manilla 42E3
Manisa 21L5
Manistee 47J3
Manitoba *prov.* 45I4
Manitoba, Lake 45I4
Manitowoc 47J3
Manizales 52C2
Manja 35E6
Mankato 47I3
Mankono 32C4
Mannar, Gulf of 27G6
Mannheim 13L6
Mannington 48A3
Manp'o 30B4
Manresa 19G3
Mansa 35C5
Mansa Konko 32B3
Mansfield 15F5
Mansfield 42C6
Mansfield 47I5
Mansfield 47K3
Manta 52B4
Manteca 49B2
Mantena 55C2
Mantes-la-Jolie 18E2
Mantiqueira, Serra da *mts* 55B3
Mantoudi 21J5
Mäntsälä 11N6
Mänttä 10N5
Mantua 20D2
Manturovo 22J4
Manuel Ribas 55A4
Manuel Vitorino 55C1
Manukau 43E3
Manyas 21L4
Manyoni 35D4
Manzanillo 50D5
Manzanillo 51I4
Manzhouli 27K2
Manzini 37J4
Mao 33E3
Maokeng 37H4
Maple Creek 46F2
Maputo 37K3
Maputo *prov.* 37K3
Maputsoe 37H5
Maqteïr *reg.* 32B2
Maquela do Zombo 35B4
Maraã 52E4
Maraba 53I5
Maracaibo 52D1
Maracaibo, Lake 52D2
Maracaju 54E2
Maracás 55C1
Maracay 52E1
Maradi 32D3
Marajó, Ilha de *i.* 53H4
Marand 26D3
Maranhão *r.* 52D4
Maraú 55D1
Marbella 19D5
Marble Hall 37I3
Marburg 37J6
Marburg an der Lahn 13L5
Marcali 20G1
March 15H6
Marcona 52C7
Mardan 27G3
Mar del Plata 54E5
Mardin 33H1
Maree, Loch *l.* 16D3
Margate 15I7
Margherita Peak 34C3
Marg'ilon 27G2
Marhanets' 23G7
Mariana 55C3
Marianna 47I5
Marianna 47J5
Ma'rib 34E2
Maribor 20F1
Mariehamn 11K6
Mariental 36C3
Mariestad 11H7
Marietta 47K5
Marietta 48A3
Marignane 18G5
Mariinsk 24J4
Mariinskiy Posad 22J4
Marijampolė 11M9
Marília 55A3
Marín 19B2
Marina 49B2
Mar"ina Horka 11P10
Marinette 47J2
Maringá 55A3
Marinha Grande 19B4
Marion 47J3
Marion 47K3
Marion 47K4
Marion 47L5
Maritime Alps *mts* 18H4
Mariupol' 23H7
Marīvān 33H1
Marka 34E3
Market Deeping 15G6
Market Harborough 15G6
Market Weighton 14G5
Markovo 25S3
Marks 23J6
Marmande 18E4
Marmara, Sea of *g.* 21M4
Marmaris 21M6
Marne *r.* 18F2
Marne-la-Vallée 18F2
Maroantsetra 35E5
Marondera 35D5
Maroochydore 42F1
Maroua 33E3
Marovoay 35E5
Marquesas Islands 6
Marquês de Valença 55C3
Marquette 47J2
Marra, Jebel *mt.* 33F3
Marrakech 32C1
Marsá al 'Alam 33G2
Marsabit 34D3
Marsala 20E6
Marsá Maṭrūḥ 33F1
Marseille 18G5
Marshall 47H3
Marshall 47I4
Marshall 47I5
Marshall Islands *country* 6
Marshalltown 47I3
Märsta 11J7
Martapura 29D8
Martigny 18H3
Martin 13Q6
Martinho Campos 55B2
Martinique *terr.* 51L6
Martinsburg 48C3
Martinsville 47L4
Martos 19E5
Martuk 26E1
Maruim 53K6
Mary 26F3
Maryborough 41K5
Maryland *state* 48C3
Marysville 49B1
Maryville 47I3
Maryville 47K4
Masai Steppe *plain* 35D4
Masaka 34D4
Masan 31C6
Masasi 35D5
Mascara 19G6
Mascote 55D1
Maseru 37H5
Mashhad 26E3
Masilo 37H5
Masindi 34D3
Masjed Soleymān 33H1
Mask, Lough *l.* 17C4
Mason City 47I3
Massa 20D2
Massachusetts *state* 48E1
Massachusetts Bay 48F1
Massafra 20G4
Massango 35B4
Massawa 33G3
Massenya 33E3
Massif Central *mts* 18F4
Massillon 48A2
Massina 32C3
Masterton 43E5
Mastung 26F4
Mastūrah 34D1
Masty 11N10
Masuda 31C6
Masvingo 35D6
Masvingo *prov.* 37J1
Matabeleland South *prov.* 37I1
Matadi 35B4
Matagalpa 51G6
Matam 32B3
Matamey 32D3
Matamoros 46G6
Matamoros 47H6
Matane 47N2
Matanzas 47K7
Mataram 29D8
Mataró 19H3
Matā'utu 39I3
Matehuala 50D4
Matemanga 35D5
Matera 20G4
Mateur 20C6
Mathura 27G4
Mati 29E7
Matías Cardoso 55C1
Matías Romero 50E5
Matlock 15F5
Mato Grosso *state* 55A1
Mato Grosso, Planalto do *plat.* 53H7
Matosinhos 19B3
Mato Verde 55C1
Matsue 31D6
Matsumoto 31E5
Matsuyama 31D6
Matterhorn *mt.* 18H4
Matterhorn *mt.* 46D3
Maturín 52F2
Matwabeng 37H5
Mauchline 16E5
Maui *i.* 46□
Maun 35C5
Maunatlala 37H2
Mauritania *country* 32B3
Mauritius *country* 7
Mavinga 35C5
Mawlamyaing 27I5
Mawqaq 33H2
Mayagüez 51K5
Maya Mountains 50G5
Maybole 16E5
Maych'ew 34D2
Mayenne 18D2
Maykop 23I7
Mayna 23J5
Mayotte *terr.* 35E5
Mayskiy 23J8
Mazar del Vallo 20E6
Mazār-e Sharīf 26F3
Mazatlán 50C4
Mažeikiai 11M8
Mazyr 23F5
Mbabane 37J4
Mbahiakro 32C4
Mbaïki 34B3
Mbale 34D3
Mbalmayo 32E4
Mbandaka 34B4
M'banza Congo 35B4
Mbarara 33G5
Mbari *r.* 34C3
Mbeya 35D4
Mbinga 35D5
Mbouda 32E4
Mbour 32B3
Mbuji-Mayi 35C4
Mburucuyá 54E3
McAlester 47H5
McAllen 46H6
McCall 46D3
McCook 46G3
Mchinga 35D4
McKinley, Mount 44C3
McMinnville 46C2
McPherson 46H4
Mdantsane 37H7
M'Daourouch 20B6
Mead, Lake *resr* 49E2
Meadville 48A2
Meaux 18F2
Mecca 34D1
Mechanicsville 48C4
Mechelen 12J5
Mecheria 32C1
Mecklenburger Bucht *b.* 13M3
Medan 27I6
Médéa 19H5
Medellín 52C2
Medenine 32E1
Medford 46C3
Medford 48E2
Medgidia 21M2
Media 48D3
Medias 21K1
Medicine Bow Mountains 46F3
Medicine Hat 44G4
Medina 34D1
Medina 55C2
Medina de Rioseco 19D3
Mediterranean Sea 20D6
Medvedevo 22J4
Medvezh'yegorsk 22G3
Meekatharra 40D5
Meerut 27G4
Megalopoli 21J6
Meiganga 33E4
Meihekou 30B4
Meiktila 27I4
Meiningen 13M5
Meißen 13N5
Meixi 30C3
Meizhou 28D5
Mek'elē 34D2
Mékhé 32B3
Meknès 32C1
Mekong *r.* 27J4
Mekong *r.* 29C6
Melaka 29C7
Melbourne 42B6
Melbourne 47K6
Melenki 23I5
Melilla 19E6
Melitopol' 23G7
Melk 13O6
Melksham 15E7
Melo 54F4
Melrose 16G5
Melton 42B6
Melton Mowbray 15G6
Melun 18F2
Melville Bay 41H2
Melville Island 40G2
Melville Island 45H2
Memmingen 13M7
Memphis 47I4
Mena 23G6
Mena 47I5
Mende 18F4
Mendefera 33G3
Mendeleyevsk 22L5
Mendi 38E2
Mendip Hills 15E7
Mendoza 54C4
Menemen 21L5
Menongue 35B5
Mentawai, Kepulauan *is* 29B8
Menton 18H5
Menzel Bourguiba 20C6
Menzel Temime 20D6
Meppen 13K4
Meqheleng 37H5
Merano 20D1
Merauke 29G8
Merced 49B2
Mercedes 54E3
Mercedes 54E4
Mercês 55C3
Mere 15E7
Merefa 23H6
Mergui Archipelago *is* 27I5
Mérida 19C4
Mérida 50G4
Mérida 52D2
Meriden 48E2
Meridian 47J5
Mérignac 18D4
Merimbula 42D6
Merowe 33G3
Merredin 40D6
Merrill 47J2
Mersa Fatma 33H3
Mersey *est.* 14E5
Mersin 33G1
Merthyr Tydfil 15D7
Merzig 13K6
Mesa 46E5
Mesagne 20G4
Mesolongi 21I5
Mesquita 55C2
Messina 20F5
Messina, Strait of *strait* 20F5
Messini 21J6
Mestre 20E2
Meta *r.* 52E2
Metán 54C3
Methuen 48F1
Metlaoui 32D1
Metu 34D3
Metz 18H2
Meuse *r.* 12J5
Mevagissey 15C8
Mexicali 49E4
Mexico *country* 50D4
Mexico, Gulf of 47H6
Mexico City 50E5
Meyersdale 48B3
Meymaneh 26F3
Mezdra 21J3
Mezen' 22J2
Mezen' *r.* 22J2
Mezhdurechensk 22K3
Mezhdurechensk 24J4
Mezőtúr 21I1
Miami 47I4
Miami 47K6
Miami Beach 47K6
Miandowāb 33H1
Miandrivazo 35E5
Mianwali 27G3
Mianyang 27J3
Miarinarivo 35E5
Miass 24H4
Michalovce 23D6
Michigan *state* 47J2
Michigan, Lake 47J3
Michurinsk 23I5
Micronesia, Federated States of *country* 29G7
Middelburg 12I5
Middelburg 37I3
Middelfart 11F9
Middle River 48C3
Middlesbrough 14F4
Middletown 48D2
Middletown 48E2
Midland 46G5
Midland 47L3
Midleton 17D6
Miðvágur 10□[1]
Mielec 23D6
Miercurea-Ciuc 21K1
Mieres 19D2
Miguel Auza 46G7
Mihara 31D6
Mikhaylov 23H5
Mikhaylovka 23I6
Mikhaylovka 30D4
Mikhaylovskiy 24I4
Mikkeli 11O6
Milan 20C2
Milas 21L6
Milazzo 20F5
Mildenhall 15H6
Mildura 41I6
Miles 42E1
Miles City 46F2
Milford 48F1
Milford Haven 15B7
Milford Sound *inlet* 43A7
Miliana 19H5
Mil'kovo 25Q4
Millau 18F4
Milledgeville 47K5
Mille Lacs, Lac des *l.* 45I5
Millerovo 23I6
Millmerran 42E1
Millville 48D3
Milpitas 49B2
Milton Keynes 15G6
Milwaukee 47J3
Mīnāb 26E4
Minahasa, Semenanjung *pen.* 29E7
Minas 27J6
Minas 54E4
Minas Gerais *state* 55B2
Minas Novas 55C2
Minatitlán 50F5
Mindanao *i.* 29E7
Mindelo 32□
Minden 13L4
Minden 47I5
Mindoro *i.* 29E6
Mindouli 34B4
Minehead 15D7
Mineola 48E2
Mineral'nyye Vody 23I7
Mineral Wells 46H5
Minerva 48A2
Mingäçevir 23J8
Minglanilla 19F4
Mingoyo 35D5
Mingshui 30B3
Minna 32D4
Minneapolis 47I3
Minnesota *state* 47I2
Minorca *i.* 19H3
Minot 46G2
Minsk 11O10
Mińsk Mazowiecki 13R4
Minusinsk 24K4
Mirabela 55B2
Miraí 55C3
Miramar 54E5
Miramichi 45L5
Miranda 54E2
Miranda de Ebro 19E2
Mirandela 19C3
Mirandola 20D2
Mirassol 55A3
Mirboo North 42C7
Miri 29D7
Mirim, Lagoa *l.* 54F4
Mirnyy 25M3
Mirpur Khas 27F4
Mirtoö Pelagos *sea* 21J6
Miryang 31C6
Mirzapur 27H4
Miskolc 23D6
Miṣrātah 33E1
Mission Viejo 49D4
Mississauga 48B1
Mississippi *r.* 47J6
Mississippi *state* 47J5
Missoula 46E2
Missouri *r.* 47I4
Missouri *state* 47I4
Mistassini, Lac *l.* 45K4
Mistelbach 13P6
Mitchell 41J5
Mitchell 46H3
Mitchell *r.* 41I3
Mitchelstown 17D5
Mito 31F5
Mitú 52D3
Mitumba, Chaîne des *mts* 35C5
Miura 31E6
Miyako 31F5
Miyakonojō 31C7
Miyazaki 31C7
Miyazu 31D6
Miyoshi 31D6
Mizen Head 17C6
Mizhhir"ya 23D6
Mizusawa 31F5
Mjölby 11I7
Mkata 35D4
Mladá Boleslav 13O5
Mladenovac 21I2
Mława 13R4
Mlungisi 37H6
Mmabatho 37G3
Moanda 34B4
Moberly 47I4
Mobile 47J5
Mobile Bay 47J5
Moçambique 35E5
Mocha 34E2
Mochudi 37H3
Mocimboa da Praia 35E5
Mocoa 52C3
Mococa 55B3
Mocuba 35D5
Modder *r.* 37G5
Modena 20D2
Modesto 49B2
Moe 42C7
Moelv 11G6
Moffat 16F5
Mogadishu 34E3
Mogi-Mirim 55B3
Mogocha 25M4
Mogoditshane 37G3
Mohács 20H2
Mohale's Hoek 37H6
Mohammadia 19G6
Mohoro 35D4
Mohyliv Podil's'kyy 23E6
Moinești 21L1
Mo i Rana 10I3
Mojave Desert 49D3
Moji das Cruzes 55B3
Mokhotlong 37I5
Mokrine 20D7
Mokolo 33E3
Mokopane 37I3
Mokp'o 31B6
Mokrous 23J6
Mokshan 23J5
Molde 10E5
Moldova *country* 23F7
Moldovei de Sud, Cîmpia *plain* 21M1
Molepolole 37G3
Molėtai 11N9
Molfetta 20G4
Molina de Aragón 19F3
Mollendo 52D7
Mölnlycke 11H8
Molong 42D4
Molopo *watercourse* 36E5
Moloundou 33E4
Moluccas *is* 29E8
Mombaça 53K5
Mombasa 34D4
Momchilgrad 21K4
Mompós 52D2
Møn *i.* 11H9
Monaco *country* 18H5
Monadhliath Mountains 16E3
Monaghan 17F3
Monastir 20D7
Monastyrshche 23F6
Monbetsu 30F3
Moncalieri 20B2
Monchegorsk 10R3
Mönchengladbach 13K5
Monclova 46G6
Moncton 45L5
Mondlo 37J4
Mondovì 20B2
Mondragone 20E4
Monfalcone 20E2
Monforte de Lemos 19C2
Mongbwalu 34D3
Mông Cai 27J4
Mongo 33E3
Mongolia *country* 27J2
Mongu 35C5
Monkey Bay 35D5
Monmouth 15E7
Monopoli 20G4
Monreal del Campo 19F3
Monreale 20E5
Monroe 47I5
Monrovia 32B4
Mons 12I5
Montana 21J3
Montana *state* 46F2
Montargis 18F3
Montauban 18E4
Montbrison 18G4
Montceau-les-Mines 18G3
Mont-de-Marsan 18D5
Monte Alegre 53H4
Monte Alegre de Goiás 55B1
Monte Alegre de Minas 55A2
Monte Azul 55C1
Monte Azul Paulista 55A3
Montebelluna 20E2
Monte-Carlo 18H5
Monte Cristi 51J5
Montego Bay 51I5
Montélimar 18G4
Montemorelos 46H6
Montemor-o-Novo 19B4
Monterey 49B2
Monterey Bay 49A2
Montería 52C2
Monteros 54C3
Monterrey 46G6
Monte Santo 53K6
Montes Claros 55C2

Montesilvano 20F3
Montevarchi 20D3
Montevideo 54E4
Montgomery 47J5
Montgomery 48A3
Monthey 18H3
Monticello 48D2
Montilla 19D5
Montluçon 18F3
Montmagny 45K5
Monto 41K4
Montpelier 47M3
Montpellier 18F5
Montréal 45K5
Montrose 16G4
Montrose 46F4
Mont-St-Aignan 15I9
Montserrat terr. 51L5
Monywa 27I4
Monza 20C2
Moora 40D6
Moorhead 47H2
Mooroopna 42B6
Moose Jaw 44H4
Mopipi 35C6
Mopti 32C3
Moquegua 52D7
Mora 11I6
Mora 33E3
Morada Nova 53K5
Moramanga 35E5
Morar, Loch l. 16D4
Moray Firth b. 16E3
Mordovo 23I5
Morecambe 14E4
Morecambe Bay 14D4
Moree 42D2
Morelia 50D5
Morella 19F3
Morena, Sierra mts 19C5
Moreni 21K2
Moreno Valley 49D4
Morgan Hill 49B2
Morganton 47K4
Morgantown 48B3
Morges 18H3
Morioka 31F5
Morisset 42E4
Morki 22K4
Morlaix 18C2
Morley 14F5
Mornington Island 41H3
Morocco country 32C1
Morogoro 35D4
Moro Gulf 29E7
Morombe 35E6
Mörön 27J2
Morondava 35E6
Morón de la Frontera 19D5
Moroni 35E5
Moroto 34D3
Morozovsk 23I6
Morpeth 14F3
Morrinhos 55A2
Morristown 47K4
Morristown 48D2
Morrisville 48D1
Morro do Chapéu 53J6
Morshanka 23I5
Morsott 20C7
Morteros 54D4
Mortlake 42A7
Moruya 42E5
Morvern reg. 16D4
Morwell 42C7
Mosbach 13L6
Moscow 22H5
Moscow 46D2
Moselle r. 18H2
Moses Lake 46D2
Moshi 34D4
Mosjøen 10H4
Mosonmagyaróvár 13P7
Moss 11G7
Mossel Bay 36F8
Mossman 41J3
Mossoró 53K5
Most 13N5
Mostaganem 19G6
Mostar 20G3
Mostovskoy 23I7
Mosul 33H1
Motala 11I7
Motherwell 16F5
Motilla del Palancar 19F4
Motril 19E5
Motru 21J2
Motul 50G4
Mouila 34B4
Moulins 18F3
Moultrie 47K5
Moundou 33E4
Moundsville 48A3
Mountain Home 46D3
Mountain Home 47I4
Mount Darwin 35D5
Mount Gambier 41I7
Mount Hagen 38E2
Mount Holly 48D3
Mount Isa 41H4
Mount Magnet 40D5
Mountmellick 17E4
Mount Morris 48C1
Mount Pleasant 47I3
Mount Pleasant 47I5
Mount Pleasant 47K3
Mount's Bay 15B8
Mount Shasta 46C3
Mount Vernon 46C2
Mount Vernon 47J4
Moura 19C4
Moura 41J4
Mourdi, Dépression du depr. 33F3
Mourdiah 32C3
Mourne Mountains hills 17F3
Mouscron 12I5
Mouydir, Monts du plat. 32D2
Moyeni 37H6
Moyobamba 52C5
Mozambique country 35D6
Mozambique Channel strait 35E6
Mozdok 23J8
Mozhaysk 23H5
Mozhga 22L4
Mpanda 35D4
Mpika 35D5
Mpumalanga prov. 37I4
Mpwapwa 35D4
M'Saken 20D7
M'Sila 19I6
Mstsislaw 23F5
Mtsensk 23H5
Mtwara 35E5
Mubende 34D3
Mubi 32E3
Muconda 35C5
Mucuri 55D2
Mudanjiang 30C3
Mudanya 21M4
Mudurnu 21N4
Mufulira 35C5
Muğla 21M6
Mühlhausen (Thüringen) 13M5
Mui Ca Mau c. 29C7
Muine Bheag 17F5
Muir of Ord 16E3
Muju 31B5
Mukacheve 23D6
Mukalla 34E2
Mulan 30C3
Mulhacén mt. 19E5
Mulhouse 18H3
Muling 30C3
Mull i. 16D4
Mull, Sound of sea chan. 16C4
Mullens 48A4
Mullingar 17E4
Mull of Kintyre hd 16D5
Mullumbimby 42F2
Multan 27G3
Mumbai 27G5
Muna 50G4
Mundesley 15I6
Mundubbera 41K5
Munger 27H4
Munich 13M6
Münster 13K5
Münster 13M4
Muqui 55C3
Murakami 31E5
Muramvya 34C4
Murashi 22K4
Muratlı 21L4
Murcia 19F5
Murcia aut. comm. 19F5
Mureșul r. 21I1
Muret 18E5
Murfreesboro 47J4
Muriaé 55C3
Müritz l. 13N4
Murmansk 10R2
Murmanskaya Oblast' admin. div. 10S2
Murom 22I5
Muroran 30F4
Muroto 31D6
Murramarang National Park 42I5
Murray 47J4
Murray r. 42A5
Murray Bridge 41H7
Murrumbidgee r. 42A5
Murrumburrah 42D5
Murska Sobota 20G1
Murwara 27H4
Murzüq 33E2
Mürzzuschlag 13O7
Musala mt. 21J3
Musan 30C4
Muscat 26E4
Muscatine 47I3
Musgrave Ranges mts 40G5
Mushie 34B4
Muskogee 47H4
Musoma 34D4
Musselburgh 16F5
Mustafakemalpaşa 21M4
Muswellbrook 42E4
Müţ 33F2
Mutare 35D5
Mutoko 35D5
Mutsamudu 35E5
Mutsu 30F4
Mutum 55C2
Muyinga 34D4
Muzaffarpur 27H4
Múzquiz 46G6
Mvuma 35D5
Mwanza 34D4
Mwene-Ditu 35C4
Mweru, Lake 35C4
Myadzyel 11O9
Myanmar country 27I4
Myeik 27I5
Myingyan 27I4
Myitkyina 27I4
Mykolayiv 21O1
Mykonos i. 21K6
Mymensingh 27I4
Myŏnggan 30C4
Myory 11O9
Mýrdalsjökull ice cap 10□2
Myrhorod 23G6
Myronivka 23F6
Myrtle Beach 47L5
Myrtleford 42C6
Myślibórz 13O4
Mysore 27G5
My Tho 29C6
Mytilini 21L5
Mytilini Strait strait 21L5
Mytishchi 22H5
Mzimba 35D5
Mzuzu 35D5

N

Naantali 11M6
Naas 17F4
Nabari 31E6
Naberera 35D4
Naberezhnyye Chelny 24G4
Nabeul 20D6
Nacala 35E5
Nachingwea 35D5
Nacogdoches 47I5
Nador 19E6
Nadvirna 23E6
Nadym 24I3
Næstved 11G9
Nafplio 21J6
Naftalan 23J8
Nafy 34E1
Naga 29E6
Nagambie 42B6
Nagano 31E5
Nagaoka 31E5
Nagasaki 31C6
Nagato 31C6
Nagercoil 27G6
Nagoya 31E6
Nagpur 27G4
Nagqu 27I3
Nagyatád 20G1
Nagykanizsa 20G1
Nahavand 33H1
Nairn 16F3
Nairobi 34D4
Naji 30A2
Najin 30C4
Najrān 34E2
Nakasongola 33G4
Nakatsu 31C6
Nakatsugawa 31E6
Nakfa 33G3
Nakhodka 30D4
Nakhon Pathom 29C6
Nakhon Ratchasima 29C6
Nakhon Sawan 29C6
Nakhon Si Thammarat 29B7
Nakskov 11G9
Nakuru 34D4
Nal'chik 23I8
Nallıhan 21N4
Nälüt 32E1
Namahadi 37I4
Namangan 27G2
Nambour 42F1
Nambucca Heads 42F3
Nam Định 29C5
Namib Desert 36B3
Namibe 35B5
Namibia country 35B6
Nampa 46D3
Nampala 32C3
Namp'o 31B5
Nampula 35D5
Namsos 10G4
Namtsy 25N3
Namtu 27I4
Namur 12J5
Namwŏn 31B6
Nan 29C6
Nanaimo 44F5
Nanao 31E5
Nancha 30C3
Nanchang 27K4
Nanchong 27J3
Nancy 18H2
Nanded 27G5
Nanga Eboko 32E4
Nangulangwa 35D4
Nanjing 28D4
Nan Ling mts 27K4
Nanning 27J4
Nanortalik 45N3
Nanping 28D5
Nantes 18D3
Nanticoke 48A1
Nanticoke 48D2
Nantucket Sound g. 48F2
Nantwich 15E5
Nanuque 55C2
Nanyang 27K3
Nanyuki 34D4
Napa 49A1
Napier 43F4
Naples 20F4
Naples 47K6
Nara 31D6
Nara 32C3
Narach 11O9
Naracoorte 41I7
Naranjal 52C4
Narbonne 18F5
Nardò 20H4
Nares Strait strait 45K2
Narimanov 23J7
Narmada r. 27G4
Narni 20E3
Narodnaya, Gora mt. 24G3
Naro-Fominsk 23H5
Narooma 42E6
Narowlya 23F6
Närpes 10L5
Narrandera 42C5
Narromine 42D4
Narsaq 45N3
Nartkala 23I8
Naruto 31D6
Narva 11P7
Narva Bay 11O7
Narvik 10J2
Nar'yan-Mar 22L2
Naryn 27G2
Nashik 27G4
Nashua 48F1
Nashville 47J4
Nassau 47L6
Nasser, Lake resr 33G2
Nässjö 11I8
Nata 35C6
Natal 53K5
Natchez 47I5
Natchitoches 47I5
National City 49D4
Natitingou 32D3
Natividade 53I6
Natori 31F5
Natron, Lake salt l. 34D4
Natuna Besar i. 27J6
Naturaliste, Cape 40D6
Naturaliste Channel 40C5
Naujoji Akmenė 11M8
Naurskaya 23J8
Nauru country 39G2
Navahrudak 11N10
Navan 17F4
Navapolatsk 11P9
Navarra aut. comm. 19F2
Navashino 22I5
Navassa Island terr. 51I5
Navlya 23G5
Năvodari 21M2
Navoiy 26F2
Navojoa 46F6
Navolato 46F7
Nawabshah 26F4
Naxçıvan 26D3
Naxos i. 21K6
Nayoro 30F3
Nazaré 55D1
Nazareth 33G1
Nazário 55A2
Nazca 52D6
Nazilli 21M6
Nazran' 23J8
Nazrēt 34D3
Nazwá 26E4
N'dalatando 35B4
Ndélé 34C3
Ndjamena 33E3
Ndola 35C5
Neagh, Lough l. 17F3
Nea Liosia 21J5
Neapoli 21J6
Neath 15D7
Nebbi 34D3
Nebolchi 22G4
Nebraska state 46G3
Nebraska City 47H3
Necochea 54E5
Nedroma 19F6
Neftegorsk 23K5
Neftegorsk 30F1
Neftekamsk 24G4
Neftekumsk 23J7
Nefteyugansk 24I3
Negage 35B4
Negēlē 34D3
Negotino 21J4
Negro r. 52G4
Negro r. 55A4
Negros i. 29E7
Nehe 30B2
Neijiang 27J4
Nei Mongol Zizhiqu aut. reg. 30A2
Neiva 52C3
Nek'emtē 34D3
Nekrasovskoye 22I4
Nelidovo 22G4
Nellore 27G5
Nelson 14E5
Nelson 43D5
Nelson 44G5
Nelson r. 45I4
Nelspruit 37J3
Néma 32C3
Neman 11M9
Nemours 18F2
Nemuro 30G4
Nemuro-kaikyō sea chan. 30G4
Nemyriv 23F6
Nenagh 17D5
Nenjiang 30B2
Neosho 47I4
Nepal country 27H4
Nerang 42F1
Nerchinsk 25M4
Nerekhta 22I4
Nerópolis 55A2
Neryungri 25N4
Ness, Loch l. 16E3
Nestos r. 21K4
Netherlands country 12J4
Netherlands Antilles terr. 51K6
Neubrandenburg 13N4
Neuchâtel 18H3
Neuchâtel, Lac de l. 18H3
Neufchâtel-Hardelot 15I8
Neumünster 13L3
Neunkirchen 13K6
Neunkirchen 13P7
Neuquén 54C5
Neuruppin 13N4
Neusiedler See l. 13P7
Neustrelitz 13N4
Neuwied 13K5
Nevada 47I4
Nevada state 46D4
Nevada, Sierra mts 19E5
Nevada, Sierra mts 46C3
Nevel' 22F4
Nevel'sk 30F3
Never 30B1
Nevers 18F3
Nevesinje 20H3
Nevinnomyssk 23I7
Newala 35D5
New Albany 47J4
New Amsterdam 53G2
Newark 48D2
Newark 48D3
Newark-on-Trent 15G5
New Bedford 48F2
New Bern 47L4
Newberry 47K5
New Boston 47I5
New Braunfels 46H6
New Britain 48E2
New Britain i. 38E2
New Brunswick 48D2
New Brunswick prov. 45L5
Newburgh 48D2
Newbury 15F7
Newburyport 48F1
New Caledonia terr. 39G4
Newcastle 17G3
Newcastle 37I4
Newcastle 42E4
New Castle 48A2
Newcastle-under-Lyme 15E5
Newcastle upon Tyne 14F4
Newcastle West 17C5
New City 48E2
New Cumnock 16E5
New Delhi 27G4
New England Range mts 42E3
Newent 15E7
Newfane 48B1
Newfoundland i. 45M5
Newfoundland and Labrador prov. 45M4
New Guinea i. 38E2
New Halfa 33G3
New Hampshire state 48F1
New Haven 48E2
New Iberia 47I5
New Ireland i. 38F2
New Jersey state 48D3
New Kensington 48B2
New Liskeard 45K5
New London 48E2
Newman 40D4
Newmarket 15H6
New Martinsville 48A3
New Mexico state 46F5
New Orleans 47I6
New Philadelphia 48A2
New Plymouth 43E4
Newport 15D7
Newport 15E6
Newport 15F8
Newport 46C3
Newport 47I4
Newport 48F2
Newport Beach 49D4
Newport News 48C4
Newport Pagnell 15G6
Newquay 15B8
New Roads 47I5
New Rochelle 48E2
New Ross 17F5
Newry 17F3
New Siberia Islands 25P2
New South Wales state 31B5
New Stanton 48B2
Newton 47H4
Newton 47I3
Newton 48D2
Newton 48F1
Newton Abbot 15D8
Newton Stewart 16E6
Newtown 15D6
New Town 46G2
Newtownabbey 17G3
Newtownards 17G3
Newtown-mountkennedy 17F4
New Ulm 47I3
New York 48E2
New York state 48D1
New Zealand country 43D5
Neya 22I4
Neyrīz 26E4
Neyshābūr 26E3
Ngaoundal 32E4
Ngaoundéré 33E4
Ngugimi 32E3
Nguru 32E3
Ngwelezana 37J5
Nha Trang 29C6
Nhill 41I7
Nhlangano 37J4
Niafounké 32C3
Niagara Falls 48B1
Niagara Falls 48B1
Niamey 32D3
Nianzishan 30A3
Nias i. 29B7
Nicaragua country 51G6
Nicaragua, Lake 51G6
Nicastro 20G5
Nice 18H5
Nice 49A1
Nicobar Islands 27I6
Nicosia 33G1
Nida 11L9
Nidzica 13R4
Nienburg (Weser) 13L4
Nieuw Nickerie 53G2
Niğde 26C3
Niger country 32D3
Niger r. 32D4
Nigeria country 32D4
Niigata 31E5
Niihama 31D6
Niimi 31D6
Niitsu 31E5
Nijmegen 13J5
Nikel' 10Q2
Nikolayevka 23J5
Nikolayevsk 23J6
Nikolayevsk-na-Amure 30F1
Nikol'sk 22J4
Nikopol' 23G7
Nikšić 20H3
Nile r. 33G1
Niles 48A2
Nîmes 18G5
Ning'an 30C3
Ningbo 28E5
Ninohe 31F4
Niono 32C3
Nioro 32C3
Niort 18D3
Nipigon, Lake 45J5
Nipissing, Lake 45K5
Niquelândia 55A1
Nirmal 27G5
Niš 21I3
Niscemi 20F6
Niterói 55C3
Nitra 13Q6
Niue terr. 39J3
Nivala 10N5
Nizamabad 27G5
Nizhnekamsk 22K5
Nizhneudinsk 25K4
Nizhnevartovsk 24I3
Nizhneyansk 25O2
Nizhniy Lomov 23I5
Nizhniy Novgorod 22I4
Nizhnyaya Omra 22L3
Nizhnyaya Tunguska r. 24J3
Nizhyn 23F6
Njombe 35D4
Njurundabommen 10J5
Nkambe 32E4
Nkawkaw 32C4
Nkhata Bay 35D5
Nkhotakota 35D5
Nkongsamba 32D4
Nobeoka 31C6
Noboribetsu 30F4
Nogales 46E5
Nogales 46E5
Nōgata 31C6
Nogent-le-Rotrou 18E2
Noginsk 22H5
Nogliki 30F2
Nola 34B3
Nolinsk 22K4
Nome 44B3
Nong'an 30B3
Noranda 45K5
Norberg 11I6
Norden 13K4
Norderstedt 13M4
Nordhausen 13M5
Norfolk 47H3
Norfolk 48C4
Norfolk Island terr. 39G4
Noril'sk 24J3
Norman 47H4
Normandia 53G3
Normandy reg. 18D2
Normanton 41I3
Norra Kvarken strait 10L5
Norristown 48D2
Norrköping 11J7
Norrtälje 11K7
Nortelândia 53G6
Northallerton 14F4
Northampton 15G6
Northampton 48E1
North Atlantic Ocean ocean 47O4
North Bay 45K5
North Canton 48A2
North Cape 10N1
North Cape 43D2
North Carolina state 47L4
North Channel lake channel 47K2
North Channel strait 17G2
North Dakota state 46G2
North Downs hills 15G7
Northern Cape prov. 36D5
Northern Ireland prov. 17F3
Northern Mariana Islands terr. 29G6
Northern Territory admin. div. 40G3
North Frisian Islands 13L3
North Haven 48E2
North Island 43D4
North Kingsville 48A2
North Korea country 31B5
North Las Vegas 49E2
North Platte 46G3
North Platte r. 46G3
North Ronaldsay Firth sea chan. 16G1
North Saskatchewan r. 44H4
North Sea 12H2
North Shields 14F3
North Taranaki Bight b. 43E4
North Tonawanda 48B1
North Tyne r. 14E4
North Uist i. 16B3
North West prov. 36G4
Northwest Territories admin. div. 44H3
Northwich 14E5
North York Moors moorland 14G4
Norton Sound sea chan. 44B3
Norwalk 47K3
Norwalk 48E2
Norway country 10E6
Norwegian Sea 10E3
Norwich 15I6
Norwich 48D1
Norwich 48E2
Noshiro 31F4
Nossob watercourse 36D2
Notodden 11F7
Notre Dame, Monts mts 45L5
Notre Dame Bay 45M5
Nottingham 15F6
Nouâdhibou 32B2
Nouakchott 32B3
Nouméa 39G4
Nouna 32C3
Nouvelle Calédonie i. 39G4
Nova Friburgo 55C3
Nova Iguaçu 55C3
Nova Kakhovka 21O1
Nova Lima 55C2
Nova Odesa 23F7
Nova Pilão Arcado 53J5
Nova Ponte 55B2
Novara 20C2
Nova Scotia prov. 45L5
Nova Sento Sé 53J5
Novato 49A1
Nova Trento 55A4
Nova Venécia 55C2
Nova Xavantino 53H6
Novaya Sibir', Ostrov i. 25P2
Novaya Zemlya is 24G2
Nova Zagora 21L3
Novelda 19F4
Nové Zámky 13Q7
Novhorod-Sivers'kyy 23G6
Novi Ligure 20C2
Novi Pazar 21I3
Novi Pazar 21L3
Novi Sad 21H2
Novoanninskiy 23I6
Novo Aripuanã 52F5
Novoazovs'k 23H7
Novocheboksarsk 22J4
Novocherkassk 23I7
Novo Cruzeiro 55C2
Novodvinsk 22I2
Novo Hamburgo 55A5
Novohrad-Volyns'kyy 23E6
Novokhopersk 23I6
Novokiyevskiy Uval 30C2
Novokubansk 23I7
Novokuybyshevsk 23K5
Novokuznetsk 24J4
Novo Mesto 20F2
Novomoskovs'k 23G6
Novomoskovsk 23H5
Novonikolayevskiy 23I6
Novopokrovskaya 23I7
Novopskov 23H6
Novorossiysk 23H7
Novorzhev 22F4
Novoshakhtinsk 23H7
Novosibirsk 24J4
Novosokol'niki 22F4
Novospasskoye 23J5
Novotroyits'ke 23G7
Novoukrayinka 23F6
Novouzensk 23K6
Novovolyns'k 23E6
Novovoronezh 23H6
Novozybkov 23F5
Nový Jičín 13P6
Novyy Oskol 23H6
Novyy Urengoy 24I3
Novyy Zay 22L5
Nowra 42E5
Nowy Sącz 13R6
Nowy Targ 13R6
Noyabr'sk 24I3
Nsanje 35D5
Nsukka 32D4
Ntungamo 34D4
Nuba Mountains 33G3
Nubian Desert 33G2
Nueva Gerona 51H4
Nueva Imperial 54B5
Nueva Rosita 46G6
Nueva San Salvador 50G6
Nuevitas 51I4
Nuevo Casas Grandes 46F5
Nuevo Laredo 46H6
Nuku'alofa 39I4
Nukus 26E2
Nullarbor Plain 40F6
Numan 34B3
Numazu 31E6
Numurkah 42B6
Nunavut admin. div. 45J2
Nuneaton 15F6
Nunivak Island 44B4
Nuñomoral 19C3
Nuoro 20C4
Nuqrah 34E1
Nuremberg 13M6
Nurlat 23K5
Nurmes 10P5
Nurmo 10M5
Nuuk 45M3
Nuweveldberge mts 36E7
Nyagan' 24H3
Nyala 33F3
Nyamtumbo 35D5
Nyandoma 22I3
Nyasa, Lake 35D4
Nyasvizh 11O10
Nyborg 11G9
Nyborg 10J8
Nyeri 34D4
Nyíregyháza 23D7
Nykøbing 11G9
Nykøbing Sjælland 11G9
Nyköping 11J7
Nynäshamn 11J7
Nyngan 42C3
Nyon 18H3
Nysa 13P5
Nyunzu 35C4
Nyurba 25M3
Nzega 35D4
Nzérékoré 32C4

O

O'ahu i. 46□
Oakey 42E1
Oakham 15G6
Oakland 49A2
Oakridge 46C3
Oakville 48B1
Oamaru 43C7
Oaxaca 50E5
Ob' r. 24H3
Obama 31D6
Oban 16D4
Oberon 42D4
Oberpfälzer Wald mts 13N6
Óbidos 53G4
Obihiro 30F4
Obil'noye 23J7
Obluch'ye 30C2
Obninsk 23H5
Obo 34C3
Obock 34E2
Oboyan' 23H6
Obrenovac 21I2
Obskaya Guba sea chan. 24I3
Obuasi 32C4
Ob"yachevo 22K3
Ocala 47K6
Ocaña 19E4
Ocaña 52D2
Occidental, Cordillera mts 52C3
Occidental, Cordillera mts 52D7
Ocean City 48D3
Oceanside 49D4
Ochakiv 21N1
Och'amch'ire 23I8
Ochil Hills 16F4
Octeville-sur-Mer 15H9
Ódáðahraun lava field 10□2
Ödate 31F4
Odawara 31E6
Odda 11E6
Ödemiş 21L5
Odense 11G9
Oderbucht b. 13O3
Odesa 21N1
Odessa 46G5
Odienné 32C4
Odintsovo 22H5
Odra r. 13Q6
Oeiras 53J5
Of 23I8
Offa 32D4
Offenbach am Main 13L5
Offenburg 13K6
Oga 31E5
Ōgaki 31E6
Ogallala 46G3
Ogbomosho 32D4
Ogden 46E3
Ogre 11N8
Ohio r. 48A3
Ohio state 48A2
Ohrid 21I4
Ohrid, Lake 21I4
Oil City 48B2
Ōita 31C6
Ojinaga 46G6
Ojiya 31E5
Ojos del Salado, Nevado mt. 54C3
Oka r. 23I4
Okavango Delta swamp 35C5
Okaya 31E5
Okayama 31D6
Okazaki 31E6
Okeechobee, Lake 47K6
Okehampton 15C8
Okha 30F1
Okhotsk 25P4
Okhotsk, Sea of 30G3
Okhtyrka 23G6
Okinawa-shotō is 31B8
Oklahoma state 46H4
Oklahoma City 47H4
Okmulgee 47H4
Okovskiy Les for. 22G5
Oktyabr'skiy 22I3
Oktyabr'skiy 23I7
Oktyabr'skiy 24G4
Oktyabr'skiy 25Q4
Oktyabr'skoy Revolyutsii, Ostrov i. 25K2
Okulovka 22G4
Okuta 32D4
Öland i. 11J8
Olavarría 54D5
Oława 13P5
Olbia 20C4
Oldenburg 13L4
Oldham 14E5
Old Head of Kinsale 17D6
Olean 48B1
Olecko 13S3
Oleksandriya 23G6
Olenegorsk 10R2
Olenino 22G4
Olevs'k 23E6
Olhão 19C5
Olifants r. 36D6
Olifants r. 36E7
Olifants r. 37J3
Olinda 53L5
Oliva 19F4
Oliva, Cordillera de mts 54C3
Oliveira dos Brejinhos 55C1
Olmos 52C5
Olney 15G6
Olney 48C3
Olofström 11I8
Olomouc 13P6
Olonets 22G3
Oloron-Ste-Marie 18D5
Olot 19H2
Olovyannaya 25M4
Olsztyn 13R4
Olten 18H3
Oltenița 21L2
Olympia 46C2
Olympus, Mount 21J4
Omagh 17E3
Omaha 47H3
Omaheke admin. reg. 36D2
Oman country 26E5
Oman, Gulf of 26E4
Omdurman 33G3
Om Hajêr 33G3
Ōmiya 31E6
Omsk 24I4
Omsukchan 25Q3
Ōmura 31C6
Omutninsk 22L4
Oncativo 54D4
Ondjiva 35B5
Ondo 32D4
Öndörhaan 27K2
Onega 22H3
Onega r. 22H3
Onega, Lake 22G3
Oneida 48D1
Oneonta 48D1
Onești 21L1
Onezhskaya Guba g. 22G2
Ongjin 31B5
Ongole 27H5
Onitsha 32D4
Onomichi 31D6
Ontario 49D3
Ontario prov. 48A1
Ontario, Lake 48C1
Onverwacht 53G2
Oolambeyan National Park 42F5
Oparino 22K4
Opava 13P6
Opelika 47J5
Opelousas 47I5
Opochka 11P8
Opole 13P5
Oporto 19B3
Opuwo 35B5
Oradea 21I1
Oran 19F6
Orán 54D2
Orang 30C4
Orange 18G4
Orange 42D4
Orange 47I5
Orange 49D4
Orange r. 36C5
Orangeburg 47K5
Orange Walk 50G5
Oranjemund 36C5
Oranjestad 51J6
Orăștie 21J2
Orbost 42D6
Ordu 23H8
Ore 32D4
Örebro 11I7
Oregon state 46C3
Oregon City 46C2
Orekhovo-Zuyevo 22H5
Orel 23H5
Orenburg 24G4
Öresund strait 11H9
Orford Ness hd 15I6
Orhaneli 21M5
Orhangazi 21M4
Orichi 22K4
Oriental, Cordillera mts 52D2
Oriental, Cordillera mts 52E6
Orihuela 19F4
Orikhiv 23G7
Orimattila 11N6
Orinoco r. 52F2
Oristano 20C5
Orivesi 11N6
Oriximiná 53G4
Orizaba 50E5
Orizona 55A2
Orkney 37H4
Orkney Islands 16F1
Orlândia 55B3
Orlando 47K6
Orleaes 55A5
Orléans 18E3
Orlov 22K4
Orlovskiy 23I7
Ormskirk 14E5
Örnsköldsvik 10K5
Orodara 32C3
Oroquieta 29E7
Orosháza 21I1
Oroville 46C4
Orqohan 30A2
Orsha 23F5
Orshanka 22J4
Orsk 24G4
Ørsta 10E5
Orthez 18D5
Ortona 20F3
Oruro 52E7
Orvieto 20E3
Ōsaka 31D6
Osby 11H8
Osh 27G2
Oshakati 35B5
Oshawa 45K5
Oshkosh 47J3
Oshogbo 32D4
Osijek 20H2
Osimo 20E3
Osizweni 37J4
Oskarshamn 11J8
Oslo 11G7
Oslofjorden sea chan. 11G7
Osmancık 23G8
Osmaneli 21M4
Osnabrück 13L4
Osorno 19D2
Osorno 54B6
Osoyoos 46D2
Osøyri 11D6
Oss 13J5
Ossining 48E2
Ostashkov 22G4
Ostend 12I5
Östersund 10I5
Ostrava 13Q6
Ostróda 13Q4
Ostrogozhsk 23H6
Ostrov 11P8
Ostrovskoye 22I4
Ostrowiec Świętokrzyski 23D6
Ostrów Mazowiecka 13R4
Ostrów Wielkopolski 13P5
Oswego 48C1
Oswestry 15D6
Otago Peninsula 43C7
Otaki 43E5
Otaru 30F4
Otawara 31F5
Otepää 11O7
Otjiwarongo 35B6
Otjozondjupa admin. reg. 36C1
Otley 14F5
Otradnyy 23K5
Otranto, Strait of strait 20H4
Ōtsu 31D6
Ottawa 45K5
Ottawa 47H4
Ottawa 47J3
Ottumwa 47I3
Otway, Cape 42A7
Ouachita Mountains 47I5
Ouaddaï reg. 33F3
Ouagadougou 32C3
Ouahigouya 32C3
Ouargaye 32D3
Ouargla 32D1
Ouarzazate 32C1
Oudtshoorn 36F7
Oued Zem 32C1
Oued Zénati 20B6
Ouesso 34B3
Ouezzane 19D6
Oujda 19F6
Oulainen 10N4
Ouled Djellal 19I6
Ouled Farès 19G5
Oulu 10N4
Oulujärvi l. 10O4
Oulunsalo 10N4
Oum el Bouaghi 20B7
Oundle 15G6
Ourense 19C2
Ouricurí 53J5
Ourinhos 55A3
Ouro Preto 55C3
Ouse r. 14G5
Ouse r. 15H8
Outer Hebrides is 16B3
Outer Santa Barbara Channel 49C4
Outlook 46F1
Outokumpu 10P5
Ouyen 41I7
Ovalle 54B4
Ovar 19B3
Oviedo 19D2
Ovruch 23F6
Owando 34B4
Owase 31E6
Owatonna 47I3
Owego 48C1
Owensboro 47J4
Owens Lake 49D2
Owen Sound 45J5
Owen Stanley Range mts 38E2
Owerri 32D4
Owo 32D4
Öxarfjörður b. 10□2
Oxelösund 11J7
Oxford 15F7
Oxford 47J5
Oxnard 49C3
Oyama 31E5
Oyem 34B3
Oyo 32D4
Oyonnax 18G3
Ozark 47J5
Ozark Plateau 47I4
Ozarks, Lake of the 47I4
Ozernovskiy 25Q4
Ozersk 11M9
Ozerskiy 30F3
Ozery 23H5
Ozinki 23K6

P

Paamiut 45N3
Paarl 36D7
Pabianice 13Q5
Pabna 27H4
Pacasmayo 52C5
Pachino 20F6
Pachuca 50E4
Pacific Grove 49B2
Padang 29C8
Padany 22G3
Paderborn 13L5
Padstow 15C8
Padua 20D2
Paducah 47J4
Pag 20F2
Pag i. 20F2
Pagadian 29E7
Paide 11N7
Paignton 15D8
Päijänne l. 11N6
Paimio 11M6
Painesville 48A2
Paisley 16E5
Paita 52B5
Pakaraima Mountains 52F3
Pakaraima Mountains 53G3
Pakhachi 25R3
Pakistan country 26F3
Pakruojis 11M9
Paks 20H1
Pakxé 29C6
Pala 33E4
Palaiseau 18F2
Palana 25Q4
Palanpur 27G4
Palapye 37H2
Palatka 25Q3
Palau country 29F7
Palawan i. 29D7
Palekh 22I4
Palembang 29C8
Palena 54B6
Palencia 19D2
Palermo 20E5
Palestine 47H5
Palghat 27G5
Palhoca 55A4
Pali 27G4
Palikir 7
Palk Strait strait 27G6
Pallasovka 23J6
Palliser, Cape 43E5
Palma de Mallorca 19H4
Palmares 53K5
Palmares do Sul 55A5
Palmas 53I6
Palmas 55A4
Palmas, Cape 32C4
Palmdale 49C3
Palmeira 55A4
Palmeira das Missões 54F3
Palmeira dos Índios 53K5
Palmeirais 53J5
Palmerston atoll 39J3
Palmerston North 43E5
Palmi 20F5
Palmira 52C3
Palm Springs 49D4
Palo Alto 49A2
Palopo 29E8
Palu 29D8
Pamiers 18E5
Pamir mts 27G3
Pamlico Sound sea chan. 47L4
Pampas reg. 54D5
Pamplona 19F2
Pamplona 52D2
Pamukova 21N4
Panagyurishte 21K3
Panaji 27G5
Panama country 51H7
Panama, Gulf of 51I7
Panama Canal 51I7
Panama City 47J5
Panama City 51I7
Panay i. 29E6
Pančevo 21I2
Panevėžys 11N9
Pangkalanbuun 29D8
Pangkalpinang 29C8
Pangnirtung 45L3
Pankakoski 10Q5
Panorama 55A3
Panshi 30B4
Pánuco 50E4
Panzhihua 27J4
Paoua 34B3
Pápa 20G1
Papakura 43E3
Papantla 50E4
Papa Stour i. 16□
Papenburg 13K4
Paphos 33G1
Papua, Gulf of 38E2
Papua New Guinea country 41J1
Par 15C8
Pará r. 55B2
Pará, Rio do r. 53I4
Paraburdoo 40D4
Paracatu 55B2
Paracel Islands 29D6
Paracin 21I3
Paracuru 53K4
Pará de Minas 55B2
Paradise 46C4
Paragominas 53I4
Paragould 47I4
Paraguaçu Paulista 55A3
Paraguay country 54E2
Paraguay r. 54E3
Paraíso do Norte 53I6
Paraisópolis 55B3
Parakou 32D4
Paramaribo 53G2
Paramirim 55C1
Paramus 48D2
Paraná 54D4
Paraná 55B1
Paraná r. 53H8
Paraná r. 55A1
Paraná state 55A4
Paranaguá 55A4
Paranaíba 55A2
Paranapiacaba, Serra mts 55A4
Paranavaí 54F2
Paraopeba 55B2
Paratinga 55C1
Paraúna 55A2
Parbhani 27G5
Parchim 13M4
Pardubice 13O5
Parecis, Serra dos hills 52F6
Parepare 29D8
Pargas 11M6
Paria, Gulf of 51L6
Parintins 53G4
Paris 18F2
Paris 47H5
Parkano 11M5
Parkersburg 48A3
Parkes 42D4
Parma 20D2
Parma 48A2
Parnaíba 53J4
Pärnu 11N7
Paroo watercourse 42A3
Paroo-Darling National Park 42E3
Paros 21K6
Paros i. 21K6
Parras 46G6
Parramatta 42E4
Parras 46G6
Parry Channel 45G2
Parry Islands 45G2
Parsons 47H4
Parthenay 18D3
Partizansk 30D4
Pasadena 49C3
Pascagoula 47J5
Pașcani 21L1
Pashkovskiy 23H7
Paso de los Toros 54E4
Paso Robles 49B3
Passaic 48D2
Passa Tempo 55B3
Passau 13N6
Passo Fundo 54F3
Passos 55B3
Pastavy 11O9
Pasto 52C3
Pastos Bons 53J5
Pasvalys 11N8
Patagonia reg. 54B8
Paterson 48D2
Patna 27H4
Pato Branco 54F3
Patos 53K5
Patos, Lagoa dos l. 54F4
Patos de Minas 55B2
Patras 21I5
Patrocínio 55B2
Patton 48B2
Patu 53K5
Pau 18D5
Pauini 52E5
Paulo Afonso 53K5
Pavão 55C2
Pavia 20C2
Pavlikeni 21K3
Pavlodar 27G1
Pavlohrad 23G6
Pavlovka 23J5
Pavlovo 22I5
Pavlovsk 23I6
Pavlovskaya 23H7
Pawtucket 48F2
Payakumbuh 29C8
Payette 46D3
Paysandú 54E4
Pazar 23I8
Pazardzhik 21K3
Pazin 20E2
Peabody 48F1
Peace r. 44G4
Pearsall 46H6
Peary Channel 45I2
Peć 21I3
Peçanha 55C2
Pechenga 10Q2
Pechora 22M2
Pechora r. 22L1
Pechorskaya Guba b. 22L1
Pechory 11O8
Pecos 46G5
Pecos r. 46G6
Pécs 20H1
Pedernales 51J5
Pedra Azul 55C1
Pedregulho 55B3
Pedreiras 53J4
Pedro Juan Caballero 54E2
Peebles 16F5
Peekskill 48E2
Pegasus Bay 43D6
Pegu 27I5
Pehuajó 54D5
Peipus, Lake 11O7
Peixe 53I6
Peixoto de Azevedo 53H6
Pekinga 32D3
Peloponnese admin. reg. 21J6
Pelotas 54F4
Pemba 35E5
Pembroke 15C7
Pembroke 45K5
Penápolis 55A3
Penarth 15D7
Penas, Golfo de g. 54A7
Pendleton 46D2
Penha 55A4
Peniche 19B4
Penicuik 16F5
Peninsular Malaysia 29C7
Penn Hills 48B2
Pennine, Alpi mts 18H4
Pennines hills 14E4
Pennsburg 48D2
Pennsville 48D3
Pennsylvania state 48B2
Penn Yan 48C1
Penonomé 51H7
Penrith 14E4
Penrith 42E4
Pensacola 47J5
Penticton 44G5
Pentland Firth sea chan. 16F2
Pentland Hills 16F5
Penza 23J5
Penzance 15B8
Peoria 47J3
Perdizes 55B2
Pereira 52C3
Pereira Barreto 55A3
Peremyshlyany 23E6
Pereslavl'-Zalesskiy 22H4
Pereyaslavka 30D3
Pereyaslav-Khmel'nyts'kyy 23F6
Pergamino 54D4
Perico 54C2
Périgueux 18E4
Perm' 24G4
Pernik 21J3
Perpignan 18F5
Perranporth 15B8
Perris 49D4
Perry 47K5
Perryton 46G4
Perryville 47J4
Persian Gulf see The Gulf
Perth 16F4
Perth 40D6
Perth Amboy 48D2
Peru country 52D6
Perugia 20E3
Pervomays'k 23F6
Pervomaysk 23I5
Pervomayskiy 23I5
Pervomays'kyy 23H6
Pesaro 20E3
Pescara 20F3
Peschanokopskoye 23I7
Peshawar 27G3
Peshkopi 21I4
Peshtera 21K3
Pesnica 20F1
Pessac 18D4
Pestovo 22G4
Pestravka 23K5
Petaluma 49A1
Petatlán 50D5
Peterborough 15G6
Peterborough 41H6
Peterborough 45K5
Peterborough 48F1
Peterhead 16H3
Peterlee 14F4
Petersburg 48C4
Petersfield 15G7
Petersville 44C3
Peto 50G4
Petoskey 47K2
Petrich 21J4
Petrolina 53J5
Petrolina de Goiás 55A2
Petropavlovsk 27F1
Petropavlovsk-Kamchatskiy 25Q4
Petrópolis 55C3
Petroșani 21J2
Petrovsk 23J5
Petrovsk-Zabaykal'skiy 25L4
Petrozavodsk 22G3
Petukhovo 24H4
Petushki 22H5
Pevek 25S3
Pezinok 13P6
Pforzheim 13L6
Phahameng 37H5
Phalaborwa 37J2
Phangnga 29B7
Phan Rang-Thap Cham 29C6
Phan Thiêt 29C6
Phatthalung 29C7
Phenix City 47J5
Phet Buri 29B6
Philadelphia 48D3
Philippines country 29E6
Philippine Sea 29E6
Phiritona 37H4
Phitsanulok 29C6
Phnom Penh 29C6
Phoenix 46E5
Phoenix Islands 39I2
Phôngsali 28C5
Phrae 29C6
Phuket 29B7
Piacenza 20C2
Piatra Neamț 21L1
Picardie admin. reg. 15J9
Picardy reg. 18E2
Picauville 15F9
Picayune 47J5
Pichanal 54D2
Pichilemu 54B4
Pickering 14G4
Picos 53J5
Pico Truncado 54C7
Picton 42E5
Piedade 55B3
Piedras Negras 46G6
Pieksämäki 10O5
Pielinen l. 10P5
Pierre 46G3
Pietermaritzburg 37J5
Pigg's Peak 37J3
Pihlajavesi l. 10P6
Pikalevo 22G4
Pikeville 47K4
Piła 13P4
Pilar 54E3
Pilar 54E4
Pil'na 22J5
Pimenta Bueno 52F6
Pinamar 54E5
Pinar del Río 51H4
Pinarhisar 21L4
Piñas 52C4
Pińczów 13R5
Pindaí 55C1
Pindamonhangaba 55B3
Pindus Mountains 21I5
Pine Bluff 47I5
Pinega 22I2
Pinerolo 20B2
Pinetown 37J5
Pingdingshan 27K3
Pingxiang 27J4
Pingxiang 27K4
Pinhal 55B3
Pinheiro 53I4
Pinjarra 40D6
Pinsk 11O10
Pionki 13R5
Piotrków Trybunalski 13Q5
Piracanjuba 55A2
Piracicaba 55B3
Piraçununga 55B3
Piracuruca 53J4
Piraeus 21J6
Piraí do Sul 55A4
Piraju 55A3
Pirajuí 55A3
Piranhas 53H7
Piranhas r. 53K5
Pirapora 55B2
Pirenópolis 55A1
Pires do Rio 55A2
Piripiri 53J4
Pisa 20D3
Pisco 52C6
Písek 13O6
Pissis, Cerro 54C3
Pisté 50G4
Pistoia 20D3
Pita 32B3
Pitanga 55A4
Pitangui 55B2
Pitcairn Islands terr. 6
Piteå 10L4
Pitești 21K2
Pitești 21K2
Pitkyaranta 22F3
Pitlochry 16F4
Pittsburgh 48B2
Pittsfield 48E1
Pittsworth 42E1
Piumhí 55B3
Piura 52B5
Pivka 20F2
Pixley 49C3
Placerville 49B1
Plácido de Castro 52E6
Plainfield 48F2
Plainview 46G5
Planaltina 55B1
Planura 55A3
Plaquemine 47I5
Plasencia 19C3
Plato 52D2
Platte r. 46H3
Plattsburgh 47M3
Plauen 13N5
Plavsk 23H5
Playas 52B4
Pleasantville 48D3
Plenty, Bay of g. 43F3
Plesetsk 22I3
Pleven 21K3
Pljevlja 21H3
Płock 13Q4
Ploiești 21L2
Plovdiv 21K3
Plungė 11L9
Plymouth 15C8
Plymouth 47J3
Plymouth 48F2
Plymouth 51L5
Plynlimon hill 15D6
Plzeň 13N6
Pô 32C3
Po r. 20E2
Pocatello 46E3
Pochayiv 23E6
Pochep 23G5
Pochinki 23J5
Pochinok 23G5
Poções 55C1
Poconé 53G7
Poços de Caldas 55B3
Podgorenskiy 23H6
Podgorica 21H3
Podgornoye 24J4
Podol'sk 23H5
Podporozh'ye 22G3
Pofadder 36D5
Pogar 23G5
Poggibonsi 20D3
Pogradec 21I4
Pogranichnyy 30C3
P'ohang 31C5
Pointe-à-Pitre 51L5
Pointe-Noire 35B4
Point Pleasant 48D2
Poitiers 18E3
Pokaran 27G4

Vallenar 54B3
Valletta 20F7
Valley 14C5
Valley City 46H2
Valmiera 11N8
Valozhyn 11O9
Valparaíso 54B4
Valuyki 23H6
Vammala 11M6
Van 26D3
Van, Lake *salt l.* 26D3
Vanadzor 23J8
Vancouver 44F5
Vancouver 46C2
Vancouver Island 44F5
Vandalia 47J4
Vanderbijlpark 37H4
Vanderkloof Dam *resr* 36G6
Van Diemen Gulf 40G2
Vändra 11N7
Vänern *l.* 11H7
Vänersborg 11H7
Vangaindrano 35E6
Vanimo 38E2
Vanino 30F2
Vannes 18C3
Vantaa 11N6
Vanua Levu *i.* 39H3
Vanuatu *country* 39G3
Varakļāni 11O8
Varanasi 27H4
Varangerfjorden *sea chan.* 10P1
Varaždin 20G1
Varberg 11H8
Varde 11F9
Varėna 11N9
Varese 20C2
Varginha 55B3
Varkaus 10O5
Varna 21L3
Värnamo 11I8
Várpalota 20H1
Várzea da Palma 55B2
Vaslui 21L1
Västerås 11J7
Västerhaninge 11K7
Västervik 11J8
Vasto 20F3
Vasyl'kiv 23F6
Vathy 21L6
Vatican City 20E4
Vatnajökull *ice cap* 10□2
Vatra Dornei 21K1
Vättern *l.* 11I7
Vavatenina 35E5
Vava'u Group *is* 39I3
Vavoua 32C4
Vavozh 22K4
Vawkavysk 11N10
Växjö 11I8
Vazante 55B2
Veddige 11H8
Veendam 13K4
Vejle 11F9
Velebit *mts* 20F2
Velenje 20F1
Veles 21I4
Vélez-Málaga 19D5
Velika Gorica 20G2
Velika Plana 21I2
Velikaya *r.* 11P8
Veliki Preslav 21L3
Velikiye Luki 22F4
Velikiy Novgorod 22F4
Velikiy Ustyug 22J3
Veliko Tŭrnovo 21K3
Velikoye, Ozero *l.* 23I5
Velizh 22F5
Vellore 27G5
Vel'sk 22I3
Venado Tuerto 54D4
Venceslau Bráz 55A3
Vendôme 18E3
Venev 23H5
Venezuela *country* 52E2
Venezuela, Golfo de *g.* 52D1
Vengurla 27G5
Venice 20E2
Venice 47K6
Venice, Gulf of 20E2
Vénissieux 18G4
Vennesla 11E7
Venta 11M8
Ventersdorp 37H4
Ventoux, Mont *mt.* 18G4
Ventspils 11L8
Ventura 49C3
Venus Bay 42B7
Vera 19F5
Vera 54D3
Veracruz 50E5
Vera Cruz 55A3
Veraval 27G4
Verbania 20C2
Vercelli 20C2
Vercors *reg.* 18G4
Verdalsøra 10G5
Verde *r.* 55A2
Verden (Aller) 13L4
Verdun 18G2
Vereeniging 37H4
Verkhnetulomskiy 10Q2
Verkhnevilyuysk 25N3
Verkhov'ye 23H5
Vermilion 46E1
Vermillion 47H3
Vermont *state* 48E1
Vernal 46F3
Verneuk Pan *salt pan* 36E5
Vernon 44G4
Vernon 46H5
Vero Beach 47K6
Veroia 21J4
Verona 20D2
Verona 48B3
Versailles 18F2
Vertou 18D3
Verulam 37J5
Verviers 13J5
Vesele 23G7
Veselyy 23I7
Veshenskaya 23I6
Vesoul 18H3
Vesterålsfjorden *sea chan.* 10H2
Vestfjorden *sea chan.* 10H3
Vestmannaeyjar 10□2
Vesuvius *vol.* 20F4
Ves'yegonsk 22H4
Veszprém 20G1
Vetlanda 11I8
Vetluga 22J4
Vevey 18H3
Vezirköprü 23G8
Viamao 55A5
Viana 53J4
Viana 55C3
Viana do Castelo 19B3
Vianópolis 55A2
Viareggio 20D3
Viborg 11F8
Vibo Valentia 20G5
Vic 19H3
Vicenza 20D2
Vichy 18F3
Vicksburg 47I5
Viçosa 55C3
Victoria 7
Victoria 20F6
Victoria 44F5
Victoria 47H6
Victoria 54B5
Victoria 54D4
Victoria *state* 42B6
Victoria, Lake 34D4
Victoria Falls 35C5
Victoria Island 44H2
Victoria West 36F6
Victorville 49D3
Videle 21K2
Viedma 54D6
Viedma, Lago *l.* 54B7
Vienna 13P6
Vienne 18G4
Vientiane 29C6
Vierzon 18F3
Viesite 11N8
Vietnam *country* 29C6
Vigan 29E6
Vigevano 20C2
Vigia 53I4
Vignola 20D2
Vigo 19B2
Vijayawada 27H5
Vila Franca de Xira 19B4
Vilagarcía de Arousa 19B2
Vila Nova de Gaia 19B3
Vilanova i la Geltrú 19G3
Vila Real 19C3
Vilar Formoso 19C3
Vila Velha 55C3
Vil'gort 22K3
Vilhena 52F6
Viljandi 11N7
Vilkaviškis 11M9
Vilkija 11M9
Villa Ángela 54D3
Villach 13N7
Villa Dolores 54C4
Villaguay 54E4
Villahermosa 50F5
Villa Insurgentes 46E6
Villajoyosa-La Vila Joiosa 19F4
Villa María 54D4
Villa Montes 52F8
Villanueva de la Serena 19D4
Villa Ocampo 54E3
Villa Regina 54C5
Villarrica 54E3
Villarrobledo 19E4
Villa San Giovanni 20F5
Villa Unión 46G7
Villavicencio 52D3
Villazon 52E8
Villefranche-sur-Saône 18G4
Villena 19F4
Villeneuve-sur-Lot 18E4
Villers-sur-Mer 15G9
Villeurbanne 18G4
Villingen 13L6
Vilnius 11N9
Vil'nyans'k 23G7
Vilyeyka 11O9
Vilyuy *r.* 25N3
Vimmerby 11I8
Viña del Mar 54B4
Vinaròs 19G3
Vincennes 47J4
Vinchina 54C3
Vineland 48D3
Vinh 29C6
Vinita 47H4
Vinnytsya 23F6
Vinson Massif *mt.* 56C4
Vire 18D2
Virgem da Lapa 55C2
Virginia 37H5
Virginia *state* 48B4
Virginia Beach 48D4
Virgin Islands (U.K.) *terr.* 51L5
Virgin Islands (U.S.A.) *terr.* 51L5
Virginópolis 55C2
Virovitica 20G2
Visaginas 11O9
Visalia 49C2
Visby 11K8
Viscount Melville Sound *sea chan.* 45G2
Viseu 19C3
Viseu 53I4
Vishakhapatnam 27H5
Visp 18H3
Vista 49D4
Vistula *r.* 13Q3
Viterbo 20E3
Vitigudino 19C3
Viti Levu *i.* 39H3
Vitória 55C3
Vitória da Conquista 55C1
Vitoria-Gasteiz 19E2
Vitry-le-François 18G2
Vitsyebsk 23F5
Vittel 18G2
Vittoria 20F6
Vittorio Veneto 20E2
Vize 21L4
Vizianagaram 27H5
Vizinga 22K3
Vlaardingen 12J5
Vladikavkaz 23J8
Vladimir 22I4
Vladimiro-Aleksandrovskoye 30D4
Vladivostok 30C4
Vlasotince 21J3
Vlissingen 12I5
Vlorë 21H4
Vöcklabruck 13N6
Voghera 20C2
Vohipeno 35E6
Voinjama 32C4
Vojens 11F9
Vojvodina *prov.* 21H2
Vokhma 22J4
Volcano Islands 28G5
Volda 10E5
Volga 22H4
Volga *r.* 23J7
Volgodonsk 23I7
Volgograd 23J6
Volgogradskoye Vodokhranilishche *resr* 23J6
Völkermarkt 13O7
Volkhov 22G4
Vol'no-Nadezhdinskoye 30C4
Volnovakha 23H7
Volochys'k 23E6
Volodars'ke 23H7
Volodymyr-Volyns'kyy 23E6
Vologda 22H4
Volokolamsk 22G4
Volos 21J5
Volosovo 11P7
Vol'sk 23J5
Volta, Lake *resr* 32D4
Volta Redonda 55B3
Volzhsk 22K5
Volzhskiy 23J6
Vopnafjörður *b.* 10□2
Voranava 11N9
Voreioi Sporades *is* 21J5
Vorkuta 24H3
Voronezh 23H6
Vorotynets 22J4
Võru 11O8
Vosburg 36F6
Vosges *mts* 18H3
Voskresensk 23H5
Voss 11E6
Vostochnyy Sayan *mts* 25K4
Votkinsk 24G4
Votuporanga 55A3
Vozhega 22I3
Voznesens'k 23F7
Vrangel' 30D4
Vranje 21I3
Vratsa 21J3
Vrbas 21H2
Vredenburg 36C7
Vršac 21I2
Vryburg 36G4
Vryheid 37J4
Vsevolozhsk 22F3
Vučitrn 21I3
Vukovar 21H2
Vuktyl' 24G3
Vukuzakhe 37I4
Vurnary 22J5
Vyatskiye Polyany 22K4
Vyazemskiy 30D3
Vyaz'ma 23G5
Vyazniki 22I4
Vyborg 11P6
Vychegda *r.* 22J3
Vyerkhnyadzvinsk 11O9
Vyksa 23I5
Vynohradiv 23D6
Vyselki 23H7
Vyshhorod 23F6
Vyshniy-Volochek 22G4
Vyškov 13P6
Vytegra 22H3

W

Wa 32C3
Waco 47H5
Waddenzee *sea chan.* 12J4
Wadi Halfa 33G2
Wad Medani 33G3
Wagga Wagga 42C5
Wahpeton 47H2
Waidhofen an der Ybbs 13O7
Wajima 31E5
Wakatipu, Lake 43B7
Wakayama 31D6
Wakefield 14F5
Wakkanai 30F3
Wałbrzych 13P5
Walcha 42E3
Wałcz 13P4
Waldkraiburg 13N6
Waldorf 48C3
Wales *admin. div.* 15D6
Walgett 42D3
Walkersville 48C3
Wallasey 14D5
Walla Walla 46D2
Wallis and Futuna Islands *terr.* 39I3
Walnut Creek 49A2
Walsall 15F6
Walterboro 47K5
Waltham 48F1
Walvis Bay 36B2
Walvis Bay 36B2
Wamba 32D4
Wamba 34C3
Wanaka, Lake 43B7
Wanganui 43E4
Wangaratta 42C6
Wangkui 30B3
Wangqing 30C4
Wantage 15F7
Wanxian 27J3
Wanyuan 27J3
Warab 33F4
Warangal 27G5
Waren 13N4
Warendorf 13K5
Warialda 42E2
Warmbad 36D5
Warminster 15E7
Warminster 48D2
Warracknabeal 41I7
Warrego *r.* 42B3
Warren 42C3
Warren 48A2
Warren 48C1
Warren 48B2
Warrenpoint 17F3
Warrensburg 47I4
Warri 32D4
Warrington 14E5
Warrnambool 41I7
Warsaw 13R4
Warwick 15F6
Warwick 42F2
Warwick 48F2
Wasco 49C3
Washington 47L4
Washington 48A2
Washington 48C3
Washington *state* 46C2
Washington, Mount 47M3
Watampone 29E8
Waterbury 48E2
Waterford 17E5
Waterford Harbour 17F5
Waterloo 47I3
Waterloo 48A1
Waterloo 48C1
Waterlooville 15F8
Watertown 47H3
Watertown 47L3
Waterval Boven 37J3
Watford 15G7
Watsonville 49B2
Wau 33F4
Wauchope 42F3
Waukegan 47J3
Wausau 47J3
Waverly 48C1
Waycross 47K5
Waynesboro 48B3
Wear *r.* 14F4
Weatherford 46H5
Webi Shabeelle *r.* 34E3
Webster 48F1
Weddell Sea 56C5
Wee Waa 42D3
Weifang 27K3
Weimar 13M5
Weinan 27J3
Weipa 41I2
Weirton 48A2
Weiz 13O7
Wejherowo 13Q3
Weldiya 34D2
Welkom 37H4
Welland 48B1
Wellesley Islands 41H3
Wellingborough 15G6
Wellington 36D7
Wellington 43E5
Wells-next-the-Sea 15H6
Wels 13O6
Welwyn Garden City 15G7
Wembesi 37I5
Wenatchee 46C2
Wenshan 27J4
Wenzhou 28E5
Werris Creek 42E3
Wesel 13K5
Wesselton 37I4
West Bank *terr.* 33G1
West Bend 47J3
West Bromwich 15F6
Westbury 15E7
West Chester 48D3
Westerly 48F2
Western Australia *state* 40E4
Western Cape *prov.* 36E7
Western Desert 33F2
Western Ghats *mts* 27G5
Western Port *b.* 42B7
Western Sahara *terr.* 32B2
West Falkland *i.* 54D8
Westfield 48E1
West Frisian Islands 12J4
West Hartford 48E2
West Haven 48E2
West Indies *is* 51J4
Westminster 48C3
Weston-super-Mare 15E7
West Palm Beach 47K6
West Plains 47I4
West Point 48C4
Westray *i.* 16F1
Westray Firth *sea chan.* 16F1
West Siberian Plain 24J3
West Virginia *state* 48A3
West Wyalong 42C4
West York 48C3
Wete 35D4
Wetzlar 13L5
Wewak 38E2
Wexford 17F5
Weybridge 15G7
Weyburn 44H5
Weymouth 15E8
Weymouth 48F1
Whalsay *i.* 16□
Whangarei 43E2
Wharton 47H6
Wheaton-Glenmont 48C3
Wheeling 48A2
Whernside *hill* 14E4
Whitburn 16F5
Whitby 14G4
Whitehaven 14D4
Whitehead 17G3
Whitehill 15G7
Whitehorse 44E3
White Nile *r.* 33G3
White Plains 48E2
White Sea 22H2
Whiteville 47L5
White Volta *r.* 32C4
Whitley Bay 14F3
Whitney, Mount 49C2
Whitstable 15I7
Whittlesea 42B6
Whittlesey 15G6
Whyalla 41H6
Wichita 47H4
Wichita Falls 46H5
Wick 16F2
Wickford 15H7
Wicklow 17F5
Wicklow Head 17G5
Wicklow Mountains 17F5
Widnes 14E5
Wieluń 13Q5
Wiener Neustadt 13P7
Wiesbaden 13L5
Wigan 14E5
Wight, Isle of *i.* 15F8
Wigston 15F6
Wigtown Bay 16E6
Wild Coast 37I6
Wilge *r.* 37I3
Wilhelm, Mount 38E2
Wilhelmshaven 13L4
Wilkes-Barre 48D2
Wilkes Land *reg.* 56A5
Willand 15D8
Willemstad 51K6
Williamsburg 48C4
Williams Lake 44F4
Williamsport 48C2
Williamstown 48D1
Williamstown 48D3
Willimantic 48E2
Williston 46G2
Williston Lake 44F4
Willmar 47H2
Wilmington 47L5
Wilmington 48D3
Wilmslow 14E5
Wilson 47L4
Wilson's Promontory *pen.* 42C7
Wincanton 15E7
Winchester 15F7
Winchester 47K4
Winchester 48B3
Windber 48B2
Windermere 14E4
Windermere *l.* 14E4
Windhoek 36C2
Windsor 15G7
Windsor 42E4
Windsor 45J5
Windsor Locks 48E2
Windward Islands 51L5
Windward Passage 51J5
Winfield 47H4
Wingate 14F4
Wingham 42F3
Winneba 32C4
Winnemucca 46D3
Winnfield 47I5
Winnipeg 45I5
Winnipeg, Lake 45I4
Winnipegosis, Lake 45H4
Winona 47I3
Winona 47J5
Winsford 14E5
Winston-Salem 47K4
Winterthur 18I3
Winton 41I4
Wisbech 15H6
Wisconsin *state* 47J3
Wisconsin Rapids 47J3
Wishaw 16F5
Wismar 13M4
Witbank 37I3
Witham 15H7
Witney 15F7
Wittenberge 13M4
Włocławek 13Q4
Wodonga 42C6
Woking 15G7
Wokingham 15G7
Wolfenbüttel 13M4
Wolfsberg 13O7
Wolfsburg 13M4
Wollaston Lake 44H4
Wollongong 42E5
Wolverhampton 15E6
Wondai 41K5
Wŏnju 31B5
Wŏnsan 31B5
Woodbine 48D3
Woodbridge 15I6
Woodbridge 48C3
Woodbury 48D3
Woodland 49B1
Woods, Lake of the 45I5
Woodstock 48A1
Woodward 46H4
Wooler 14E3
Woolgoolga 42F3
Woomera 41H6
Woonsocket 48F1
Wooster 47K3
Worcester 15E6
Worcester 36D7
Worcester 48F1
Workington 14D4
Worksop 14F5
Worland 46F3
Worthing 15G8
Wotu 38C2
Wrangel Island 25T2
Wrexham 15E5
Wrightwood 49D3
Wrocław 13P5
Września 13P4
Wuchang 30B3
Wuhai 27J3
Wuhan 27K3
Wuhu 28D4
Wuliang Shan *mts* 27J4
Wuppertal 13K5
Würzburg 13L6
Wuwei 27J3
Wuxi 28E4
Wuyi Shan *mts* 28D5
Wuyuan 28C3
Wuzhong 27J3
Wuzhou 27K4
Wymondham 15I6
Wyndham 40F3
Wyndham-Werribee 42B6
Wyoming *state* 46F3
Wyszków 13R4
Wythall 15F6
Wytheville 48A4

X

Xai-Xai 37K3
Xambioa 53I5
Xam Nua 28C5
Xankändi 26D3
Xanthi 21K4
Xátiva 19F4
Xiamen 28D5
Xi'an 27J3
Xiangfan 27K3
Xiangkhoang 29C6
Xiangtan 27K4
Xianyang 27J3
Xiao Hinggan Ling *mts* 30B2
Xichang 27J4
Xifeng 30B4
Xigazê 27H4
Xi Jiang *r.* 27K4
Xilinhot 27K2
Xinglongzhen 30B3
Xingu *r.* 53H4
Xinguara 53H5
Xingyi 27J4
Xining 27J3
Xinqing 30C2
Xintai 27K3
Xinxiang 27K3
Xinyang 27K3
Xinzhou 27K3
Xique Xique 53J6
Xo'jayli 26E2
Xuddur 34E3
Xuwen 27K4

Y

Ya'an 27J3
Yabuli 30C3
Yadrin 22J5
Yagodnoye 25P3
Yagoua 33E3
Yahualica 50D4
Yaizu 31E6
Yakima 46C2
Yako 32C3
Yakovlevka 30D3
Yakutsk 25N3
Yakymivka 23G7
Yala 29C7
Yalova 21M4
Yalta 23G7
Yalvaç 21N5
Yamagata 31F5
Yamaguchi 31C6
Yamal Peninsula 24H2
Yamba 42F2
Yambio 33F4
Yambol 21L3
Yamoussoukro 32C4
Yampil' 23F6
Yamuna *r.* 27H4
Yana *r.* 25O2
Yan'an 27J3
Yanbu' al Baḩr 34D1
Yangdok 31B5
Yangtze *r.* 27I3
Yangtze *r.* 27L3
Yangyang 31C5
Yanji 30C4
Yankton 47H3
Yantai 28E4
Yaoundé 32E4
Yap *i.* 29F7
Yaqui *r.* 46E6
Yar 22L4
Yaransk 22J4
Yaren 39G2
Yarim 34E2
Yaroslavl' 22H4
Yaroslavskiy 30D3
Yarra Junction 42B6
Yarram 42C7
Yarrawonga 42B6
Yartsevo 23G5
Yashkul' 23J7
Yasnogorsk 23H5
Yass 42D5
Yatağan 21M6
Yatsushiro 31C6
Yavari *r.* 52E4
Yavoriv 23D6
Yazd 26E3
Yazoo City 47I5
Ydra *i.* 21J6
Yefremov 23H5
Yegorlykskaya 23I7
Yegor'yevsk 23H5
Yekaterinburg 24H4
Yekaterinoslavka 30C2
Yelabuga 22K5
Yelan' 23I6
Yelets 23H5
Yell *i.* 16□
Yellow *r.* 27K3
Yellowknife 44G3
Yellow Sea 28E4
Yell Sound *strait* 16□
Yel'sk 23F6
Yemen *country* 34E2
Yemtsa 22I3
Yemva 22K3
Yenagoa 32D4
Yenakiyeve 23H6
Yenice 21L5
Yenişehir 21M4
Yenisey *r.* 24J2
Yeniseysk 24K4
Yeniseyskiy Kryazh *ridge* 24K4
Yenotayevka 23J7
Yeovil 15E8
Yeppoon 41K4
Yerevan 26D2
Yereymentau 27G1
Yergeni *hills* 23J7
Yershov 23K6
Yertsevo 22I3
Yesan 31B5
Yesil' 26F1
Yeşilova 21M6
Yessentuki 23I7
Yevlax 23J8
Yevpatoriya 23G7
Yevreyskaya Avtonomnaya Oblast' *admin. div.* 30D2
Yeysk 23H7
Yi'an 30B3
Yibin 27J4
Yichun 30C3
Yilan 30C3
Yimianpo 30C3
Yinchuan 27J3
Yingkou 27L2
Yingtan 28D5
Yining 27H2
Yirga Alem 34D3
Yitulihe 30A2
Yiyang 27K4
Ylivieska 10N4
Ylöjärvi 11M6
Yogyakarta 29D8
Yokadouma 33E4
Yokkaichi 31E6
Yoko 32E4
Yokohama 31E6
Yokosuka 31E6
Yokote 31F5
Yola 32E4
Yŏnan 31B5
Yonezawa 31F5
Yong'an 28D5
Yŏnghŭng 31B5
Yŏngju 31C5
Yonkers 48E2
Yopal 52D2
York 14F5
York 48B1
York 48C3
York, Cape 41I2
Yorke Peninsula 41H7
Yorkshire Wolds *hills* 14G5
Yorkton 44H4
Yoshkar-Ola 22J4
Youghal 17E6
Youngstown 48A2
Yozgat 26C3
Yreka 46C3
Ystad 11H9
Ysyk-Köl *salt l.* 27G2
Ytyk-Kyuyel' 25O3
Yuba City 49B1
Yucatán *pen.* 50F5
Yucatan Channel *strait* 51G4
Yucca Valley 49D3
Yueyang 27K4
Yukon *r.* 44B3
Yukon Territory *admin. div.* 44E3
Yulin 27K4
Yuma 49E4
Yumen 27I3
Yungas *reg.* 52E7
Yurga 24J4
Yuriria 50D4
Yur'ya 22K4
Yur'yevets 22I4
Yur'yev-Pol'skiy 22H4
Yushu 27I3
Yushu 30B3
Yuxi 27J4
Yuzawa 31F5
Yuzha 22I4
Yuzhno-Kuril'sk 30G3
Yuzhno-Sakhalinsk 30F3
Yuzhno-Sukhokumsk 23J7
Yuzhnoukrayinsk 23F7
Yverdon 18H3

Z

Zaandam 12J4
Zabaykal'sk 27K2
Zabīd 34E2
Zābol 26F3
Zacapa 50G5
Zacatecas 50D4
Zacharo 21I6
Zacoalco 50D4
Zadar 20F2
Zadonsk 23H5
Zafra 19C4
Zaghouan 20D6
Zagreb 20F2
Zagros Mountains 26E3
Zāhedān 26F4
Zahlé 33G1
Zaḩrān 34E2
Zaječar 21J3
Zakho 33H1
Zakopane 13Q6
Zakynthos 21I6
Zakynthos *i.* 21I6
Zalaegerszeg 20G1
Zalai-domsag *hills* 20G1
Zalantun 30A3
Zalău 21J1
Zalim 34E1
Zambezi *r.* 35C5
Zambia *country* 35C5
Zamboanga 29E7
Zamora 19D3
Zamora 52C4
Zamora de Hidalgo 50D5
Zamość 23D6
Zanesville 47K4
Zanjān 33H1
Zanzibar 35D4
Zanzibar Island 35D4
Zaozernyy 25K4
Zaozhuang 27K3
Zapadnaya Dvina 22G4
Zapadnyy Kazakhstan *admin. div.* 23K6
Zapadnyy Sayan *reg.* 24J4
Zapata 46H6
Zapolyarnyy 10Q2
Zaporizhzhya 23G7
Zaqatala 23J8
Zaragoza 19F3
Zarand 26E3
Zaranj 26F3
Zarasai 11O9
Zárate 54E4
Zaraysk 23H5
Zaraza 52E2
Zārdab 23J8
Zaria 32D3
Zarichne 23E6
Zărnești 21K2
Żary 13O5
Zavetnoye 23I7
Zavidoviči 20H2
Zavitinsk 30C2
Zavolzhsk 22I4
Zawiercie 13Q5
Zaysan, Lake 27H2
Žďár nad Sázavou 13O6
Zdolbuniv 23E6
Zeerust 37H3
Zeil, Mount 40G4
Zelenodol'sk 22K5
Zelenograd 22H4
Zelenogradsk 11L9
Zelenokumsk 23I7
Zell am See 13N7
Zemetchino 23I5
Zemmora 19G6
Zenica 20G2
Zenzach 19H6
Zernograd 23I7
Zeya 30B1
Zgierz 13Q5
Zhabinka 11N10
Zhanaozen 26E2
Zhangjiakou 27K2
Zhangye 27J3
Zhanibek 23J6
Zhanjiang 27K4
Zhaodong 30B3
Zhaotong 27J4
Zhaoyuan 30B3
Zhaozhou 30B3
Zharkent 27H2
Zharkovskiy 22G5
Zhashkiv 23F6
Zheleznogorsk 23G5
Zhengzhou 27K3
Zhenlai 30A3
Zherdevka 23I6
Zhezkazgan 26F2
Zhitikara 26F1
Zhlobin 23F5
Zhmerynka 23F6
Zhob 27F3
Zhongwei 27J3
Zhovti Vody 23G6
Zhuanghe 31A5
Zhukovka 23G5
Zhukovskiy 23H5
Zhuzhou 27K4
Zhydachiv 23E6
Zhytkavichy 11O10
Zhytomyr 23F6
Žiar nad Hronom 13Q6
Zibo 27K3
Zielona Góra 13O5
Zigong 27J4
Ziguinchor 32B3
Žilina 13Q6
Zima 25L4
Zimbabwe *country* 35C5
Zimnicea 21K3
Zimovniki 23I7
Zinder 32D3
Ziniaré 32C3
Zinjibār 34E2
Zirc 20G1
Zitácuaro 50D5
Zittau 13O5
Zlín 13P6
Zmiyevka 23H5
Znamenka 23I5
Znam"yanka 23G6
Znojmo 13P6
Zolochiv 23E6
Zolochiv 23G6
Zolotonosha 23G6
Zolotukhino 23H5
Zomba 35D5
Zongo 34B3
Zonguldak 21N4
Zorgho 32C3
Żory 13Q5
Zouérat 32B2
Zrenjanin 21I2
Zubova Polyana 23I5
Zubtsov 22G4
Zuénoula 32C4
Zug 18I3
Zugdidi 23I8
Zunyi 27J4
Županja 20H2
Zürich 18I3
Zuru 32D3
Zuwārah 32E1
Zuyevka 22K4
Zvishavane 35D6
Zvolen 13Q6
Zwedru 32C4
Zwelitsha 37H7
Zwettl 13O6
Zwickau 13N5
Zwolle 13K4
Zyryanka 25Q3

Collins World Atlas

Collins
An imprint of HarperCollinsPublishers
77-85 Fulham Palace Road
London
W6 8JB

First Published 1986
Second Edition 1991
Third Edition 1993
Fourth Edition 1994
Fifth Edition 1997
Sixth Edition 2003

Seventh Edition 2005
This edition produced for Remainders Ltd. in 2005
by HarperCollins Publishers

Copyright © HarperCollinsPublishers 2005
Maps © Bartholomew Ltd 2005

Collins ® is a registered trademark of HarperCollinsPublishers Ltd

All rights reserved. No part of this publication may be reproduced, stored in a retrieval system, or transmitted, in any form or by any means, electronic, mechanical, photocopying, recording or otherwise without the prior written permission of the publisher and copyright owners.

The contents of this edition of the Collins World Atlas are believed correct at the time of printing. Nevertheless the publisher can accept no responsibility for errors or omissions, changes in the detail given, or for any expense or loss thereby caused.

Printed in Spain

British Library Cataloguing in Publication Data.
A catalogue record for this book is available from the British Library.

ISBN 0 00 763336 X

All mapping in this atlas is generated from Collins Bartholomew digital databases. Collins Bartholomew, the UK's leading independent geographical information supplier, can provide a digital, custom, and premium mapping service to a variety of markets. For further information:
Tel: +44 (0) 141 306 3752
e-mail: collinsbartholomew@harpercollins.co.uk

We also offer a choice of books, atlases and maps that can be customized to suit a customer's own requirements. For further information:
Tel +44 (0) 141 306 3209
e-mail: business.gifts@harpercollins.co.uk
or visit our website at: www.collinsbartholomew.com

Collins. Do More. www.collins.co.uk

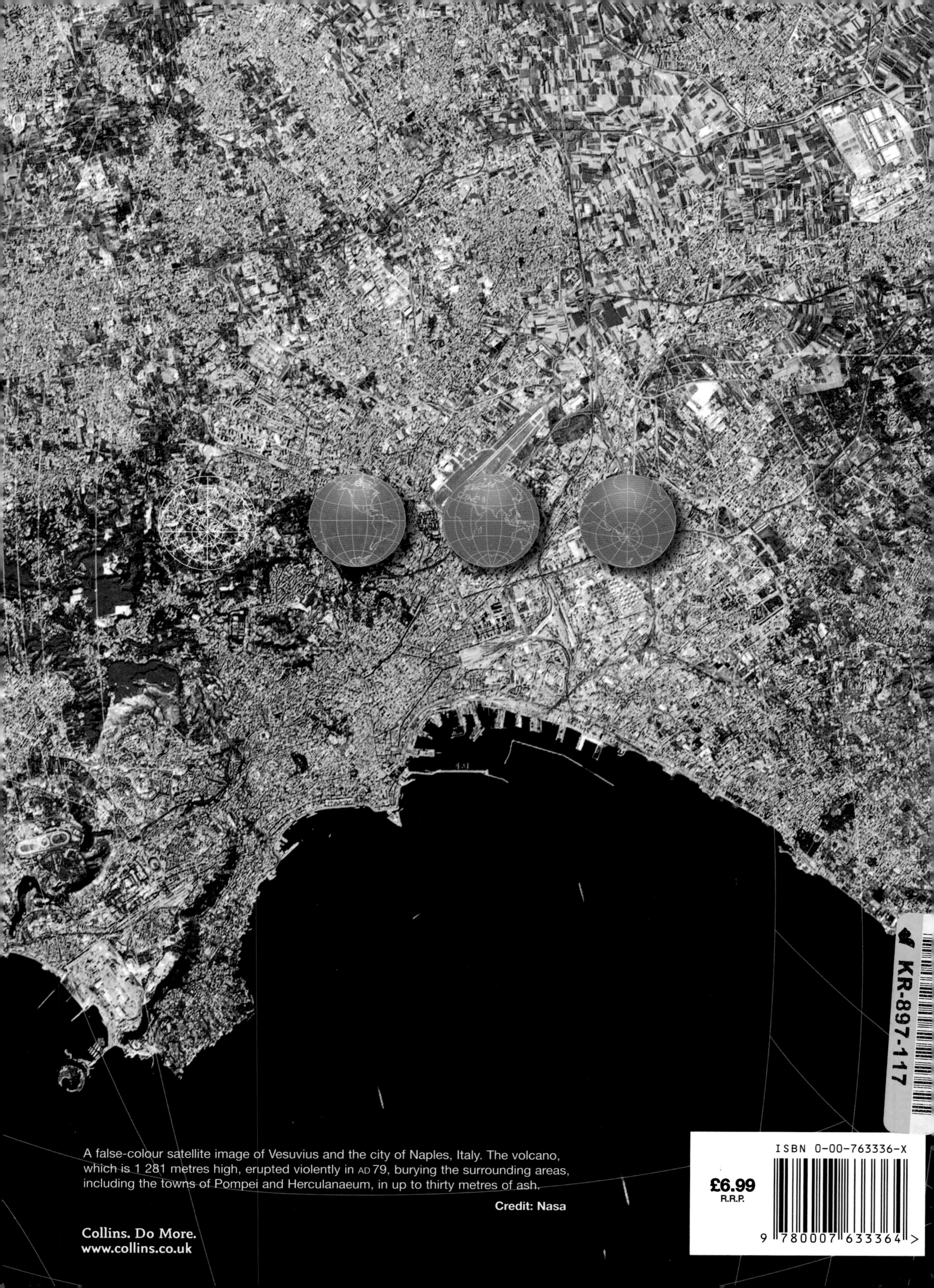

A false-colour satellite image of Vesuvius and the city of Naples, Italy. The volcano, which is 1 281 metres high, erupted violently in AD 79, burying the surrounding areas, including the towns of Pompei and Herculanaeum, in up to thirty metres of ash.

Credit: Nasa

Collins. Do More.
www.collins.co.uk